For Business Ethics

For Business Ethics is a daring adventure into the world of business ethics. It offers a clear and accessible introduction to business ethics and also expands business ethics beyond its current narrow confines. It is ground-breaking in the sense that it invites a distinctively critical approach to business ethics, an approach that the authors argue is part and parcel of ethics.

Jones, Parker and ten Bos overview utilitarianism, deontology and virtue ethics, and uncover the possibility of subversive and critical business ethics in these theories. They expand the definition of business ethics while questioning the meaning of ethics, the possibility of ethics in an era of corporate capitalism and the function of business ethics in civil society.

With a thought-provoking glossary and recommendations for further readings, *For Business Ethics* is an essential purchase for students and practitioners alike. It is at once an introduction to business ethics and a challenge to anyone who wishes to take part in or change contemporary organised society.

Campbell Jones is Director of the Centre for Philosophy and Political Economy and Senior Lecturer in Critical Theory and Business Ethics in the Management Centre, University of Leicester, UK.

Martin Parker is Professor of Organisation and Culture in the Management Centre, University of Leicester, UK.

René ten Bos is a philosopher and management teacher who works for Schouten & Nelissen. He is also Professor in Philosophy and Organisational Theory at the Radboud University, Nijmegen, the Netherlands.

For Business Ethics

Campbell Jones,
Martin Parker and
René ten Bos

Routledge
Taylor & Francis Group

LONDON AND NEW YORK

First published 2005
by Routledge
2 Park Square, Milton Park, Abingdon, Oxon OX14 4RN

Simultaneously published in the USA and Canada
by Routledge
270 Madison Ave, New York, NY 10016

Routledge is an imprint of the Taylor & Francis Group

© 2005 Campbell Jones, Martin Parker and René ten Bos

Typeset in Perpetua and Bell Gothic by
Keystroke, Jacaranda Lodge, Wolverhampton
Printed and bound in Great Britain by
TJ International Ltd, Padstow, Cornwall

British Library Cataloguing in Publication Data
A catalogue record for this book is available from the British Library

Library of Congress Cataloging in Publication Data
Jones, Campbell, 1973–
For business ethics : a critical text / Campbell Jones, Martin Parker and
René ten Bos.— 1st ed.
    p. cm.
Includes bibliographical references and index.
1. Business ethics. I. Parker, Martin, 1962– II. Bos, René ten. III. Title.
HF5387.J65 2005
174′.4—dc22   2004027821

ISBN 0–415–31134–9 (hbk)
ISBN 0–415–31135–7 (pbk)

'Freedom is the ontological condition of ethics. But ethics is the considered form that freedom takes when it is informed by reflection.'

Michel Foucault

Contents

CONTENTS

Acknowledgements

We thank all of the students, managers and others that we have discussed these ideas with, and especially those who have disagreed with us. We also thank those who have commented directly on this text, in particular Steffen Böhm, Stephen Dunne, Shayne Grice, Simon Lilley, Sam Mansell, Carl Rhodes, Sverre Spoelstra and Edward Wray-Bliss.

Campbell Jones thanks Sophie for everything. Martin Parker names Jude, Ben, Max, Zoe and Spike, with love. René ten Bos is saying hello to Juliette, Julia and Boris.

Collectively, we would like to thank the nameless others who have made this book possible, and the spaces in our institutions that respect this kind of work.

We dedicate this book to all those others in this world still not recognised, and for whom the notion of 'business ethics' is little more than idle chatter.

Chapter 1

Introduction: against business ethics

THIS STRANGE BOOK

Before you read this book you should be aware of two things. First of all we, the authors, don't like textbooks. Most of the **textbooks** that we have ever read have been too long, rather dull, and full of abstract examples and even more abstract theories. But most importantly, they don't *do* anything interesting and relevant. They try to tell the student everything about a subject, and almost always end up saying not very much. They are little more than lists and tables, and often there isn't much in those lists or tables. You can memorise the list for an exam, of course, but we wonder what you actually learn from that kind of book. It seems to us that this is what most business ethics textbooks are like.

We should also make a second, and perhaps more worrying, admission. To be quite honest, we are not particularly fond of '**business ethics**'. Most of what we read under the name business ethics is either sentimental **common sense**, or a set of excuses for being unpleasant. Some of business ethics is easy talk and simple rules – 'nice people do nice things, nasty people do nasty things'. The rest of it is a laughably transparent attempt to make things look a whole lot better than they actually are. For us, and hopefully soon also for you, business ethics in its present form is at best window dressing and at worst a calculated lie.

Given that we don't like textbooks or business ethics you might wonder why we would think of sitting down and writing a textbook on business ethics. Even more improbable, a business ethics textbook with a title like *For Business Ethics*. But, despite appearances, we want to argue that it is not us, but the world we live in that is strange. Further, we think that most of the knowledge that is produced by academics and consultants and appears in business ethics textbooks is also strange. So, one of our goals is to invite you into this world of strangeness. To put it another way, we propose one of the things that has always been the demand of critical thought – to think about things, to look at alternative perspectives, and in the end to make the world that we are familiar with look a little bit more strange than it usually does. In other words, to expose the 'common sense' of business ethics as neither common nor sensible.

Because of this, we are going to ask a bit more of you as a reader than is often asked in textbooks. Specifically, we are going to ask you to read the whole of the book from start to end, even if you find some parts of it confusing and some bits hard. We have tried to write as simply and straightforwardly as we can, and we hope that things will come across reasonably clearly. We have also prepared a glossary that provides discussions of most of the key terms that we mention throughout the book. But no matter how hard we try, we are aware that reading this book is not going to be an easy experience. We hope that you will eventually agree that this is not because we are intentionally troublesome sorts, but because business ethics and the world that produces it are, to put it bluntly, in a miserable state.

In the classic definition that we inherit from the ancient Greeks, **ethics** is a question of the meaning of 'the good life'. When understood in this way, ethics asks questions about what is 'good' and 'bad'. We want to argue that very often business ethics has given easy and self-interested answers to such really big questions. So one of the things that we will need to do is to slow 'business' and 'ethics' down, to slow down your reading and thinking, and to interrupt some of the ideas about 'business ethics' that you might have already acquired. Because whether you have taken a course in business ethics before or not, you will still have some idea about what is 'good' and 'bad' in **business**. That is unavoidable. But as you read this book we will ask you to examine these ideas again, and that process may be uncomfortable. You may well want to dismiss our ideas without further thought.

But, uncomfortable as it may be, we want you to enjoy a certain discomfort, or at least to begin with, to understand it. That discomfort is part of a training that involves considering different understandings of what is good and bad. Similar discomfort was keenly felt by Socrates about two and a half thousand years ago when he called on his **community** to think about ethics. It was also felt by those that put him to death for asking such irritatingly difficult questions. We should recall the suggestion that Socrates made to his fellows, on being sentenced to death: 'to let no day pass without discussing goodness and all the other subjects about which you hear me talking and examining both myself and others is really the very best thing that a man can do, and that life without this sort of examination is not worth living' (Plato, 1954: 71–72). In this book we want to propose that the discipline of business ethics is rarely subjected to that examination, but that it would be worthwhile. Indeed, without that sort of examination, we would go so far as suggesting that 'business ethics' is not interested in ethics at all.

AGAINST BUSINESS ETHICS

What, then, is the problem with business ethics? One way of expressing it would be to say something like the following. It is simply a matter of getting let down. Business ethics holds a great promise, in that it promises ethics and speaks of justice. But at the same time it seems compromised to its very core, and seems to resist the very thing that it advances

(Jones, 2003a: 241; see also Parker, 2002a: 92–93). Part of the problem, then, is that business ethics promises far more than it delivers. And this delivery problem is due to the way that business ethics has taken what we would call a narrow or restricted version of business and ethics. While business ethics claims to be open and critical, we feel it to be narrow and uncritical. So in this book we will do our best to outline an argument for a broadened or expanded business ethics. Which is perhaps doing little more than taking business ethics seriously, more seriously than it takes itself.

In this opening chapter we will try to outline the problems that we have with business ethics, which is a way of pointing out how business ethics fails to take itself seriously. Very simply, we have six problems with the discipline of business ethics. Each of these problems relates to a 'foreclosure', by which we mean that something has been closed down before it should have been. Premature responses to questions look like answers, but if we take these answers for granted then we no longer think about the questions. Against these foreclosures, our own view is that ethics is an opening and not a closure, and hence all of these foreclosures represent serious problems.

FIRST PROBLEM: FORECLOSING PHILOSOPHY

Our first problem with business ethics relates to the way that business ethicists do **philosophy**. Business ethics is that part of business education that makes the most explicit claim to be interested in philosophy. But if we look at the philosophy that is done in business ethics, it seems clear that twentieth century philosophy is almost completely excluded. In Chapters 3, 4 and 5 of this book we will look at the three streams of ethical thinking that have dominated business ethics. We find that one originates from the ancient Greeks, one from a late eighteenth century German and another from two eighteenth and nineteenth century Englishmen. Despite the fact that ethics has been hotly debated in philosophy throughout the twentieth century and has been one of the major sources of philosophical reflection up to the close of the millennium, the discipline of business ethics has insulated itself from these developments, either ignoring them altogether or misrepresenting them so that it looks as if twentieth century philosophy has nothing interesting to say about ethics. For this reason, we and others have been arguing that recent philosophers actually have a lot to say about business ethics (see, for example, Borgerson, 2004; Freeman and Phillips, 1999; Jones, 2003a; 2003b; Parker, 2003a; 2003b; Roberts, 2001; 2003; Rosenthal and Bucholz, 1999; ten Bos, 2002; 2003; Wicks and Freeman, 1998; Wray-Bliss, 2002; 2003).

In this book we propose to extend the challenge to the foreclosure of philosophy that we generally find in business ethics. The first way that we do this is by rereading business ethics in the light of developments in contemporary thought. This is one of the tasks of the first half of the book. The other way that we contest the foreclosure of business ethics is by turning to sources that have been pretty much ignored in the development of business ethics, and this is the major task of the second half of the book. Hence

3

part of our expanded conception of business ethics will be based on, first, a broadened reading of traditional ethical theory and, second, a broadened canon of ethical theory. We propose to bring philosophy back into business ethics, but perhaps a better way of thinking about this is that we are simply taking the philosophical claims of business ethics seriously. That is to say, we all know that business ethics poses questions of ethics, and ethical questions are an important part of philosophy. So whilst business ethics has often said it is philosophically informed, in this book we propose to take it at its word.

SECOND PROBLEM: FORECLOSING SOCIETY

The second major problem that we have with business ethics is its **individualism**. Individualistic explanations of social action focus exclusively, or largely, on the characteristics of individuals, and ignore or downplay the role of social context. This is like trying to explain something about a person without referring to the situations that have shaped them in ways that are common to other people – gender, ethnicity, class, age and so on. The most common way that individualism manifests itself in business ethics is when corporate scandals or other obvious wrongdoing are attributed purely to the evil or selfish **character** of individuals. Often it is tempting, when we see gross corporate misconduct, to explain this by pointing the finger at the person who did the wrong act. But we want to argue that individualism itself can also be a problem, particularly when it hides from view the context in which acts of misconduct take place.

When we say that we want to challenge the individualism of business ethics, we are not saying that individuals never do bad things, and we certainly think that we, as individuals, have a **responsibility** for our acts. But we want to stress that individual action always takes place in a social context. Another way of putting this is that individual action always takes place in relation to social structures, like organisations or economies, to mention just two obvious examples. This is not to say that structures entirely cause or determine individual actions, but rather to note that social action is always social, always taking place when an individual produces and is produced by a social context. We will discuss this problem in more detail in Chapter 5, when we examine the place of character and community in ethical explanation. But for now it is enough to be clear that individualism is one of the problems that we have with business ethics.

This means that, although you are obviously an individual reading this book, we will invite you throughout to think both about yourself and your social context, and when you assess the ethics of others, we invite you to consider them in their context. Sometimes we need to criticise the actions of individuals. That is clear. But sometimes we also need to criticise social structures and arrangements, and to see the way that those structures influence action, making some types of action possible and others impossible. If we want to explain the scandals associated with business, it is important that we see both the individuals responsible for certain choices and the context in which their actions took place. To put it simply, people are often encouraged to behave in ways that others might later decide are immoral. We want to understand more about how people are encouraged to behave in these ways, and hence judge structures, as well as the people. We therefore will directly discuss organisational and economic structures in Chapters 7 and 8.

THIRD PROBLEM: FORECLOSING 'THE ETHICAL'

In addition to philosophical foreclosure and individualism, business ethics far too often rests on a very narrow definition of what counts as 'the ethical'. Some aspects of business obviously present ethical dilemmas. Most people would agree that matters such as bribery, pollution and child labour raise ethical issues. And business ethicists do indeed debate the rights and wrongs of these 'ethical issues'. But by designating certain things as 'ethical' issues, what often then happens is that other things are treated, either explicitly or implicitly, as if they did not involve ethical questions. As a result, business ethics has treated many of the day to day practices of contemporary organised life as if they do not present ethical concerns. Hence, a range of issues, even including basic things such as the employment contract, are treated as if they are not of concern for business ethics. For example, it is generally assumed that once you have a university qualification you will spend most of the rest of your life working for wages within an organisation. Yet, as a television comedy like *The Office* illustrates, many people find the 9 to 5 routines of work to be anything but satisfying and meaningful. Perhaps it is work itself that is a problem? Business ethics, most of the time, claims to be about good and bad within business. This is all very well, but it does not exhaust the range of matters that concern people about the role of businesses in the contemporary world.

To contest this narrowing, throughout the book we raise ethical problems with a number of things which are considered business as usual. For example, when a company with shareholders gives some of the profits it has made to investors who have not been involved in producing the value, this is seen as a reward for risk. But why should the surplus generated by workers be given to someone else who almost certainly already has a lot of money in the first place? Or think about some other examples. Why do poor nations have to export food when their own populations are starving? Why are third world workers paid so little to make things that are sold for huge profits in the first world? We suggest that the ways that we live and the choices that we make involve major ethical decisions, even if these concerns are largely ignored by the business ethics literature. Indeed, the narrowness of business ethics suggests something quite sinister about the ethics of the business ethics literature. Why are certain topics considered to be common sense? What is it that business ethics is leaving in the shadows?

FOURTH PROBLEM: FORECLOSING THE MEANING OF 'ETHICS'

Related to the narrowing of the ethical to a specific set of issues, we face a fourth problem, which is one about the meaning of 'ethics'. Quite often business ethics texts will provide a 'definition' of business ethics, that tells us what business ethics is supposed to mean. The problem with this is that business ethics means quite a lot of quite different things. In fact, one of the major problems when we start looking at business ethics is that words like ethics do not have a transparent meaning. Indeed, if we all agreed what 'ethics' was, we would not need to argue about it quite so much. In the first half of this book we will look at a range of different meanings of business ethics, particularly looking at the meanings of business ethics in common sense and popular discourse (Chapter 2), and in the philosophies of **utilitarianism** (Chapter 3), **deontology** (Chapter 4) and **virtue** ethics (Chapter 5). As we look at these different ways of thinking about ethics we will find that the differences are not just a matter of talking about the same thing in different ways. Rather, these different ways of talking about ethics seem to be talking about different things, about different ways of imagining ethics itself.

In Chapter 6, we therefore turn directly to the question of the meaning of ethics. In that chapter we suggest that, if we are to understand talk about ethics, we need to understand the captivating and charming nature of the idea of ethics, but we also need to see beyond this to think critically about the meaning of ethics. We therefore strip ethics back to its most basic element, which is something about a relationship with other people and with difference more generally. From this we set out towards the task in the rest of this book, which is to contribute to introducing a new language for thinking and talking about business ethics.

FIFTH PROBLEM: FORECLOSING POLITICS

The fifth problem with business ethics is the way that it tends to deny the role of **politics**. This is partly related to the third problem we mentioned above, of narrowing 'the ethical'. But it goes further than this, and relates to a basic question of what business ethics is willing to question and challenge. More often than not, business ethics is assumed to be something that does not really trouble basic assumptions about the normal practices of business. Even when we see a crisis such as the collapse of Enron and the complicity of Arthur Andersen in collecting huge consultancy fees in return for lying about the accounts, business ethics usually does not see this as indicating any basic problems with the operation of corporations in general or of the right of private companies to enforce audit law. Rather, much of business ethics prefers to explain such things as small problems in a wide sea. The point is that very rarely does business ethics even imagine the possibility that the sea may be destroyed or that we might, one day soon, not be able to breath the air in the sky.

6

In this book we will challenge this foreclosure of politics. We will argue that business ethics could treat scandals such as Enron and Arthur Andersen as a symptom of broader problems in contemporary business practice. Such a move is dangerous, of course, because it unsettles a number of cherished assumptions. It makes us think that the world that we live in might not be the best of all possible worlds. In fact, today, there is a widespread recognition that all is not well in the world, but there seems little will to do anything about this. Perhaps this cynicism is part and parcel of the problem. People who doubt the solutions that are offered for various sorts of problems are often accused of being cynical. But cynicism also involves what has been described as a manifestation of an 'enlightened false consciousness' which knows perfectly well what is wrong in the world yet refuses to do anything about it (Sloterdijk, 1988: 5).

In this sense, business ethics, as it is often practised, might itself be an instance of cynicism. Against this, we want you to consider how business ethics might be different from the way it is at the moment. What if we took business ethics seriously? We believe that this is a radical **possibility**, and one that needs to be considered. To take business ethics seriously will likely set us against much in the world today, and encourage us to consider political alternatives. But because business ethics usually refuses to consider such alternatives, it is often little more than a cynical apology for the status quo. As such, it helps to perpetuate wrongdoings in business rather than understanding or changing them. In doing so, business ethics does not just avoid politics – it assumes a politics that accepts the status quo. It is, we suggest, a bad omen that many of the very same companies that have caused moral outrage about their behaviour have ethical codes and social responsibility statements.

A second task of the second half of the book will therefore be to reconsider the place of politics in business ethics. In Chapter 7 we will look at the role of modern **bureaucracy** in promoting or denying ethics, and in Chapter 8 we will ask what ethics means in an age of global capital. By asking questions about modernity, bureaucracy, **globalisation** and **capitalism**, we are dealing with issues that are sometimes discussed in business ethics texts, though they are much more commonly seen in disciplines like politics and sociology. Business ethics can learn a lot from these disciplines, and it must. These issues threaten to expand, if not explode, business ethics in its narrow form.

SIXTH PROBLEM: FORECLOSING THE GOAL OF ETHICS

This brings us to a tension that we will deal with throughout the book. Business ethics is often caught between two conceptions of what it is for. On the one hand, it can be a reassuring and satisfying set of ideas that reminds us how to do the right thing. On the other hand, it can be something that threatens us by exposing us to difference, and that challenges us to think and act differently. More often than not, business ethics has taken the first path, and in this respect is a source of solutions rather than problems.

7

Business ethics often acts as a **technology** (see **techne**) for the reduction of un-decidability. It has become something that claims to show us what to do, almost to the extent that we simply need to know the right **rules** in order to do the right thing. In this way, it has become much the same as described by the German philosopher Theodor Adorno, as a form of mathematised and codified knowledge in which thought is removed and 'which robots can learn and copy' (1973: 30) – textbook knowledge for puppets, not knowledge that you gain by thinking for yourself.

For us, ethics always involves a certain dislocation from common sense. Ethics shakes you, jolts you out of your complacent acceptance of 'what is'. This problem has been put differently by different thinkers. Emmanuel **Levinas** (1974) argues that ethics is not a question of 'being' someone, but a question of understanding difference and calling one's self into question. Jacques **Derrida** (1995) argues that ethics always involves a certain difficulty, an experience of 'not knowing what to do'. And Giorgio Agamben (1993b) argues that ethics is not a matter of stable solutions but one of endless openness and difficulty. Throughout the book we will discuss these and other thinkers who have argued that ethics is not a matter of solutions but is perhaps better thought of as a set of problems.

So this book will not be a comforting one, not an easy way of passing a course without having to think too much. This book was not titled 'The Five Minute Ethicist', or 'Seven Steps to Happiness'. But who in their right mind would expect that a consideration of the meaning of the good life would be easy, or comforting?

FOR OR AGAINST BUSINESS ETHICS?

Before we proceed, we should say something more about whether we are for or against business ethics. On the one hand, we are obviously not happy with 'business ethics'. But part of our discontent is that it fails to take things seriously, first of all not taking itself very seriously. So it might seem strange for us to call our book *For Business Ethics* if it is actually an argument against business ethics. This draws attention to a number of things. The first of these is that, despite what we might have suggested, 'business ethics' is not a stable or uncontested discipline. Indeed, the very fact that we are writing this book is indicative of that contest. But others have also contested business ethics, or have tried to open business ethics out to new perspectives (see, for example, Crane and Matten, 2004; Griseri, 1998; Jackall, 1988; Parker, 1998; Verstraeten, 2000; Watson, 1994). So we do not want to give the impression that we are the only ones to express concern with the state of business ethics. As we criticise business ethics we are drawing on the ideas of many others.

You will notice that as we move through the book we are making an active effort to shift the discipline of business ethics. We begin with almost direct opposition in this chapter (which is, after all, titled 'Against Business Ethics') to a plea in favour of business ethics in the final chapter ('For Business Ethics'). You will also notice that in the first half of the book we discuss many established ideas in business ethics, and are often quite critical of the ideas advanced there. But in the second half, as we seek to further expand and open up business ethics, we become increasingly affirmative of the idea of business ethics. This movement rests on a belief that business ethics is profoundly compromised at present, but is still something that could be very promising, that could contribute to making the world a better place.

Rather than dismiss talk of ethics out of hand, as some of our critical colleagues have suggested (Thompson et al., 2000), in this book we will make an effort to do the work of figuring out what can be salvaged from the current condition of business ethics. Sometimes the answer is that there is not very much, for example in the case of 'common sense business ethics' that we discuss in the next chapter. In other cases, such as the orthodox tradition of business ethics that we discuss in Chapters 3, 4 and 5, we find that there is some potential, but this potential is best seen through a critical rereading of this tradition. In some other cases, mostly covered in the second half of the book, we find that there is a whole wealth of thinking about ethics that has the potential to redeem business ethics and to enable it to take its place as a critical social science and a progressive social practice. So if it appears strange that we argue both for and against business ethics, it is because there is more than one business ethics. We are arguing against its current, restricted form, and for a broader form which is both more serious and more joyful, and is redeemed of its current fall into platitudes and the tyranny of unexamined common sense. So, let's begin in the next chapter by thinking about 'common sense'. What is the common sense of business, ethics and business ethics?

Chapter 2

Common sense business ethics

INTRODUCTION

We started by asserting the miserable state of much of business ethics (and the world too) and suggested that we were going to change things. 'Fair enough,' you might be thinking, 'but since I don't know what business ethics is in the first place, I can hardly share your impatience with it.' So, mindful of this need, this chapter will try to explain something about the 'common sense' of business ethics. When we write 'common sense', we are referring to the ways that most business ethicists, most of the time, think, write and practise business ethics. If you want to check what we are suggesting, then go and have a look, and compare what they are claiming to what we write here.

Perhaps unsurprisingly, some of this common sense is quite similar to the sort of common sense that people use when they are thinking about everyday ethical issues. However, on other issues, this common sense is not that common at all. In fact, when viewed from an everyday perspective, much of the common sense of business ethics is uncommon nonsense, but more of that later. Let us begin at the beginning, even if this is Chapter 2. Imagine that this chapter is a distilled essence of much of the material found in 1001 other business ethics books. How do the authors of these books write about their subject matter? And why do we have difficulties with what they have to say? We will start by asking some very basic questions:

1 What is business?
2 What is ethics?
3 What is business ethics?

We will think about how business ethicists answer these questions in order to find out what their common sense is, and we will wonder throughout if this common sense really makes sense.

WHAT IS BUSINESS?

Business is, in an older sense, a particular trade or activity that a person is engaged in. The correct response to the question, 'what is your business here?', would be a description of a particular task, not an organisation. Nowadays, the term has become rather more generalised, and seems to mean an entire complex of trades and activities. 'Business' typically refers to jobs and organisations in the private sector. Business is about profit making and being enterprising. Most importantly, enterprises, companies or firms are organisations that respond to the 'market', which is to say that they work for customers who expect to get what they want, at prices they will pay. Throughout this book, we will refer to these organisations by using the word 'businesses'. Those businesses which fail to satisfy their customers will be eaten by those that do not, so that the laws of business are similar to the laws of evolution. Only the strong and clever survive, and there is no virtue in being a loser.

Let us just run through this one more time, because this is perhaps the most important starting point for common sense business ethics. This is a division of the world of work into two parts. One is a business sector which is brutal but realistic. It offers high rewards, but relies on hard work and job insecurity. The other is a world which is not business, which refers to organisations such as schools and hospitals or families and friends. The not-business world is often believed to be kinder and slower, sheltered as it is from the harsh winds of market realities. By implication, then, the sort of ethics that might apply to that which is not business are not really useful for those in business (see Carr, 1968, for an extension of this argument). That is why we need something called *business ethics*, a special sort of ethics, for a special sort of situation. Note that most people would probably think that this move is not in accordance with common sense. After all, they would normally think consistency of moral comportment and moral judgement across different situations to be a value when thinking about whether someone was ethical or not. If a person admitted that their ethics depended on the situation that they found themselves in, we might decide that they did not have strong principles, or call them hypocritical. Nonetheless, this captures something of the logic that is needed when we establish a particular form of ethics called business ethics.

In most cultures, business has been seen to be a rather dirty and vulgar matter. Jesus Christ threw the moneylenders out of the temple; taking interest ('usury') is prohibited by Islam; Confucius said that 'the superior person knows what is right; the inferior person knows what will sell'; and Buddhists warn that if you harm another person when you are doing business you will inevitably end up harming yourself (this is 'karma'). But suspicion towards business is not restricted to religious sources. Indeed, if we look at contemporary books and films, we can see that many representations of business are negative. Corporations and their inhabitants are presented as conspiratorial places populated by immoral individuals. The bad guy wears a suit, and is probably working for the mafia, the devil or some other suspicious power. But if you read a management textbook, you will get a very different image altogether. Managers, executives,

11

entrepreneurs, leaders – these are all positive words, with qualities like charisma, dynamism, energy, drive and so on. Indeed, business and management is one of the most popular areas of study at universities nowadays, and we expect that a lot of you who are reading this book will be doing your business ethics module on such a course.

These sorts of courses will tend not to be too critical of their subject matter. After all, if you were studying physics, you wouldn't expect the lecturers to be suggesting that physics was a waste of time, or even immoral. In practice what teachers do is to 'sell' their subject, to try and get students to care about it, and invest their time and effort into finding out more about it. So it is hardly surprising that most of the material which makes up business courses – in strategy, marketing, organisational behaviour, operations, accounting and finance and so on – tends to celebrate business, or at the very least to treat it as basically unproblematic.

Often, this sort of celebration turns on the idea that business and management is a sort of science. That is to say, that it might have been done badly in the past – when children went up chimneys, and the same chimneys spewed pollution across the land-scape – but that it is being done better now. Now, the story goes, we are increasingly expert in doing business and management because we understand more about people and we understand more about markets. The two key sciences here are psychology and economics, the former claiming to tell us what goes on in the heads of individuals, the latter claiming to tell us what happens when we collect together the choices made in a lot of heads.

So something about the common sense of business can be found in the idea that business is an applied science resting on increasingly scientific understandings of people and markets. If harmony can be found between people's internal desires and their collective preferences, human beings will be happy, wealthy and wise. In practical terms, if a marketer finds something that people really want, sells it and becomes rich and generates jobs, everybody wins. Customers are happy, the marketer is happy and employees are happy. Achieving this sort of win-win situation is precisely what business is good at, and what management textbooks can teach you about. Or can they?

It is all very well to claim that you know the truth about people and markets, but what would this sort of claim mean? Many people claim to know the truth, but some of them think they are Napoleon, or that little green monsters live at the bottom of their garden. One answer might be that the truth about people and markets has been established through scientific enquiry, but this certainly is not the sort of science that helps bridges stay up. No-one can legitimately claim to be able to predict with any meaningful degree of precision what either people or markets actually do. They might have some rules of thumb, but this certainly has not stopped people from stealing from pension funds or stopped markets from crashing. So when someone writes about the rules governing human motivation, or the laws of the hidden hand of the market, they don't mean 'rules' and 'laws' in the sense that we know that if a gas is compressed it heats up. Indeed, these sort of claims might actually be more like opinion and prejudice. So when you read or hear a statement which suggests a certain knowledge about business, you might want to stop for a moment and think about what this statement and the knowledge it contains might actually be based on.

This is very important for the common sense of business ethics because, for example, if someone says that 'people are self-interested' or that 'markets are efficient', they are also making claims about the sorts of things that 'should' then be done. After all, if someone else were to say 'people are co-operative' or 'planning is efficient', the sorts of 'shoulds' that follow would be entirely different. Yet business people, and many business academics too, do often make claims about human nature and markets as if they were entirely true, and accepted by all, and based on irrefutable fact. For example, consider these claims:

People want challenging jobs.
Leadership is important for business.
Customers do not wish to pay high prices.
Competitors are trying to outperform you.
An ardent belief in the goals of a business is a precondition for excellent performance.

Perhaps you share some of these assumptions too, or perhaps you don't. Is it really true that people want challenging jobs or that leadership is crucial to business? The crucial point, however, is not whether you agree or disagree, but that you realise that assumptions about 'what *is*' lead to assumptions about 'what *ought* to be'. So, when we are presented with so-called 'facts', these will always involve ideas as to how things should be. Perhaps the statements we have just listed represent some commonsensical understandings in the world of business. But does that make them true? Is this what makes them indisputable? Or do they contain a normative agenda?

We do not want to accept these and other similarly entrenched understandings as unassailable truths. What we hope you to get from this book is that once in a while even our most commonsensical understandings can and should be questioned. It is the only way, we suggest, to take them seriously.

WHAT IS ETHICS?

If business is a term which usually carries a sort of baggage with it, then this is even more so for ethics. When we claim that something is 'good' or 'bad', 'right' or 'wrong', 'moral' or 'immoral' and so on, we are making some very firm assertions about other people's behaviour. To condemn or praise someone else's action is one of the most powerful things that we can do with language, and that others can do to us. For example, TV soap operas, and the inevitable talk that people have about last night's episode, are often largely concerned with such judgements: 'They shouldn't have done that.' 'It was the right thing to do, but I'm not sure about their reason for doing it.' 'They wouldn't have done that if they had known what would happen.' Most of the time, we praise and condemn others, and hope that they will praise us. No-one really wants to be in the wrong, and so they find ways to justify their actions to others: 'I couldn't help myself.' 'They deserved it.' 'I didn't realise that they were listening.'

When we praise or condemn, what are we doing? Well, we might just want to say that, in our humble opinion, such and such was wrong. In other words, that I think something, but do not really expect everyone to agree with me. Now that sort of claim is a small and modest one that cannot really be contested. We might ask that person why they believe as they do, but if they keep saying that it is just their opinion, then there is not really any point in trying to persuade them otherwise. You say apples, I say pears. That's it. But this is not what actually happens most of the time when judgements are made. Usually, when asked why they think the way they do, people will attempt to generalise particular forms of behaviour; they will say, 'doing X is always wrong' or 'you should consider Y before doing Z', or something like that. People tend to look for some sort of consistent rule they can invoke in order to persuade the other to think like they do. As we shall see in later chapters, this is pretty much what moral philosophers have done. They have attempted to formalise the sorts of arguments that ordinary people make, and give them a shape and logic that everyone might then agree with.

However, as you will no doubt have noticed, neither philosophers nor ordinary human beings have come up with any sort of law that seems to apply to everyone, all of the time, in all places. If they had, you would know about it. Books on business ethics would be very short, because as an author you would just have to explain the law to everyone, and they would be able to decide whether they should be good or bad. And they would know that everyone else could make the same judgement of them, too. The world would be a straightforward place where heroes and villains could be clearly distinguished and where good and evil fought for supremacy. Incidentally, much of the legal system would also disappear, because we could all decide for ourselves and would not need judges to decide for us. Neither would we need to talk about soap operas, since we would already know who the good and bad people were, which might make the human drama rather less compelling.

As you will also have noticed, these sorts of views of the world do exist, but are usually held in place by something other than the arguments of human beings or philosophers. Instead, many people would suggest that some sort of non-human agent – a god or any other mystical force – has ordained that the universe be like this and that they themselves are involved in an eternal battle against evil and disorder. Indeed, this is typically insisted on in the holy texts that many people read and reread.

Against all this, you may want to argue that it is sometimes rather puzzling why God or the gods did not just make everybody good in the first place, which would have saved all of us a lot of trouble. That there is trouble, however, seems undeniable. And, once again, this has something to do with freedom. If we did not have the capacity to do evil, then there would not be any freedom at all in doing the good. But why would we then make such a fuss about the good? Would in this case the good not appear as something unavoidable, or as something that comes to us with the inevitability of a law of physics created by God himself? The problem is that in such a case morality would lose all its connection to freedom. In this book, we will see that many philosophers have stressed the lawless and unruly nature of morality. Put another way, to us morality is not merely a domain where common sense, law or religious force will prevail without further ado. In the moral domain, there is always the shadow of freedom, and this will involve difference, disruption and unrest.

One of the topics that we will also address is the relationship between community or tradition on the one hand and morality on the other. We will have much more to say about this in Chapters 5 and 10, but already here we would like to point out that moral assumptions are in significant ways shaped by social contexts. Imagine showing an episode of a soap opera in a series of different countries and then getting people to talk about it. Though there would probably be similarities, there are likely to be just as many differences. What would be seen as plainly right in Kenya might not be so straightforward in Indonesia. A virtuous New Zealander might display characteristics that would be seen as suspicious in the Netherlands and the Welsh make jokes that New Zealanders and the Dutch do not find funny at all.

Think also, for example, of *American Beauty*, an Oscar-winning Hollywood film starring Kevin Spacey about a middle-aged man who falls in love with the 16-year-old girlfriend of his daughter, gives up his career to start working in a fast food restaurant, and smokes more marijuana with the boy next door than is probably good for either of them. Most of the European reviewers tended to interpret the film as a brilliant satirical indictment of the American way of life, indeed of consumerism and business life in general. Most American reviewers, on the other hand, saw the film as a rather sobering reminder of the moral vulnerability of American family life.

The point is that what you think is ethical common sense is very likely to be shaped by who you are and where you are, and when people make generalisations about what is right and wrong, they sometimes forget this. They assume that their common sense is, and should be, shared; that what they call democracy is always good, or that the writings of **Marx** are unchallengeable, or that the holy church cannot be wrong. And when they start to notice that others disagree and that their arguments do not work, they shout louder, and claim that the others are misguided, bad or even sick.

Yet there is another, and perhaps even bigger, problem waiting to trip up common sense generalisations about conduct. We might agree that people in different places believe different things, but what if people in the same places believe different things? Our workplaces, neighbourhoods and cities are not homogeneous. Instead we have young and old, black and white, gay and straight, right wing and left wing, working class and middle class, men and women, and so on, and so on. Whether you like it or not, people are, for all their similarities, also very different. And, if they are so different, is it then really sensible to believe in some form of ethical generalisation that could apply to all of them, all of the time? Is there a rule that could equally be followed by an elderly woman living with her relatives on the outskirts of Moscow and a young man who has

15

just enrolled into the army in Sri Lanka? Even the most 'obvious' rules seem to be a little difficult to generalise if we take such radical differences seriously.

If we stop and try to think of an example of a good or a bad action, we often come up with examples and of rules such as 'don't kill people'. Most people would agree that this is an example of a bad action, but what does this mean? Does it mean that killing is always wrong, under any circumstances, ever? What if the old woman is suffering from an agonising illness that leaves her in constant pain and will inevitably lead to her death? What if political action involves the reduction of support for the poor and the homeless and causes people to die in the streets? What if the young man was suddenly facing an enemy who was pointing a gun at him? What about capital punishment for serial killers? What if killing your enemy and bringing their head to your family would bring you great honour within your society? What about abortion? What if killing one person would save the lives of a hundred others? What if your God told you to sacrifice your son? It seems as if there are always possible exceptions to what seems to be an obvious and clear rule. This is an aspect of the disruptive nature of ethics we referred to above.

So, if the common sense of ethics is that there is a clear line between 'good' and 'bad', 'right' and 'wrong', 'moral' and 'immoral', then it seems that it might not fit very well with what human beings actually do. It might be that there is no point in worrying about ethics, and we should just do what we like. No rules, only choices, and only the strong survive. Or, it might persuade us that we should simply try harder to find a better set of ethical rules. Which is to say that we should listen to philosophers or politicians more carefully in the future in the hope that we really do get somewhere with all these problems. This might be the case, too, and we will explore some of these ideas in the next three chapters. But note one thing before we move on. If prophets have spent thousands of years attempting to bring us rules for human conduct, and the very best thinkers on the planet have done the same, is it reasonable to believe that a little book like this will do any better? Could anyone do any better?

WHAT IS BUSINESS ETHICS?

Over the last 25 years or so, business ethics has become an accepted part of management both inside and outside universities. First in the USA, and now in the rest of the world, there are a growing number of books, journals, institutes, professors, consultants and university courses in business ethics. Much like all the other management sub-disciplines, there is a claim to centrality in this expansion. Just as marketers claim that everything follows from marketing, or accountants that organisations would be nothing without the numbers, so do business ethicists claim that the values and purposes of business organisations matter above all else. The rise of business ethics is an interesting case study in the history of ideas, and of the claims to expertise and legitimacy that are needed in order to launch a supposedly 'new' area of enquiry. Constructing such legitimacy requires that certain questions need to be addressed. Were businesses not ethical before business ethics? What expertise do professional ethicists have that ordinary mortals do not? And, perhaps most importantly, will business ethics actually make businesses ethical?

So what are the forms of common sense that can be found in business ethics? To be a business ethicist – or any other sort of expert for that matter – you must claim (at least) three things. First, that something is needed; second, that you are the kind of person who can do it; third, that you can achieve something with your expertise. So, business ethicists must claim that the various customers of their knowledge do not have the resources to deal with moral matters on their own, and hence need guidance from experts. A core assumption of business ethics seems to be that people in business are somehow 'morally insufficient' (Parker, 2002a; ten Bos, 2002). Why would that be the case?

A very common opening argument is to suggest, implicitly or explicitly, that there is some kind of crisis of ethics. This is a diagnosis of the present age which compares it unfavourably with the past. It is suggested that people do not trust businesses anymore, that negative images of organisations are common in the media, that hyper-competition is making employees and organisations perform whatever the costs, that globalisation is causing competing belief systems to collide, or that the environment can no longer sustain unbridled capitalism. Or, simply, that people are not as good now as they used to be in the old days. Think about directors' pay, oil spills, creative accounting, offensive marketing, workers' rights, stakeholder rights, global inequality, anti-corporate protest, sweatshop labour, green consumers, consumer boycotts, ethical investors, insider trading and so on. It is implied that these sort of things did not use to happen in the past. Now if this is the case, then managers are in a different and potentially dangerous world and are much in need of guidance. As is clear, this is a diagnosis that essentially relies on a story of ethical decline. This sort of story suggests that progress involves the loss of community and traditional forms of moral regulation. The small scale, high trust and face-to-face interactions that once constrained small businesses have now been replaced with huge and anonymous corporate structures. Unlike local factories and corner shops, the players in global marketplaces now have fewer meaningful responsibilities to people or places. Business is good, but has some awkward consequences. Business ethics will help you deal with them.

In a sense, the actual accuracy of this kind of history is unimportant. It does not matter if we believe that people used to behave better in the old days, or that communities really existed. What seems to matter is that this story helps to provide a space for business ethics to step into. Ethical analysis, education and regulation are now needed, when previously they were not. Importantly, this is a history that is often simultaneously used to legitimise management and the business school in general. More effective business and management then becomes the answer, and more management research and investment is always needed.

This is rather like being told that we 'need' estate agents, or pet psychologists, or more TV channels. The creation of the need is an essential move in legitimising the product. It is not until someone has persuaded you that other people are sniffing and raising their eyebrows that you think you need a deodorant. In the same way, businesses, and busy people, now 'need' ethics, when presumably they did not need it before. The argument that ethics is needed is also supported by pointing out that it is important for all businesses to think hard about ethics because heightened public awareness and state legislation demand it. Both are the sticks that threaten unethical businesses all over the world. This is pretty much the same as saying that ethics is a part and parcel of contemporary business practice, and whether you like it or not, it is something every-one who takes interest in business needs to know about. In a strangely self-fulfilling way, the fact that people talk about business ethics proves that it is needed.

And so, the need created, the question that then arises is who is to fulfil it. Business ethicists have two cards to play here. The first is a body of ethical knowledge which they largely appropriate from moral philosophy. This is an ancient and impressive list, stretching back to Plato and **Aristotle**, and incorporating big words (utilitarianism, deontology, virtue ethics) and big names (**Kant**, **Mill**, **Bentham**). The usefulness of such grand language should not be underestimated, since it can be sufficiently obscure to impress and since it allows the business ethicist to sound fairly clever. Without moral philosophy, it might have been more difficult to legitimate business ethics as a discrete and credible domain of enquiry within universities.

The second card that business ethicists have to play is in stressing the application and relevance of their knowledge. Tactically, this is important in order to avoid accusations of irrelevance by a busy practically-minded audience that wants to get things done by the end of the week. This issue largely boils down to stressing the role of business ethics as a bridge between the intellectual world of the academy and the practicality of management decision making in the real world. This is clearly a delicate balancing act between 'ethics' and 'business'. Too far in the direction of ethics and there is little connection to the real world of business, too far in the direction of business and the discipline just echoes management common sense with no 'unique selling proposition', as the marketers put it. As a result, many business ethics teaching texts stress their practicality and usefulness, and the experience of their authors in business or consulting on ethics. On this view, business ethics is both academic and realistic, but this is a smooth blend, not a mess of contradictions and dead ends.

This approach is then underlined by a common approach to teaching business ethics, which is to ask the student to be the manager making the difficult decision. 'What would you do in this situation? Give reasons for your decisions.' This stress on the autonomy or free will of the individual decision maker is not to be conflated with the kind of freedom that a thinker like **Foucault** has in mind. He did not harbour any illusions about a world where you can choose what to do without any constraint whatsoever. That is not to say that he denied the possibility of freedom. It is rather that freedom comes only when you are able to question at least some of your constraints. This is, indeed, what he refers to as the ethical. As we already suggested in Chapter 1, in the standard textbooks on business ethics, little attention is paid to the constraints on what people do. They are routinely swept under the carpet. Hence, in these textbooks decision makers appear to be in a kind of free-floating situation where nothing could possibly interfere with their autonomous free will. We think that such detached circumstances are, to say the least, completely delusory.

Be this as it may, the standard picture that we get of the decision-making process goes like this: the manager collects the evidence, models a set of potential answers, and then makes a decision on what actions should be taken. These decisions might concern key business issues – sexual harassment and diversity, health and safety, whistleblowing, intellectual property, the environment, and so on. All important issues, of course, and, as many business ethicists have understood, ones that need addressing. So looking at them makes a lot of sense. That is not our problem with many business ethicists. It is rather *how* they look at these issues. Frankly, we do not think that it is helpful to think about these issues as if they are just a matter of autonomous moral choice. The belief that this is possible is based on a willingness to exclude many matters as if they were a form of background noise. This noise includes organisational and financial structures, the position of the manager and management education, the relationships between first world and third world, the nature of work and employment, and so on. Incredibly, the common sense of global capitalism and **market managerialism** typically ends up being 'outside' business ethics.

Finally, and perhaps most importantly, there is then the question of whether business ethics will actually make businesses more ethical. Here, business ethicists are generally more cautious, and justifiably so. For a start, they do not raise expectations too high. Their goals very rarely include any form of radical social change. The heart of the matter is gentle and polite reform, or a moral education for top decision makers. What they do should not be too distressing or upsetting. The emphasis is on working with and within contemporary business organisations in order that their worst excesses can be tempered. Indeed, since the vast majority of business ethicists also assert that ethics makes for good business, or at least that there is no contradiction between ethics and business, sometimes even reform seems irrelevant. Ethics becomes a specific part of a business and marketing strategy, something done in order to make more money. Yet, if someone told us that they were merely being good so that they would be rewarded, or so that people would think better of them, we would probably not be impressed. In fact, we might decide that they were not being ethical at all.

Business ethics is rarely ambitious in its aims. It reasons with business people, and does not expect too much from them. It suggests personal development, or perhaps sensible reform, as reasonable ends. Such modesty is very good to hear in the often hysterically breathless arena of management in general; but if so little is expected, then perhaps little is likely to be achieved. And this, frankly, will be of little use to someone working in an export processing zone in Thailand. To summarise, the common sense of business ethics is that people need ethics nowadays, that business ethicists are the people they need to give it to them, and that these business ethicists won't shake things up too much.

WHAT IS COMMON SENSE?

Much of what we have said so far in this chapter is based on an understanding that philosophy and common sense are sometimes at odds with each other – sometimes, but not always. It is well known that many philosophers not only believed in common sense but also that the world should be organised by this principle. The Scottish school of common sense philosophers is well known and in some respects paved the way for the utilitarians that we will meet in the next chapter.

Thomas Reid (1710–1796) was one of them. He claimed that there was nothing wrong with the common sense of human beings. More particularly, against idealists such as Berkeley and Hume who argued that all human understanding is entrapped in a world of ideas and impressions, he maintained that we see the world as it is and that there is no use in raising doubts against this. A really existing subject (a 'me', a 'you' . . .) sees a really existing object (this chair, this tree . . .). This is perhaps what most managers or business people, when asked, would claim is the case as well. Reid provides them with a philosophical justification (which is not to say that they need one in their day-to-day affairs). While it is perhaps true, Reid insists, that the existence of the subject and the object cannot be proven, we nevertheless know that they exist. They are, so to speak, 'ultimate facts' or, perhaps better, our consciousness of them is an ultimate fact that is not itself in need of proof but rather the foundation of all proof. Knowledge and argument should be based on such self-evident facts.

Now, this may well work in the world of business. We are not sure. But most philosophers are not inclined to take common sense seriously. In his *Critique of the Power of Judgement* (1790), Immanuel Kant, a German philosopher whose ideas we will discuss in Chapter 4, argues that common sense is merely a subjective principle that is based on feeling rather than on objective knowledge, even though it claims universal validity. For Kant, reason that is based on common sense can only be vulgar and unsophisticated. It is an undisciplined form of thinking that is based on the 'free play' of reason and imagination. Based on this free play, common sense claims to know for all of us what is good, useful, beautiful, reasonable, and so on. Yet, it only provides us with a motley of appearances and ideas rather than with any sustained knowledge of these subjects.

A more recent and even more devastating critique of common sense has been provided by Gilles Deleuze, a French philosopher. In his *Difference and Repetition* (1968), Deleuze claims that even philosophy itself, in spite of Kant's efforts, is still by no means safe from common sense. Some entrenched common sense understandings that are widely accepted among philosophers are:

1   By nature, all human beings strive for knowledge.
2   Common sense is what we all share.
3   Thought is by nature good as it is always directed towards the truth.
4   The truth of a problem can only be found if we solve it.

5 Error is alien to thought in the sense that it must have been caused by something
   outside it.

Deleuze maintains that these are common sense assumptions that are still active in
most modern philosophy. As such, they are un-philosophical or pre-philosophical. This
is why philosophers should devote some time to get rid of common sense assumptions
in their own work. This is exactly what Deleuze tried to do through his entire career.
He questioned, for example, the idea that thought itself is good or that stupidity or error
betrays lack or incompleteness of thought. The philosopher as a philosopher cannot
believe beforehand that thought is really about avoiding error and that it is therefore
good. This assumes, after all, that we already know what thought is: a kind of radio or
television quiz where the brain is the quizmaster who sees to it that no errors will slip
through undetected (see Deleuze, 1968: 150). But is it? Is thought only a matter of telling
right from wrong? Is it really only a matter of division? Deleuze uses his thought to think
against thought itself. He constantly wonders whether stupidity or error are not essential
aspects of thought, rather than its denial.

Such subversion of commonsensical and therefore well-accepted understandings is
what we have in mind in this book as well. Business ethics clearly is *about* the good, but
is this to say that it *is* good? Do we really think that, when business leaders show that they
have moral worries, this will improve the moral performance of their organisation?
Should we really take for granted that notions such as 'corporate responsibility',
'organisational citizenship' or 'codes of conduct', to mention just a few, will bring the
good? And why would we accept that people in business would value the good? Indeed,
do we actually want to be good if we work for a business organisation? Just in the way
that Deleuze uses thought against itself, we may use business ethics against itself. One
of the points that is rarely made in business ethics but that we will insist upon throughout
these pages is that the bad is not excluded by ethics but is rather an inalienable part of it.

WHAT IS PHILOSOPHY?

Not everybody would agree with what we have maintained in the previous section.
Indeed, not even all philosophers would agree with this. As a matter of fact, philosophers
tend to agree on very little. Some say that there is nothing wrong with common sense,
where others think it is stupid and dangerous. But they also disagree about a fundamental
question: should we make a distinction between fact and value? Is there an objective
good or bad in the world? Is being more important than having? Is ethics more important
than religion? The list of debating points is almost endless.

In the widest sense, a philosopher is someone who asks questions that other people
haven't asked, or asks questions about the answers that people think they already know.
Socrates, an ancient Greek philosopher, was keen to stress that philosophers were like
idiots or children. They needed an attitude of naïve disbelief in order to question the sorts
of common sense that prevented people from thinking. Nowadays, many philosophers

have become people who try to decide how different sorts of arguments work, and how they can be compared and judged. Their disbelief in common sense has sometimes resulted in a very formal and analytical kind of philosophy.

Another distinction that is frequently made is the one between matters of fact and matters of value, or 'is' statements and 'ought' statements. In the realm of fact we have a broad set of concerns with truths, the external world, law-like statements, criteria of validity, testability and so on. These are essentially ideas about what sorts of things exist, and what sort of techniques we can use to understand these things. The former area is usually called 'ontology', the latter 'epistemology'.

So, for example, an ontologist might ask whether the 'book' that you hold in your hand right now is one thing, something that contains the essence of book-ness, or if it is a collection of things (pages, ink, glue, a reader, a writer), or even the relationship between those things? When they do ontology, philosophers will generally not be inclined to use devices such as the electron microscope or field glasses to understand the world. Such instruments are quite useless when you ask questions such as: what would the 'openness' to the world of an animal or even a rock be? Now, you may think this is a puzzling, essentially unanswerable question (and some philosophers, have maintained exactly this), but it has been of central concern for famous philosophers such as Plato or, more recently, Martin Heidegger. The point to note is that ontological questions cannot in principle be answered by the use of instruments.

Even if philosophers resort to instruments, then this will only work if they have a good theory of knowledge – an epistemology – which allows them to make reliable claims about the ways in which the world can be known through our senses. So epistemologists might ask, how do you know that there is a book in your hand? Do you believe in everything that you see and feel? The scientific method relies on epistemological assumptions about the world. In constructing a hypothesis, thinking about how to test it, and then deciding whether the test has confirmed or disconfirmed the hypothesis, scientists are using a set of epistemological assumptions about how reliable knowledge can grow. Importantly, these sort of assumptions were considered to be highly radical when they were first put forward, simply because they challenged the common sense of established authorities – that the earth was flat, that the sun rotated around the earth, or that the King's authority came from God.

Both ontology and epistemology are concerned with 'objects' or 'events', that is to say, with what we can say 'is' in the world. But this is really only half of what human beings do, since most of the time we run around thinking more about 'ought' than 'is'. So here we begin to stray into questions about value – morality, politics, beauty, our attitudes towards the world of things and events and towards each other. In the most general of terms, this area is divided into two – aesthetics and ethics. The former is the study of what is beautiful and what is ugly; and the latter (as you already know by now) is the study of what is good and what is bad. So in both of these latter areas, philosophers have been concerned to come up with general rules or descriptions of the sort of things that are beautiful or not (aesthetics) and the sort of things that are good or not (ethics).

Nowadays, most people would agree that you cannot, simply through the force of argument, change someone's aesthetic taste. It is no good rationally explaining to someone that they should not like Beethoven or poetry and should buy some thrash metal or play Scrabble instead. However, that is generally not the case for ethics. If someone puts forward a point of view that we think wrong, or find offensive, then we would be less likely to stop at saying 'well, that's your opinion'. It is almost as if we are prepared to let someone enjoy whatever music they enjoy, but have a tendency to want to change their beliefs about right and wrong. This might be because we consider taste to be less important than morality, or it might be that we really do think that matters of right and wrong rather than beauty and ugliness are amenable to rational and persuasive argument. Which, perhaps, is why we might then turn to moral philosophers for guidance on what sorts of arguments are likely to be persuasive when we attempt to answer these sort of questions: 'What should we do?' 'Why should we do it?' 'What rights, duties or obligations do I, and others, have?' 'Do ends justify means?'

So, that seems tidy enough then. Or is it? There might be some facts that are not values (eggs come from chickens), and some values that are not based on facts (I like eggs), but most ethical issues are actually a combination of both. In order to answer the question 'should we factory farm chickens?', we need to both know some facts about chickens, farming and factories, and then have an opinion about those facts. Do chickens suffer, or don't they? Are big supermarkets damaging animal welfare by pushing down prices to farmers? What is a fair profit for a farmer? So perhaps the answer is simply to collect all the facts, and then make a judgement. But is it possible to collect *all* the facts? You cannot, after all, talk to the chickens.

In practice then, our values inform how we collect facts, and the facts that we deem to be important affect our values. Hence, facts are made. Everybody seems to select their own facts when it comes to ethical debate. This is certainly what makes things difficult, but it is important not to avoid such problems. In part, this is because it would be easy to fall into the trap of believing that ethics was a simple matter. It might be possible to think that 'solving' ethics simply involves finding the right equation and then applying it. This might be comforting, but even philosophers aren't that clever. So if we accept that facts and values are often hard to disentangle, we can start to see that ethics is perhaps better thought of as part of the messy business of human life, not something which can be abstracted from it, sorted out and then given back to human beings as a set of instructions.

This raises the possibility that ethics isn't a question of philosophers telling people what to do, but is also the study of what people actually do. Along these lines a distinction is often made between descriptive and prescriptive ethics. The former is primarily concerned with describing the strategies that people use to reach ethical decisions. As we have already noted, if you watch a soap opera it is easy to begin noticing the way that the characters talk about each other and themselves. They classify certain behaviours as right, others as wrong. In order to do this they accept certain kinds of evidence as fact, and make certain assumptions about motivation and intention. Most crucially, they define

COMMON SENSE BUSINESS ETHICS

right and wrong through the application of certain (fairly) predictable rules. Studying these rules involves doing descriptive ethics. It is like being a sociologist or anthropologist collecting some 'facts' about moral talk and behaviour.

At other times we might be less concerned with the 'facts' of what people do, and more concerned to suggest what they should do. This means attempting to formulate some kind of law, rule or code to guide action. Importantly, the law is not to be based on an arbitrary whim, but somehow rooted in a broadly persuasive set of arguments about human beings and their behaviour. This doesn't mean that a prescriptive ethics must use human beings as the origin of its logic. God, the life force, or the nature of the universe will do just as well. Yet a prescriptive ethics needs to be oriented to human actions, and needs to contain formulations that persuade people to think and behave in the ways suggested by the theory.

Again, though, don't be fooled into thinking that there are clear dividing lines between description and prescription, any more than there are between facts and values. If you think about it, this is simply because any prescription, any value, must originate in a certain sort of description, or set of facts. Think back to earlier in this chapter. When someone claims that human beings are, by nature, selfish, they are making a claim about facts. They are asserting something about the fundamental nature of humanity. They might well then use this assertion in order to go on and claim that individual selfishness and greed is good, because it leads to efficient markets and organisations. So, in this argument, the facts help to support a particular value. But what if we disagree with this person? What can we say to them? Well, following the rough distinction between facts and values, we might ask them two rather different things. One is 'how do you know that human beings are selfish?' The second is, 'why do you think that selfishness is good?' One question asks them for evidence, the other asks them for argument. The point here is that it is difficult to keep prescription and description separate. It might be a good idea to keep 'is' and 'ought' separate, but it rarely happens, which is itself a demonstration of the point.

CONCLUSION

In this chapter we have tried to introduce some major themes in business ethics, and to provide an idea of how and why we proposed to rethink business ethics in this book. We have invited you to challenge some commonsensical understandings of business, ethics and business ethics. Our point is not that these understandings are stupid or plain wrong, but rather that ethics always implies further thought. It is a task that one can never bring to an end.

Later, we discussed the limitations of common sense, but also the limitations of philosophy. In doing this, we have tried to show how ethics belongs to and differs from other philosophical and non-philosophical disciplines. And we have done this in a fairly critical fashion. But at this point you may ask: 'Who are we to do this?' 'Do we know so much better than other people?' 'Why do we need all this critique?' 'Should ethics be critical at all?'

These questions are complicated. Criticism, especially academic criticism, always seems to be quite arrogant and controversial. The shadow of the ivory tower is always long. Yet, the point of this book is to bring into the open what often lies hidden in the world of business ethics. We wanted to show you what seems to be assumed in much of business, ethics and business ethics. More particularly, we wanted to emphasise the importance of thought. Because, if people do not examine their prejudices and convictions, then how can they really be said to be thinking hard about something? How can they claim to be doing something new and worthwhile, rather than just repeating things that they have been told? It seems to us that much of business ethics clings to assumptions about human nature, organisations, markets and ethics. And further, it might be that these assumptions are highly political, in the sense that they tend to benefit the sorts of people that have already done rather well under present arrangements. In the next three chapters we will deal with three sorts of thinking that were new for their times. All were attempts to bring some order to common sense, to philosophise and to hope that the world might then be different.

Chapter 3

'Business ethics' I: consequences

INTRODUCTION

Children are clumsy. They throw cushions and smash vases, they spill tomato sauce onto carpets. Sometimes, their outraged parents accuse them of being careless and having no thought for others. Then, they will (red faced and defensive) turn to their parents and say 'but I didn't *mean* to do it!' And the parent will (wisely and calmly) respond, 'Ah, but you didn't think about what was likely to happen.' And then the parent and child, each knowing that they are right, will carry on being outraged and upset until they are eventually distracted by something on television and later become friends again.

This is moral philosophy at work. It might not look like it, because you might expect that philosophy would be something 'harder', something expressed in complex language and involving intricate arguments. Well, that can be true as well, but the basics of one of the defining controversies of the last two centuries of moral philosophy are pretty much captured in this familiar exchange. Are we good because of what we *intend* to do, or because of what happened as a *consequence* of what we did? This chapter will consider moral philosophers who have argued that we are good because of the good effects of our actions. The next chapter considers those who argue that we are good because of our intentions. We are doing it this way round because the majority of arguments in business ethics are about consequences, not about intentions. What has been referred to as 'consequentialism' is perhaps *the* moral philosophy of capitalist business as such. More precisely, a specific version of consequentialism underlies capitalism. This version is known as utilitarianism. Actions are good when they prove to have utility, that is to say, when they increase the total sum of happiness in a given society. This seems to be pretty obvious, but is it? Is happiness all that counts in capitalist business? Should everyone be happy in and with this world? And what precisely is entailed by strange notions such as 'the total sum of happiness'? In what sense is the child described in the opening lines of this chapter considered to be detracting from the total sum of happiness in the world? What would a parent possibly mean by that?

UTILITARIANISM

Let us start with what some people make of human beings. For example, the statement:

> Nature has placed mankind under the governance of two sovereign masters, *pain* and *pleasure*.

This seems to be a fairly straightforward thing to say about people. It doesn't involve making claims about God, doesn't use a vague word like 'justice', or make a generalisation that couldn't be supported such as 'all people are selfish'. At face value, all that it suggests is that people feel pain and pleasure. Indeed, expressions such as 'governance' and 'sovereign masters' suggest that this is somehow unavoidable.

In fact, this is the opening sentence of Jeremy Bentham's book, *An Introduction to the Principles of Morals and Legislation*, first published in 1789. What Bentham was doing in this book, and many of his other works, was attempting to discover a rational foundation for law, and public affairs generally. Bentham was endlessly outraged that the governors of eighteenth century England were more concerned with lining their pockets and protecting their ancient privileges than with serving something that we would now call the public good. Bentham's ideas and arguments suggest that there is a more reasonable way of organising things. At the heart of his philosophy is a desire to replace tradition by reason. Reasonable people, Bentham believes, are interested in facts. This is why he begins his book with what seems to be a hard fact: people like pleasure and dislike pain.

In the sentences that follow this quote, he proposes a moral lesson to be drawn from this fact:

> Nature has placed mankind under the governance of two sovereign masters, *pain* and *pleasure*. It is for them alone to point out what we ought to do, as well as to determine what we shall do. On the one hand the standard of right and wrong, on the other the chain of causes and effects, are fastened to their throne.
>
> (Bentham, 1789: 87)

Since people are governed by pain and pleasure, a rational ethics would attempt to maximise pleasure and minimise pain. This seems like an eminently logical proposition, and indeed it is. At a stroke, it reduces ethics to a choice between happiness and unhappiness. In Bentham's thought, there is an ongoing concern with transparency: ethics should be formulated in such a way as to make decision making on ethical and legal issues a fairly straightforward rather than mind-boggling business. Bentham is not a thinker of what some contemporary philosophers refer to as 'undecidability'. He felt attracted by the easiness and plausibility of Francis Hutcheson's famous formulation, written down in 1725, of the goal of all ethics: 'That action is best which procures the greatest happiness for the greatest number' (Hutcheson, 1725: 125).

What else could ethics be about? It is, as even a contemporary philosopher like Warnock (1971: 27) has claimed, 'the simplest of all suggestions'. Hutcheson, who lived from 1694 to 1747 and taught at the University of Glasgow, is credited as the person who was the first to make this suggestion. He was, with David Hume, one of the precursors of utilitarianism and a teacher of Adam Smith, who, as we will see below, already had his reservations about his teacher's apparently simple and obvious formula. Utilitarianism, as put forward in the writings of Bentham and his followers, did not share Smith's reservations. It is defined as an ethics which aims for maximum 'utility'. In other words, like jam, you should spread happiness around as much as possible.

The addition 'as much as possible' is particularly important here: there is no illusion whatsoever that the jam can be equally spread over all parts or individuals in a given society. Bentham believed in the formula of maximum utility because he thinks that it encapsulates a useful answer to questions such as: What kind of conduct is morally optimal when we are facing different courses of action all of which will affect people in more or less positive ways? Now, this is a very serious question – but is it a question that we would still want to ask when it comes to business? Do we still believe in the possibility of a moral optimum with respect to business? Bentham clearly did, but we suggest that you can only agree with him if you are willing to assume that happiness, being the obvious goal of all ethics, can be divided into chunks that can be added to each other. That is to say, you can only believe this when you are willing to reduce happiness to something that is quantitative and something about which one can calculate. This is what became known as Bentham's 'felicific calculus'. Pleasures and pains should not be considered in terms of quality or intensity. Such things are, presumably, far too complex for people who should make decisions. In other words, for Bentham, the decision-making process can only be enhanced if one brings pleasures and pains together under a unified language of numbers.

In utilitarianism, there is no question of concentrating on utility only amongst a few people. The aim, after all, is to achieve 'the greatest happiness of the greatest number'. However, all this is not to say that *everybody* has the right to get their share of the jam. If policy makers ponder a certain course of action, they should always have in mind what might increase the total sum of happiness and this is obviously not the same as making everybody happy. Happiness is a technical goal rather than a fundamental right. This implies that the utilitarian policy maker would opt for actions that might be at the expense of a few while benefiting the most. And it is at this point that somebody like Adam Smith would have raised doubts about Bentham's moral technology, for he claims that our concern for the individual should not be sacrificed on the altar of maximum utility (Smith, 1759: 129–130).

It is interesting to look at how utilitarian thought has influenced historical practice. The pursuit of happiness is an inalienable right in the American Declaration of Independence, but it is well known that it is nowhere in the American Constitution and that it has therefore no legal basis. As Kingwell (1998: 210–212) has shown, this has caused lots of trouble with the regulation of markets and businesses in the United States.

Over and over again, jurists have tried to find a possible legal protection of individual rights in the law, but that has proved to be far from easy. Utilitarian-minded judges have often tried to keep the idea of a right to happiness at bay – especially when it served the interests of business. Kingwell refers in particular to the so-called Louisiana Slaughterhouse Cases of 1869, 1872 and 1883. The problem here was about the Butchers' Union Live-Stock Landing and Slaughterhouse Company which, in an effort to achieve monopoly in the business of slaughtering, sued everybody in Louisiana who independently planned to start his or her own company, thus trying to achieve a monopoly in the business of slaughtering. In 1872, the company lost their case, because the judges considered the individual right to freely follow a chosen profession an inalienable part of the right to happiness. The Butchers' monopoly was therefore considered illegal.

Eleven years later, however, this decision was overturned for reasons that are, we suggest, profoundly 'utilitarian'. The judges now claimed that when it is the inalienable right of an individual to freely choose an occupation of his or her liking, then it is also an inalienable right of a business owner to own a corporate body. This right, however, is obviously violated when nobody wants to work in that corporate body. It undermines, so to speak, the right to pursue happiness. This insight allowed the judges to cross off both rival claims to pursue happiness and hence to look at what might be most useful to the state of Louisiana. Of course, they judged that individual butchers had either to work for the Butcher monopoly or to look for a job somewhere else. This not only shows that the right to pursue happiness has no clear-cut expression in US law, even though it is often used as a kind of polemical effect, but also that the fundamental problem of bringing happiness into law is that my happiness might not be in accord with your happiness. This latter problem may especially occur when we are talking about business. Since Bentham we have, as Kingwell (1998: 212) wryly remarks, an 'industry of happiness' that allows us to reduce ethics to a technical matter – something which consultancies and management gurus are only too keen to acknowledge. Yet, at the same time as there are many conflicting kinds of happiness in the world of business, the right to pursue individual happiness is somehow a category that evades the imperatives of industry, of law, perhaps even of capitalist society as such.

So then, Hutcheson's formula is not so clear or simple as he or Bentham might have liked. It might not even be so practical, as is shown in this example. But before engaging with Hutcheson's idea in more detail, it should be noted that his suggestion is a radical one insofar as it suggests that everybody's interests must be taken into consideration. Given that Bentham was writing at a time when laws were being passed to benefit wealthy landowners and self-serving functionaries, this was a dangerous and democratic idea – one that threatened the interests of a few in order to benefit the many.

Bentham appears to have believed that a 'moral science' (1789: 88) might be possible, and that it would be based on values firmly grounded in facts, and that it would indeed solve public problems. It was a question of replacing hierarchical tradition with reasonable logic and it is, as we have noted, primarily concerned with consequences, not intentions.

29

In part, this is because Bentham's version of utilitarianism was really a guide to policy, to what should be done in order to maximise public benefit. If this meant that people played 'push-pin' (an old nursery or brothel game) rather than reading poetry, then so be it (cited in Mill, 1869a: 123). If it meant that money was spread more evenly, then so be it. A good governor will be someone whose business has good consequences. We don't need to be too worried about whether they come from the right family, or have tastes that do not suit someone from their class.

These are radical ideas because they are concerned with **the future**, rather than the past. This is why utilitarianism is sometimes called an ethics of consequences, which is because of its orientation to the ends of action rather than to the intentions of the actors or the means that they use. In other words, the good business owner might well upset some people in achieving their ends, and may make enemies, but this is less important than their actions being justifiable according to the greatest happiness of the greatest number. In fact, this entails that society – or what Bentham himself refers to as 'the community' – is conceived as a 'fictitious body', the limbs of which are individual persons (Bentham, 1789: 88). The happiness of this community can also be divided into singular 'parts of happiness', that is to say, the happiness of each individual. So, the community is understood as a sum of persons that each bring in their own 'piece' of happiness. In Chapter 5, we will see alternatives to this conception of community. Yet, it is important to see that it operates on its own principle of justice: everybody to count for one, nobody to count for more than one. That is, your and my happiness are to be counted as equal in the addition of the total sum of happiness. Each policy maker should take this into account, but once again it should be stressed that this is not the same as granting all individuals the right to happiness.

For Bentham, maximising utility is a calculating exercise that is all part of the planning of society, and he was active in a wide variety of public policy projects. He drew up plans for new architecture for prisons, reforms of the legal system, new principles for education, and so on. He died in 1832 and, in a typically anti-sentimental gesture, he donated his body to a school of anatomy – being the first person ever to do so. One can now see his skeleton in the foyer of the Administration Building of the University of London.

REFINING UTILITARIANISM

The other key figure in the development of utilitarianism was John Stuart Mill. Born in 1806 and a child prodigy, he received an education that was partly planned by Bentham, a friend of Mill's father. According to Mill's autobiography of 1873 (the year of his death), he was taught Greek at the age of three, Latin and mathematics at eight, logic at twelve and political economy at thirteen. Until he was fourteen he saw no one of his own age. He spent most of his life working as an administrator for the East India Company, an arm of the British Empire that effectively governed India. What John Stuart

Mill did was to apply Bentham's principles of social justice to individual action. If Bentham was a blunt radical, then Mill was both more refined and more elitist. He expressed suspicion of what we might now call the 'dumbing down' rule of the majority, and consequently attempted to rank pleasures according to their importance. He was not prepared to agree that the pleasure of the pig is the same as the pleasure of the philosopher. In one sense, he modified and humanised some of Bentham's rather unbending principles, but in another he actually pushed Bentham's radicalism in a more conservative direction. His most important work in this regard was his book *Utilitarianism*, first published in 1861. Like Bentham he was also a man of action: a member of parliament and active in various reform movements, including writing a book with his wife, Harriet Taylor, entitled *The Subjection of Women*, which developed radical ideas about gender equality from utilitarian principles (Mill, 1869b).

Utilitarianism is undoubtedly a central form of thinking for any large-scale form of administration, and is one of the key features of twentieth century business. With a strange twist, in order to maximise pleasure or happiness it is necessary to coolly calculate the likely consequences of different actions, and not be carried away with what Bentham called 'metaphor and declamation' (1789: 88). The decision maker, the administrator, the manager must be strategic in the analysis of pleasure. Carrying out the procedure is the key point here – weighing the good (pleasure) and the bad (pain) that may result from a given action and then deciding on that basis. Like the figure of the law who holds the scales of justice, the utilitarian business manager must adjudicate as to whether the pile of good is bigger than the pile of bad. And remember that if Justice is blind, it does not matter whether she likes her conclusions, she is still bound by the process. Utilitarianism is therefore a highly rationalistic project, one that can be carried out on a case-by-case basis by reasonable people who are capable of setting self-interest aside in order to assess the greater good. This doesn't mean that self-interest and the greater good may not happen to be the same – after all, the decision maker is also one of those people who would prefer pleasure to pain – but such a coincidence is not essential.

Two forms of utilitarianism are usually distinguished – 'rule' and 'act' – with Mill generally associated with *rule utilitarianism* and Bentham with *act utilitarianism*. Rule utilitarianism places a premium on adhering to certain rules which increase utility. This would effectively involve adhering to certain guides to behaviour because they can be argued to normally lead to the greatest good of the greatest number. Such rules might be 'don't lie', 'keep promises', 'avoid hurting people' or similar injunctions. They would be selected because they were likely, if followed, to create a world in which there was more pleasure and less pain. The 'purer' form of utilitarianism is act utilitarianism. It is important to note that the two can easily produce entirely different imperatives. Compare act and rule utilitarian defences of two maxim: 'Don't ever lie' (in the former example) versus 'lying is sometimes justifiable' (in the case of telling children who it is that fills their Christmas stockings). Act utilitarianism places no emphasis on generalised rule following and instead insists on judging every situation as it arises. So act utilitarianism provides a kind of contingent 'golden rule' – a rule that is designed to be adapted to circumstances.

If we consider this form of utilitarianism it becomes possible to appreciate the radical potential of these ideas. Mill was keen to suggest that Bentham's thought was 'subversive' and 'critical' because it involved 'an assault on ancient institutions' (1869a: 80–81). Rather than accepting what Mill described as 'modern corruption grafted onto ancient barbarism', any given choice should be assessed for its likely consequences for producing pain or pleasure understood in the most general of terms. This will prevent mindless rule-following, it will ensure each situation is given specific attention and, importantly, it will allow us to accept that ends do justify means on many occasions.

This last point is absolutely crucial to the business manager. Anyone who is making decisions about large numbers of other people will need to be able to 'take the long view' – not to get bogged down in the detail of immediate claims and counter-claims. Indeed, it is difficult to see how managerial jobs could be justified at all if it were not for some form of act utilitarian argument. The only alternatives would seem to be an unapologetic autocracy of the sort that Bentham was criticising, or an entirely procedural bureaucracy in which people follow rules with no regard to their results. It is hardly surprising then that utilitarian arguments still resonate so strongly several hundred years after they were first put forward.

The adult who accused the child of not thinking about consequences was expressing a utilitarian ethic. So is the manager who closes one factory in order to safeguard another two. Or the teacher who refuses to accept a late essay, because of the example it would set for others. All of us sometimes reason that ethics is about consequences. 'I did it because I thought that X would happen.' Further, we can often use utilitarianism to explain why we sometimes have to do things that some other people think are wrong. This is important, because when it happens, it is often important for people to give an account of themselves as being ethical. Consequentialist ethics allows them to do just that. It allows someone to claim that they were serving a higher good or specific plan, and that particular ends justify these particular means. This is obviously an important thing to do, because if we did not do it we would spend a lot of time feeling guilty.

Utilitarianism is also an ethics of planning. This is a particularly useful and intelligent way of thinking, because how rational would we be if we never thought about con- sequences? Can you imagine any sort of reason which was not based on a calculation about means and ends? Bentham and his followers have clearly captured something massively important about ethical reasoning, particularly for anyone who lives in an organised society and makes decisions. Exactly the sort of person that business ethics is aimed at, you might think. Which raises the issue of how utilitarian ethics, at the same time as being potentially progressive, can also be quite dangerous.

THE UTILITY OF UTILITARIANISM

'The greatest good of the greatest number.' What could be more attractive for anybody who takes an interest in ethics? What else could ethics be about? Indeed, what would be more commonsensical? Yet, most philosophers have been sceptical about the utility of utilitarianism. Some of them even developed a downright condescending attitude towards it. Marx is a telling example. In a footnote in *Capital*, he writes:

> The principle of utility was no discovery made by Bentham. He simply reproduced in his dull way what Helvétius and other Frenchmen had said with wit and inge-nuity in the eighteenth century. To know what is useful for a dog, one must investigate the nature of dogs. This nature is not itself deducible from the principle of utility. Applying this to men, when one would judge all human acts, movements, relations, etc. according to the principle of utility, it would all be about human nature in general, and then about human nature as historically modified in each epoch. Bentham does not trouble himself with this. He assumes, with a most naïve dryness, that the modern narrow-minded bourgeois, more particularly, the English bourgeois, is the normal human being. . . . If I had the courage of my friend Heinrich Heine, I should call Mr Jeremy a genius in the way of bourgeois stupidity.
>
> (Marx, 1867: 758–759)

One way of describing this objection is to say that the word 'good' used by utilitarians reflects a normative prescription, not just a description. Bentham makes a lot of assump-tions about the good, and Marx asks why would we share them. Why would we share assumptions about the good that are only the assumptions of a certain privileged class from a rainy island to the west of mainland Europe? In other words, utilitarian philosophers assume that it is quite clear what the good is, but is it? It is for this kind of reason that **Nietzsche** (1889: 78) parodies Mill for his 'offensive clarity'.

Assumptions about the good are always problematical. If, for example, good is individual pleasure, as opposed to something like generalised pleasure, or duty or the values that hold in a particular society, then straightforward hedonism would be legitimated as 'morally' superior to pain. My desire for fast cars, cheeseburgers, casual sex, tequila, cigars and recreational drugs would all be perfectly acceptable within the ethical calculus. Presumably, however, there would be some point in arguing that it would be good for me to be prevented from harming my body through abusing these various acts and substances – despite the short-term pleasure they give me. Well perhaps, but what if I really *do* want a big fat cigar, and am perfectly happy to acknowledge that it will shorten my life by five minutes? Would the utilitarian deny me that pleasure? Or might I have a cheeseburger now as long as I promise to go for a run later? Here, we move from simple personal hedonism to some idea about collective good, in which case the fact that other tax payers might be picking up my hospital bills needs to be fed into the equation. It would appear that my immediate wishes for pleasure might be ignored, or considered less important, in favour of some longer time frame, and/or wider conception of the stakeholders involved in my pleasures and pains.

However, it would also be perfectly possible to say that my desires could be made into a list of preferences – a hierarchy of needs – in which food came higher than drugs. This is pretty much what Mill suggested must be the case, in order that 'higher' needs could be distinguished from 'lower' ones. Otherwise, being a happy pig would be better than being an unhappy Socrates, and being a drunk student would be better than being one reading a book like this. Mill, in other words, was not prepared to accept that, as Bentham put it, 'quantity of pleasure being equal, push-pin is as good as poetry' (in Mill, 1869a: 123). The ethical thing to do would be for the decision maker to try to optimise as many of my preferences as possible, but also to order them in some way.

Yet this assumes that I am aware of (and can articulate) all of my preferences – that they are transparent to me – and that I am capable of choosing between them, or am prepared to let someone else choose for me. In very prosaic terms, it might be good for me to go to the dentist, or eat less, or stop smoking, but I am unlikely to volunteer these as preferences high on the list, or perhaps even recognise them at all. This is not to mention preferences that might be strongly felt by me but distasteful to others: racism, fox hunting or whatever. So if the definition of 'good' is not contained within utilitarianism, then where does it come from? The only answer, it seems, must be that it is what is 'good' for whoever judges. So if the judge likes cigars and push-pin too, they will be less likely to define them as 'bad' and more likely to construct arguments that define them as pleasurable, which, in turn, would render them more or less morally acceptable. Hence, 'the greatest good' might be better rephrased as:

> The greatest good, taking into account reasonable personal preferences, based on commonly accepted time horizons, and judged by someone with the maximum degree of impartiality.

WEIGHING THE GOOD

However, unwarranted assumptions about the good are by no means the only problems with respect to utilitarianism. Another problem relates to the comparability and measurability of pleasures and pains. How can we compare, and then add up all these pleasures and pains? Suppose that we are able to establish what 'the greatest good' is, something which is highly questionable, what are we to make of the 'greatest number'? Is that not simple enough? Well, perhaps the problem could be solved with an appeal to the biggest number of happy people. Does this mean that we can say that two happy people are somehow more important than one unhappy one? That might be fine if you were one of the happy ones, but we doubt whether you would be so satisfied with this sort of ethical reasoning if you were the unhappy one. But what if a person is only slightly unhappy and another person very happy?

The problem here is one of weighing. Pleasures and pains, goods and bads do not come in neat comparable lumps. After all, it is difficult to see how the desire for a light snack can be compared with, or contrasted to, the desire to avoid death or torture. The felicific calculus proposed by the utilitarians contains a major problem. Most forms of calculation involve units of number which can be regarded as equivalent. One is the same as another one. On this basis, units can be added together, subtracted and compared. In some cases, this is clearly relevant to utilitarianism. If more people vote for one particular candidate than another one, then simple counting gives us a democratic decision. However, pleasure or good does not normally come in units. My pleasure or pain is singular, which is to say that it is mine and unique to me, but not a unit. If my leg hurts, who is to say that this pain is the same as the pain in your leg? The utilitarian decision maker, such as a health service manager, might, in any concrete situation, have to decide which one of us should get the operation that cures the pain, but they can only ever have our accounts of our separate pain to inform their decision. So perhaps they will listen to the one of us who is most persuasive, or give the operation to the one who has longest to live, or the most children, or the best genes. As you can see, we are immediately bringing criteria into our decision that require all sorts of judgements that seem to have little to do with the original utilitarian formulation. What if my pain was caused by overindulging in recreational drugs when I was a student, whilst the other person's pain was caused by rescuing a kitten from a tree?

But anyway, even if dubious judgements about the good can be compared to other dubious judgements, then what importance do we give to the raw numbers in our equation? Often it is the case that many people want to do something that many other people see as morally undesirable: selling guns, sacking people, polluting the environment, for example. When confronted with a crowd baying for an arrest after a horrible crime, we might begin to wonder whether the crowd is always in the right. So perhaps there might be circumstances when we might well need to defend 'minorities' against what Mill called the 'tyranny of the majority'. Indeed, for Mill, there was a danger that Bentham's adherence to the dominant opinion would actually lead to social stagnation since there would be no 'organised opposition to the ruling power' (1869a: 116). In order to defend individuals against majority rule from within a utilitarian line of argument, then we would need to put forward some sort of rule utilitarianism in which 'fair treatment for all' became a higher good than 'majority rule'. In which case, we must surely have a rule to decide when the big numbers count, and when they can be discounted in favour of political correctness. Fair treatment for homosexuals, but not for drink driving offenders, or people who torture kittens? Perhaps we would be better saying:

The greatest good of the greatest number, subject to the protection of the socially accepted rights of legitimate minorities.

POLITICAL ARITHMETIC

What Bentham and, to a lesser extent, Mill were really up to is what one of their precursors, William Petty (1623–1687) described as 'political arithmetic'. Petty was the man who paved the way for the typically Victorian obsession with numbers. The idea behind his political arithmetic was profoundly Pythagorean: the entire world, and especially the social world, could be reduced to and expressed in terms of numbers. Petty believed that the social and political problems of his time could only be solved if one was able to replace the inevitable human factors (passion, belief, hatred, and so on) by non-human factors (numbers, amounts, and so on). He anticipated that the context in which problems occurred could be appeased considerably. The often intran-sigent parties involved would finally be able to meet on a terrain where they could speak the same language. For Petty, this terrain was profoundly linked up with money. All human behaviours represent a value and this value could be expressed in terms of money. This mentality has been satirised in an unforgettable way by Charles Dickens in his novel *Hard Times* (1854).

It is tempting to link Bentham's quantitative understanding of pleasure to Petty's plutocracy: in both cases, the intellectual fundament of all human action, including moral action, becomes addition and subtraction. Henceforth, addition is in the mind of the politician, the business owner, the manager, the consumer, and so on, and they all know that the good life is a life that can be achieved by doing some solid piece of calculation. Moreover, as Michael Power (1998: 17) has pointed out, a world that is reduced to numbers or an amount of money is a world in which it is difficult to cheat each other. Petty and Bentham were guided by the idea that morality in human affairs could be enhanced by their political arithmetic. Nowadays, and in the face of the endless list of financial scandals that we are rapidly growing to accept as normal, this might strike you as a ludicrous idea, but they seriously believed in it.

Our earlier claim that a certain version of utilitarianism lies at the heart of capitalism now becomes particularly clear. Experts who know what addition and counting is all about – accountants, financial managers, and so on – hold fabulous positions in and around business enterprises and other organisations. Their calculating view of anything that is going on in the organisation is privileged. Their understanding of the truth with respect to the organisation is clearly more important than that of the human resource director or the average employee. Their position, however, is increasingly under pressure. If financial scandals such as Enron or Parmalat have showed one thing clearly, then it is that the accountancy function is entangled in paradoxes. On the one hand, there is this appearance of simplicity of which Petty and Bentham stressed the moral value; on the other hand, privileged positions cannot be maintained by simplicity alone. Perhaps this explains why the accountants have always been allured by magic and mystery. This was something that could not have been anticipated by Petty, Bentham and Mill, but it proffers us perhaps one explanation for the complications that these companies have run into. The world of transparency envisaged by Petty and

Bentham has deteriorated into a misty world that 'breeds confusion, illusion, and delusion' (Warburton, 2000: 7).

THE PROBLEM OF INFORMATION

So far, we have established that utilitarianism has a problem with establishing what the good is and also with weighing pleasures and pains. But there is another problem as well: how do we get the information on which to base our decisions? If the utilitarian decision machine is fed bad information, then surely it will produce bad decisions; so the quality of data is decisive if the equation is actually going to produce the greatest good. Ideally, then, we need complete knowledge of any given situation, or at least knowledge which is as good as we can discover at any given time. However, a moment's thought indicates how difficult this is. It is improbable (to say the least) that we would be able to gather together all the individuals (or stakeholders) who may be affected by a decision, get the required information from them, and then come to an accurate judgement of the consequences of each different action. Unless, of course, the decision was a very straightforward one involving very few factors. Think of a chess game, which involves two players, a few pieces and clearly agreed rules. In such a case, most people can use their reason to think about the consequences of action, and a few people are extra-ordinarily good at it. Now imagine the chess game had thousands of different pieces, all of whom were also players, a board that had areas that you could not see, and sets of different rules that applied at different times. How good do you think your predictions would be then?

And, to make matters worse, the utilitarian game is not just about you winning and others losing, it is an attempt to generate collective benefit – which takes us to another information problem. If, following the arguments above, we find it difficult to define the good for ourselves, then why should we assume that others will find it any easier? It is difficult to see how we are going to get reliable information concerning what is good for others if they are not really sure themselves. Do they want higher taxes in order to pay for their children to read books like this? Do they want fast roads that kill little hedgehogs? Do they want low-priced clothing or an end to sweatshops? Put another way, the relation between individual and collective goods is not as straightforward as utilitarians might have us believe. People do not always know what they want, or how to get it, or what the consequences of getting it might be. In fact, the only way in which a decision maker could gather reliable information on what people wanted would be if all those people had good information too. This might be a nice idea, a model of a society in which every-one knew everything, but it is hardly a realistic picture of what human beings are like.

Furthermore, to do the utility calculus correctly we also need to be able to predict the future. Even if decision makers and their subjects had good information about people and things at the present moment, they need to be able to make reliable inferences about what will happen if I do X rather than Y. Perhaps the easiest way to demonstrate this is through some hypothetical time travelling. What if an evil psychopath had murdered Mrs Hitler's lovely little boy a century ago? Then, the only way to judge this action would be as an act of calculating evil. Now, we might decide that such an action could have helped to save millions of lives, and hence had consequences that resulted in the greatest good. So does the moral meaning of an action lie entirely in its consequences? If so, then we are never really in a definitive position to decide whether something is good or bad, because it is always too early to say. We can only judge such things from the current moment, and from our inadequate and partial assumptions about what *might* happen. This seems fair enough most of the time, particularly in simple situations, but (as the stakeholder example above illustrates) most business problems are complex. Like the fabled butterfly that flaps its wings over the Amazon and, by a chaotic chain of causes and effects, causes rain in Stoke-on-Trent, simple situations have a habit of becoming complicated ones. We cannot predict the future, we can only guess. But if our guesses are wrong, does that mean that we are immoral?

CONCLUSION

So, what are we left with after all these criticisms? Do we stick with the elegant and brief 'greatest good of the greatest number', or agree with the less economical but more accurate

> The greatest good (taking into account reasonable personal preferences, based on commonly accepted time horizons, and judged by someone with the maximum degree of impartiality) of the greatest number (subject to the protection of the socially accepted rights of legitimate minorities) based on the information available at the current moment, and reasonable assumptions about what is likely to happen in the future.

Not quite so elegant, but probably a better reflection of what utilitarians might actually do when they apply their philosophy. Mill, who had recognised most of these problems, felt that the point was that utilitarianism was the most logical general framework for morality and law, but that the details would need to be continually modified in a 'progressive' way by working out the 'secondary principles' that follow from the principle of utility (1861: 25). As Mill was well aware, but reluctant to fully acknowledge, utilitarians' attempts to make ethics 'scientific' and 'logical' do not actually get us very far. Utilitarianism has some very substantial advantages for administrators who wish, or need, to justify their decisions but, in effect, can be used to justify almost anything. This is because it is extremely easy to manipulate, consciously or not, the information that goes into the equation in order to get the 'right' answer at the other end. The greatest happiness principle may sound like the most impartial form of reason, but can just as easily play the role of merely disguising self-interest or prejudice. Just as Mill justified and celebrated the role of the East India Company in running India for colonial purposes as 'the government of a semi-barbarous dependency by a civilised country' (1861: 364, 428), so can today's manager justify high pay for corporate executives or the need for **efficiency** savings through sweatshops in China.

Bentham's utilitarianism was designed to be a form of enlightened social engineering which replaced the interests of the fat minority with that of the vast majority. It is, if you like, a sort of morality based on statistics which avoids 'vague generalities' about justice, tradition and God in favour of specific categories and relations. The power of this sort of thinking should not be underestimated but, as Mill said of Bentham's philosophy:

> It can teach the means of organising and regulating the merely *business* part of social arrangements. . . . He committed the mistake of supposing that the business part of human affairs was the whole of them; or at least that the legislator and the moralist had to do with.
>
> (Mill, 1869a: 105)

Mill's extension of these ideas into the sphere of personal morality is more imaginative about the emotional, or non-rational, aspects of human beings and the consequent dangers of relying on mere hedonism. Though he sees the limitations in Bentham, his solution is to suggest that government needs to be carried out by an elite who have the intelligence and taste to avoid pandering to the basest urges of the common people. But despite Mill's acknowledgement of the 'cold, mechanical and ungenial air which characterises the popular idea of the Benthamite' (1869a: 120), his revisions did little to change the reception of many of these notions. By the middle of the nineteenth century, the word 'utilitarian' had come to mean someone uninterested in culture and emotion, and motivated by rather narrow ideas concerning progress. Utilitarians seemed to behave as if they were machines valuing logic over anything else. It is ironic that these people, who set out to capture the 'questioning spirit, the disposition to ask the *why* of everything' (Mill, 1869a: 79), would end up with such a dry and disenchanting understanding of ethics. They wanted people to make decisions for themselves rather than to trust in God, tradition or authority. To this end, they developed an ethics that could be adopted by any reasonable individual.

All the problems we have discussed so far are really methodological ones. They are pointing out some of the ways in which utilitarianism might actually end up being rather difficult to operate, and that its judgements might not be as impartial as they seem. But remember the distinction between fact and value which led utilitarians to claim that human beings were ruled by pleasure and pain, and hence that we should value pleasure. What if this is *not* a very good description of human beings? This is probably the biggest problem of all. And the paradox comes precisely from the sorts of action that demonstrate a few sacrificing themselves for the many. What if I choose death, or at least the risk of death? This is, after all, the best example of an action that is often celebrated, in war memorials for example, as being the exemplar of moral action. But exactly what relation has this got to 'the twin sovereigns' of pain and pleasure? It is possible to argue (after the fact) that more pleasure will be produced for others if I sacrifice myself, but in practice my sacrifice actually proves that people are *not* ruled by the 'twin sovereigns', and can actually choose to ignore them at certain moments. In other words, extreme cases seem to demonstrate that the 'fact' about human beings that utilitarianism claims to be based on might not apply in all cases. If all we did was avoid pain and maximise pleasure, why would we sometimes feel that we had a 'duty' to do something, or that our 'conscience' often encourages us not to take the easy path? In fact, what would society be like if all that people did was to avoid pain and seek pleasure? Would you want to live in that sort of world? Would you want to be that sort of person?

Chapter 4

'Business ethics' II: intentions

INTRODUCTION

At the start of the last chapter we discussed the way that children sometimes defend their actions by insisting that they 'didn't mean to do it'. The logic of that defence seemed to make a certain sense, even if we could see that, regardless of intentions, the consequences of action are sometimes objectionable. This is the kind of situation that is considered important according to an ethics of consequences, the kind of ethics we were discussing in the last chapter.

But consider the opposite case, in which a child *did* mean to do well, but the consequences from a utilitarian point of view were rather disappointing. On their parent's birthday the child prepares a 'special' breakfast, breaks a cup, forgets the butter and spills the tea. The parent smiles indulgently as they bite into burnt toast, and congratulates themselves on bringing up such a splendid child. In such a case, even if the consequences are a disaster, the fact that the child *intended* to do something good far outweighs any cost-benefit analysis of outcomes.

In this chapter we are going to turn to this second type of thinking about ethics, which is concerned with intentions rather than consequences. As you will see, when we turn to intentions, then ethical considerations take on quite a different form. In a way, ethics of intention are going to be much more complex, because we are not looking only at actual behaviours, but at the things that are going on inside the heads of people in ethical situations. So we need to put aside a language of utility and outcomes, and look at what people mean to do, and why they mean to do things. This will lead us to think about the kinds of things that people feel bound to do not out of utility but out of duty. In this chapter we will try to organise our discussion around an explanation of the work of a philosopher who, at the end of the eighteenth century, provided a profound and original understanding of intentions and duties, Immanuel Kant. But before we get to Kant himself, we will discuss the work of a contemporary business ethicist who has made quite a career out of presenting himself as a defender of 'Kantian business ethics'. We think that this latter-day 'Kantian' is responsible for a set of serious misunderstandings of Kant, so we will use this introductory discussion as a way to see what should be avoided when reading a philosopher such as Kant.

To our mind, the single most important contemporary defender of the Kantian perspective in business ethics is the American philosopher, Norman Bowie. He has published a number of articles and a book in which he presents Kant as a philosopher who has much wisdom in store for business ethicists. We cannot but applaud Bowie's initiative. He has been tremendously successful in introducing Kant's thought in areas where one would not expect it. It does not seem likely that one could successfully combine the gaudiness of American business life with the rigour of late eighteenth century Prussian morality.

But perhaps the sort of Kant that pops up in Bowie's text may not be the sort of Kant that would pop up in the minds of those who have cast more than a superficial glance at the writings of this severe philosopher. To give you an idea of this severity, consider this passage from the introduction to his *Critique of the Power of Judgement*, where he claims that domestic and agrarian arts and political economy:

> contain only rules of skill, which are thus only technically practical, for producing an effect that is possible in accordance with natural concepts of causes and effects which, since they belong to theoretical philosophy, are subject to those precepts as mere corollaries of it [of natural science], and thus cannot demand a place in a special philosophy called practical. By contrast, the morally practical precepts, which are grounded entirely on the concept of freedom to the complete exclusion of the determining ground of the will from nature, constitute an entirely special kind of precept: which are also, like the rules that nature obeys, simply called laws, but which do not, like the latter, rest on sensible conditions, but on a supersensible principle, and require a second part of philosophy for themselves alone, alongside the theoretical part, under the name of practical philosophy.
>
> (Kant, 1790: 61)

This kind of writing is, of course, quite hard. To grasp what is being said here, you need to know that for Kant 'practical philosophy' is concerned with values such as freedom, morality and beauty. 'Theoretical philosophy', on the other hand, is concerned with facts and the determinate, law-like relationships pertaining to them. From this it follows that various human activities such as chemistry and economics, to mention a couple that Kant alludes to, are excluded from the domain of morality since they are primarily motivated by an understanding of how things work in the real world. This understanding is, Kant believes, merely a technical matter. For Kant, 'the principles of morally practical reason are essentially different from those of technically practical reason' (Kant, 1790: 320).

Given this distinction, it is very difficult to see how business could be anything else than a technical matter. According to Kant's own criteria, business practices are very likely to be excluded from moral arguments. It seems that those who agree with people like Bowie in wanting to transfer concepts and principles from Kant's philosophy into the domain of business will have an awful lot of explaining to do. They are blending areas of thought that Kant kept quite rigorously apart. Perhaps Kantian ethics has nothing to say to business.

But we do not wish to suggest that a simple distinction between technique and morality should be taken for granted. Our remarks so far are merely intended to cast at least some doubt on the prospect of widespread Kantian practices, and also to draw attention to the difficulties of applying a body of philosophy to contemporary business. Given Kant's own complex terminology, it is rather unlikely that his ideas will be widely adopted. Bowie is aware of this. In an article on the possibilities of Kantian leadership practices, he claims that such practices are not really compatible with the shareholder model of corporate governance that prevails in the United States (Bowie, 2000: 190). In this chapter, our understanding of Bowie's use of Kant is therefore not that Bowie is unrealistic, or simply does not read the philosopher properly, but that, being a business ethicist, Bowie must represent Kant in such a way as to make him accessible to a business ethics audience. The consequence of this is that Bowie's account of Kant's philosophy highlights certain aspects of this philosophy while downplaying or simply ignoring others. Even when he writes, for example, 'I do not believe that Kantian theory is simply the articulation of a set of absolute rules and principles' (1999a: 6, see also 24), these cautions very often disappear in his analyses, or are overwhelmed by different readings of Kant also present in his work. We believe that this slippage and the resulting imbalance in Bowie's work is related to his wish to write for people who take more interest in the 'technical' aspects of Kantian morality than in its more 'practically moral' aspects. Where Kant was always keen to respect the dichotomy between technique and morality, Bowie encourages us to blur the boundaries between them in order to bring 'business' and 'ethics' together.

To put our argument simply: it seems to us that in Kant's major writings on ethics – Groundwork of the Metaphysics of Morals (1785), the Critique of Practical Reason (1788) and the Metaphysics of Morals (1797) – there is much more uncertainty and unrest than Bowie suggests. Indeed, we would suggest that there is no ethics if troubling questions such as these are treated as settled. In the first section of this chapter we give Bowie's rendering of Kant's ideas and argue that it emphasises 'technical' aspects. In the second section, we compare what Bowie has to say with our reading and argue that Kant's philosophy emphasises uncertainty and unrest as hallmarks of morality. In the final section, we try to put the Kantian endeavour in a broader context by arguing that central to his concerns are notions of human limitation and finitude. In doing so, we hope to offer Kant back to business ethicists, but understood very differently than he has been to date.

BOWIE'S VERSION OF KANT

It is perhaps important to point out that Bowie is by no means a marginal figure in the world of business ethics. He has authored or co-authored several bestselling books, he is a frequent contributor to scholarly journals such as *Business Ethics Quarterly* and the *Journal of Business Ethics*, he has links to all the important institutions in the world of business academics (including the London Business School and Harvard University), he is the founder of the Society of Business Ethics and was a director of the American Philosophical Association. He has also worked as a consultant for many well-known companies (e.g. General Motors, 3M and Arthur Andersen). Bowie is clearly a busy man, and throughout this period (1993; 1998; 1999a; 1999b; 2000) he has suggested that Kant means business.

Bowie starts with the observation that according to Kant the highest good is good will. Acting out of good will is equal to acting out of duty. What we have here is a standard deontological rendering of Kant's position on ethics: it is the duty and not the consequences of the act that makes the act good. In the world of business ethics, but also elsewhere, Kant is invariably described as the arch-enemy of utilitarian ethical systems (see Petrick and Quinn, 1997: 49–50; Willmott, 1998: 156). But how accurate is this characterisation? Allen Wood has pointed out that the widespread deontological reading of Kant can perhaps be attributed to a one-sided interest in his *Groundwork of the Metaphysics of Morals*. In his later *Metaphysics of Morals*, Kant is actually very much interested in ends, not in the utilitarian sense, but in ends that are 'derived from a formal principle, which tells us which ends are objectively worth pursuing and hence give rise to a rational desire for them' (Wood, 2002: 13; see also Timmons, 2002; Wood, 1999). Such ends include human dignity and happiness. Kant is therefore not really opposed to an ethics that is oriented to the rational pursuit of ends. Indeed, we will see below that ends are crucial for the kind of rationality he advocates. His point is merely that ethical theories cannot be justified by such ends. So, the standard deontological reading of Kant should at least be qualified. But before we get bogged down in Kantian intricacies too quickly, we should return to Bowie's understanding of Kant.

Deontology is an ethics of duties. Bowie notes, following Kant's *Groundwork of the Metaphysics of Morals*, that there are two kinds of duties: hypothetical imperatives and categorical imperatives. The first sort of imperative is always based on certain specific conditions. They can typically be formulated as 'if/then' statements: 'If you want to become a brilliant philosopher, you will have to study very hard' or 'If you want to have profitable business in the long term, you will have to adopt the concept of corporate social responsibility'. In both examples, your duty depends on what you wish to be the case. Categorical imperatives, on the other hand, are not based on conditions. You simply have to do them unconditionally, without any 'ifs' or 'buts'. Why would this be the case?

Two reasons are provided. First, it is good will, the highest good in the world, which wants you to categorically accept and carry out a particular duty. Second, it is the faculty of reason within you that allows you to recognise the good will within you and to act according to what it dictates. Being a reasonable person, you will want to comply with this duty. This implies that you are able to choose what reason suggests to be good, despite temptations to the contrary. It is this good will that rationally, and freely, accepts a categorical imperative. Bowie offers three formulations of this imperative which he derives from Kant:

1 Act only on maxims that you can will to be universal laws of nature.
2 Always treat the humanity in a person as an end, and never merely as a means.
3 So act as if you were a member of an ideal kingdom in which you were both subject and sovereign at the same time (Bowie, 1999b: 4; cf. Kant, 1785: 57, 79, 83).

Given these three formulations and his definition of the will, it is no surprise that Bowie considers the categorical imperative as a rational test with which you can find out whether your acts are morally permissible. Is, for example, a little white lie permissible if the results are massive profits for everybody in your company? Well, the answer to this question depends on whether you would be willing to accept somebody else's white lie. If so, then white lies seem to be morally permissible. Bowie (1993: 345), however, points out that it is unlikely that anybody would be willing to be lied to by somebody else. It would therefore be highly illogical for someone to accept practices such as lying or bluffing, particularly if they would undermine the general trust that is needed by business. This all conforms to the first version of the categorical imperative.

As a matter of fact, however, there might be practical circumstances in which you accept lying. For example, when you do not want to hear very bad news or listen to open and honest criticism. In such circumstances, Kant and Bowie might argue, you are not capable of rationality; that is, you are not in control of your own will and may well be guided by fear. It is only the presence of rational autonomy and sovereignty that allows you to act on the basis of laws that you recognise as rational. This is, indeed, what gives human beings their dignity, and if you claim this dignity for yourself, then you must accept that others will claim the same. As a consequence, you have to show them the kind of respect that you expect them to show to you. This is to say that, you will have to treat them as ends in themselves rather than as means to your ends. If you cannot, for whatever reason, see the logic of this, or if nobody is willing to accept this logic, then our entire ethical (and legal) system falls apart. As Bowie points out, the only reason not to abide by a contract that you have signed is if you consider your own signature to be irrelevant, but then you should not expect others to obey the contract either.

Bowie is well aware that these ideas could well prevent managers from doing things that might benefit their businesses in the short term. If a manager chooses to follow categorical imperatives, then they should refrain from undermining somebody else's autonomy. The manager should not allow himself or herself to coerce or cheat any other person. Business practices under a Kantian regime have only one ultimate reason for being: to develop the humane, rational and moral capacities of people in and outside the organisation. It is hard to believe that, with these noble ideals in mind, business practices such as making people redundant would still be legitimate, but Bowie apparently thinks that laying people off is not necessarily anti-Kantian.

In the following quote, he makes a telling distinction between those who are 'naïve Kantians' and those who are not:

> A naïve Kantian response would label them [layoffs] as immoral because, allegedly, the employees are being used as mere means to enhance shareholder wealth. However, that judgment would be premature. What would be required from a Kantian perspective is an examination of the employer/employee relationship, including any contractual agreements. So long as the relationship was neither coercive nor deceptive, there would be nothing immoral about layoffs.
>
> (Bowie, 1999b: 8)

Bowie might be right here. Accepting Kantian practices does not mean that unpleasant things will not sometimes happen. Moreover, part of an open and reasonable relationship between employer and employee is that both parties are aware that the relationship might end. So it might be that American business practices would not necessarily contradict Prussian morality. After all, part and parcel of these practices is an understanding that employer–employee relationships are relationships between the kind of free and autonomous individuals that a Kantian philosopher probably has in mind. What we have here are relationships that preserve the freedom of both parties: just as the manager can demote or fire an employee, so too can the employee quit whenever they like. This idea of the essential freedom of the employee is one that Bowie uses in several places, but we would like to raise some questions about it.

You can certainly imagine the ethical relationship between employer and employee without any reference to real-life situations. This is generally in line with Kant's own procedure, though we will suggest later that Kant is much less certain about the possibilities of rational and autonomous behaviour than Bowie. But if we pause and think for a moment about some real-life situations, we would notice that in most organisations employees are not really completely free to make their own choices. Not only are they managed through various formal and informal rules within the organisation, but also they also usually do not have the financial security to leave whenever they like. Second, we may also wonder whether organisational relationships would pass the test of the third formulation of the categorical imperative cited above: 'act as if you were a member of an ideal society in which you are both ruler and ruled at the same time'. We might accept that the threat of dismissals and other accepted business practices do not undermine people's autonomy or freedom, but would such practices help others achieve autonomy? Can a manager really believe that sacking people provides them with new career opportunities? We think that Kant's **utopia**, the 'kingdom of ends', could hardly include 'downsizing' and involuntary 'career re-adjustments'.

As we have already noted, for Kant, ends are important, but not the hedonistic consequences that concern utilitarians. He thinks of ends in the immaterial sense of the word: happiness and dignity are more likely to be encouraged in the ideal kingdom than power and opulence. In different places in his work, Kant indicates that the search for happiness is an absolute necessity for a free and rational being. Indeed, determining ends in your life is something that you do on the basis of reason and is not a consequence of human nature. An end is always an object of choice belonging to a rational being. This, Kant believes, holds even under circumstances that are opposed to the exercise of your reason, for you can never be forced to have certain ends, or values. Admittedly, you can be forced to perform particular acts, but this in no way should affect your rational freedom. Who in the world would be able to impose ends on you? Indeed, for Kant, the very idea that you can be coerced to adopt ends is contradictory.

So Bowie does not consider the possibility that several standard business practices (dismissals, bluffing, and so on) contradict the third formulation of the categorical imperative. He hides these problems and emphasises that at least *some* business practices are in alignment with this categorical imperative: empowerment, green business, diversity policies, and so on. This allows him, for example, to claim that while bluffing may undermine the general stability that business is in need of, which is a very Kantian argument, bluffing would be morally permissible if everyone involved has 'open access to all relevant information' (Bowie, 1993: 346–347). Bowie also relates his Kantian insights to the well-known distinction between what McGregor (1960) called Theory X and Theory Y. Theory X assumes that people are lazy and need firm control, Theory Y that people are motivated and need encouragement. Crucially, McGregor suggests that people will tend to behave in the ways that managers treat them – so treat people badly and they will behave badly. Bowie suggests that Kant would support a Theory Y world view.

Well perhaps, but we are in doubt as to whether Kant himself would endorse Theory Y, or any other theory that encouraged treating people as objects to be organised. Here we face the problem that the second version of the categorical imperative cuts to the heart of the employment contract. If, in capitalist societies, most people must sell their labour power on the market, and accumulation of capital is the goal of business, then most people come to be routinely treated as commodities which are the means by which businesses make profits. This practice of treating people as human resources, whether in a 'hard' Theory X fashion, or in a 'soft' Theory Y fashion, will always be a problem for a Kantian, because it reduces people to means and reduces their rational autonomy and hence the dignity of being human. Would you want to be used like that?

It therefore seems to us that an indelible optimism pervades Bowie's 'Kantian' writings. No philosophical or political doubt seriously threatens his overall project of aligning business and Kantian philosophy, despite the cautions that Kant clearly raises in his texts. Indeed, perhaps at his most extreme, Bowie concludes that business has a valuable contribution to make to a better world: 'International business, if done from the Kantian perspective, can contribute to the long hoped for, but elusive, goals of world peace' (Bowie, 1999b: 15). But unrestrained international free trade is almost the opposite of Kant's project for perpetual peace, which rests more on the grounds of reasoned social and political discourse and treaties between sovereign republics (see Kant, 1795). Kant's project for world peace looks more like declarations and social disputation about human rights, while Bowie's looks more like economic globalisation by companies largely unrestricted as to their actions. Given that Kant recognises the great pain that people can cause to others if they think only of their own ends, one might wonder what Kant would have said about Bowie's optimism.

DUTY, CERTAINTY AND MORAL CONFLICT

At the end of the *Critique of Practical Reason*, Kant asks himself what would happen if we were able to achieve a purely rationalised and **technocratic** morality. He argues that there would be an absence of any conflict between inclinations and a properly moral disposition. Although we might act in the proper fashion, we would not be doing so out of an ethical duty. In such a situation, Kant writes:

> Transgression of the law would, no doubt, be avoided: what is commanded would be done; but because the disposition from which actions ought to be done cannot be instilled by any command, and because the spur to activity in this case would be promptly at hand and external, reason would have no need to work itself up so as to gather strength to resist the inclinations by a lively representation of the dignity of the law.
>
> (1788: 258)

This lack of conflict would not be a good thing because a certain sort of struggle is required to develop moral strength. Without it

> most actions conforming to the law would be done from fear, only a few from hope, and none at all from duty, and the moral worth of actions, on which alone in the eyes of supreme wisdom the worth of the person and even that of the world depends, would not exist at all. As long as human nature remains as it is, human conduct would thus be changed into mere mechanism in which, as in a puppet show, everything would gesticulate well but there would be no life in the figures.
>
> (Kant, 1788: 258)

Kant was thus in doubt about the effects of a perfectly rationalised ethics on the moral disposition of the individual. Elsewhere in the *Critique of Practical Reason*, he argues that the moral subject would probably act like a marionette or automaton whose emotional life was caused by an 'alien hand' (1788: 221). Kant realised that his ethics did not prevent the possibility that acting according to duty might be done for entirely 'external' reasons. You might do your duty not because you have the right disposition to do it, but because somebody else orders you to do something and you think it is correct to obey them. Acting *according to* duty, however, is not the same as acting *out of* duty. There is a difference between a person who acts according to duty because they think it is good to follow

48

orders and a person who cultivates a moral disposition. For Kant, it is only such a disposition that makes an act or person moral. But he continued to wonder whether the kind of ethics he developed would really contribute to the dignity of the person, let alone to the dignity of mankind as a whole. What if people did do the right things without having the right disposition?

Kant thought that an ethics that merely concentrated on telling you how you should do the right thing would be limited, and in the *Metaphysics of Morals* he makes clear that this question is one that fits better into discussions about law and morality. One aspect of this is important here. The law, Kant argues, is concerned with absolute rules and is satisfied if it can provide us with clues as to how people can be forced, by the police for example, into following these rules. The idea of an inner disposition or internal compulsion is, as Kersting (1993: 103) has pointed out, fairly irrelevant when it comes to the law, but it is all-important in discussions about ethics and morality. Why?

The answer to this question is that from Kant's ethical perspective it does not matter so much that you are doing something but it does matter *why* you are doing it. The child who spoils the birthday breakfast may do as much damage to the house as the child who throws tomato sauce at their brother out of anger. What is different in these two cases, for the Kantian, is the intention that motivates the action. The emphasis on the grounds of an action is closely related to Kant's understanding of freedom. In his opinion, we cannot think about freedom without the notion of 'inner compulsion'. This means that only by acting upon your inner compulsion, that is, on your innermost motives, are you able to free yourself from outer compulsion. For Kant, freedom is the ontological condition of ethics. Kant urges you to decide for yourself rather than to have somebody else or something else make a decision on your behalf. Without inner compulsion, freedom and with it the entire possibility of human dignity will be irretrievably lost.

So perhaps Kantian ethics is not so much about checking whether your actions are in line with certain universal imperatives, as is suggested by Bowie, but more about looking 'into the depths of one's own heart'. Hence the 'first command of all duties to oneself' is to 'know your heart' (1797: 562). And what one finds there is hardly the kind of certainty and transparency that common sense business ethics longs for because 'a human being cannot see into the depths of his own heart so as to be quite certain, in even a *single* action, of the purity of his moral intention and the sincerity of his disposition' (Kant, 1797: 523). Kant takes motive as a key element in deciding about the moral worthiness of a particular act but – and this is very important – he never suggests that we are able to perfectly know our own motives. This is what makes Kantian ethics much more difficult than Bowie suggests it is. You have the ethical duty to gain self-knowledge but you should not think that this self-knowledge is easily obtained. You are not transparent to yourself.

In the *Metaphysics of Morals* Kant discusses the duty you have towards yourself to avoid self-deception at all costs. One of the 'inner lies' to which you can easily fall prey is indeed to think that you perfectly understand your motives. Such self-knowledge would entail that understanding yourself can at some point in time be completed, which seems very unlikely. Perhaps self-knowledge is instead a duty that we can never fully abide by, and what is needed is a permanent enquiry into the relationship between moral perfection and our own actions. Again and again, Kant emphasises the difficulty of this requirement: 'Moral cognition of one's self, which seeks to penetrate into the depths (the abyss) of one's heart which are quite difficult to fathom, is the beginning of all human wisdom' (Kant, 1797: 562). But what you might encounter during such an enquiry is a tendency towards self-deception. A fine example of this self-deception is that you pretend to know all about your motives for acting in a particular way. But who knows themself well enough to say exactly what is going on inside their mind?

The image that Kant tries to convey is one of a struggling heart. There are many impulses struggling against each other when we want to do our duty, and it is never entirely clear what the outcome of this struggle will be. Our inability to become morally perfect is, if anything, an inability to gain true self-knowledge. For example, in the *Groundwork of the Metaphysics of Morals* Kant claims that experience cannot establish with certainty whether a duty was carried out by us in a begrudgingly 'dutiful' manner or 'out of a devotion to duty' (1785: 61). That is why he goes on to suggest that reason, rather than experience, should establish what does and what does not constitute moral purity. Kant accepts that reason alone will result in the description of moral acts that are almost impossible to live up to, but this perhaps should best be seen as a thought experiment with ethics that is necessary if we are to have any guiding principles in this difficult territory.

FREEDOM

Kant therefore expresses a great deal of doubt about an ethics that is constituted by special cases and selfishness disguised as duty. Insofar as common sense business ethics is permeated by exactly these utilitarian elements, it probably does not constitute the sort of ethical thinking that Kant himself had in mind. He appeals to reason in order to establish the ideal of moral perfection. Attempts to water down this idea and follow the muddy practice of our everyday world are irrelevant to this experiment and merely serve to cheer people up or contribute to the daily chatter. Kant is a firm believer in the notion of moral progress and he sets out to formulate an idea of pure morality that might, at least on a theoretical level, help people to think about this progress. But Kant does not believe that this experiment could offer a description of actual practices.

Bowie seems to be much more optimistic, in spite of all his cautionary remarks, about the possibilities of having the idea of pure morality implemented within businesses. This follows, we think, from an overly technocratic interpretation of the three formulations of the categorical imperative. But Kant would argue that everyday practices do *not* in themselves result in moral purity. The only thing that an individual can do is to learn to know his or her own heart as best they can and to try to come to grips with the eternal struggle that takes place within it.

For Kant, it would be sheer arrogance to deny the existence of such a struggle in the heart. Only conceitedness of the worst kind would not understand gaining moral virtue as a difficult process, and something that cannot be resolved by appeal to a simple equation. This is why Kant insists on a permanent discontent with morality and describes virtue as 'a moral disposition in conflict' (1788: 208). Ethics is painful, not only because it urges you to consider the darker aspects of your moral disposition but also because it is intrinsically related to a restriction and constraint of the self. There are many passages in his work that show a deep awareness of the problematic nature of ethics, for example. Kant concedes that instinct is probably much more effective for survival, wealth and happiness than reason or reason-based ethics. An ethics that does not understand this overestimates reason's powers and must, as a consequence, misunderstand the struggle that is a hallmark of morality. Small wonder then that many people feel annoyed by ethics, because the reasonable person often uses their will to achieve a certain denial and self-limitation, or at least feels that they should.

But why, if Kant is realistic about human beings, does he place such a strong emphasis on will and duty? Why does Kantian philosophy seem so severe and rigid? Moral virtuousness, Engstrom (2002) explains, is so sternly conceived because it is related to *freedom*. In both the *Groundwork of the Metaphysics of Morals* and *The Metaphysics of Morals*, Kant is at pains to explain to us that our senses or impulses cannot be the basis of moral dignity. The same holds for habits, which he defines as 'a permanent inclination without any maxim' and therefore not a principled way of thinking. Neither can the maxims that Kant has in mind be based on custom or tradition because you would then lose your freedom when accepting them. To act out of duty is to act out of freedom. Engstrom alerts us to the paradoxes that are involved here: 'The less a human being can be compelled physically (i.e. coerced), and the more he can be compelled morally (through the representation of mere duty), the freer he is' (Engstrom, 2002: 293). In the *Critique of Practical Reason*, Kant writes that freedom of the will is the only principle underlying moral laws and the duties ensuing from them. Habit, tradition and culture merely open the door to a huge diversity of different justifications, so freedom must be independent of such contexts. Kant describes this as an inner freedom that grounds all virtue.

Kant is not so naïve as to think that diverse social contexts can be kept at bay once and for all. On the contrary, the very fact that morality in daily life is a struggle indicates that social contexts are indeed a very important influence. But influence is not the same as determination. In other words, you may be influenced by your friends and by society but this should not imply that they determine the kind of actions that you are going to undertake. If there is one central theme in Kantian ethics, then it is this: never become a plaything of fortune! He rails against what he calls 'self-imposed tutelage', a phrase which is now typically translated as 'self-incurred minority' (1784: 17). When he calls us to 'have courage to make use of your own understanding' (1784: 17), he realises that this is a difficult challenge, but this challenge is central to the ethical struggle:

> It is so comfortable to be a minor! If I have a book that understands for me, a spiritual advisor who has a conscience for me, and so forth, I need not trouble myself at all. I need not think, if only I can pay; others will readily undertake the irksome business for me.
>
> (Kant, 1784: 17)

Kantian ethics demands that one should always resist coercion and arbitrariness, inclination and determination – even by textbooks! But one aspect of this resistance is a willingness to acknowledge that other values will always influence you. This kind of self-knowledge, an understanding of your own weakness, is essential if we are to combat our otherwise irrational tendencies. So, while Kant undoubtedly tries to lift ethics and morality up to a rationalised and ideal sphere, he is never oblivious to daily complexities. Moral virtue (and the inner freedom that is its precondition) can be imagined by any rational thinker, but final perfection is impossible and in practical terms will always be contested.

What we may infer from this is that Kantian ethics is, as far as we can see, not really interested in the social control of individual behaviour. More precisely, the Kantian experiment is more about how enlightened people try to reason and find direction in their lives. There is no doubt that we may criticise the experiment – and Kant has often been criticised – but our point here is that his primary intention is totally at odds with what business ethicists are typically after. Kant is always oriented towards autonomous individuals and never towards controlling collective behaviour. Indeed, we suggest that business ethicists such as Bowie use a highly technocratic interpretation in order to make him fit into business ethics more easily. His ideas can certainly be used to help imagine more ethical forms of business and society, but can also be quite disruptive for such concerns because Kant insists that being good is an unending personal struggle. It is also clear that Kant emphasises that individuals do have feelings and emotions, even though he has often been accused of ignoring exactly these aspects of human life that are con- sidered by others to be essential to morality (e.g. **Bauman**, 1993). Kant's emphasis on the essentially contested character of morality is, as we have seen above, strongly related to his understanding of the role that emotions have to play, and to the experience of finitude.

THE EXPERIENCE OF LIMITATION

Kant's ethical work, indeed all of his writing, is based on the idea that there is a sort of discrepancy between the world and the human beings living in it. Humans have aims and intentions, but the world is bewildering and aimless. That we have intentions in our lives and formulate goals is, for Kant, exactly what makes us capable of reason and virtue. In other words, the discrepancy we are talking about here is one between the world as it is and the world as we would like it to be. The problem is that the wish to bridge the gap between 'is' and 'ought', between 'facts' and 'values', is often an example of a massive arrogance and delusion. Complaints about the evils in the world tend to deteriorate into assertions about the hidden goals of God, the struggle between good and evil, or the laws of human nature. For Kant, such answers clearly exceed the boundaries of human reason (because they cannot be proved) and he thinks that they are arrogant and stupid. It is this harsh judgement that makes him so eager to explain the boundaries of knowledge.

One of the central points of another of Kant's books, the *Critique of Pure Reason*, is that there is no point in simply complaining about the limitations of thought. These limitations constitute a fact of reason rather than something we can change, and it is therefore more reasonable to accept them. But even if we accept the imperfection of reason, we should not assume that being as reasonable and virtuous as we can be will make us happy. There is a kind of common sense in assuming that good things happen to good people, or to put it a little differently, that the promise of virtue is happiness. At first glance, this may all seem to be perfectly straightforward utilitarianism – morality has only one goal and that is to create a world in which people are happy. Kant is under no illusions about the importance of happiness. He writes: 'a rational being's consciousness of the agreeableness of life uninterruptedly accompanying his whole existence is *happiness*' (1788: 156), and in the *Metaphysics of Morals* that 'it is unavoidable for human nature to wish for and seek happiness' (1797: 519).

But to believe that happiness is a common and rational end of human life, given the limited nature of human reason and the poor state of the world, is also to create a serious problem. All this seeking after happiness does not seem to have done much for human virtues in the real world. At this point, it is important to point out that Kant's conception of happiness is in no way related to a utilitarian version of pleasure, or a hedonistic form of consumption, and he would no doubt condemn the modern hunt for rapid satisfactions. For Kant, achieving happiness is one thing and achieving virtuousness an entirely different thing. His ideas about happiness are always ideas about rational happiness – the condition of a rational human being who attempts to ensure that everything goes according to their own free will. But the quest for happiness which follows Kantian guidelines is very difficult, because it is always hampered by the limitations of human reason. Kant posits happiness as the pre-eminent human end but rejects the idea that science could one day bridge the gap between 'is' and 'ought' and guarantee that happiness.

But rather than complaining about this state of affairs, we should be grateful for it. Kant begins with the idea that pure morality is related to rule-like dispositions such as the categorical imperative, but clearly understands that impurity and a propensity to breaching the rules is always likely. Moreover, if we are to take seriously Kant's own warnings about the morality of puppets we must accept that a morally transparent world is one that would paradoxically exclude all morality. If everything was clear, there would be no choice, no struggle and no ethics. It is here that we can fully grasp the partiality of Bowie's understanding of Kant. The very effort to create moral transparency through a fetishistic form of bureaucratic rule following would be condemned by Kant as profoundly immoral. Why would Kant do this? Why does he dislike moral transparency?

The answer is that his very understanding of freedom and autonomy is based on an acceptance of human limitation. You can only act freely if your knowledge is fallible and if your power is deficient. If you knew everything and could do everything you would have no need for moral struggle. That is, freedom is conditioned by human imperfection, because if we were perfect we would have no need for choice. To put it even more poignantly, freedom has its roots in our lack of knowledge. If we could know perfectly the consequences of our acts, then we would no longer be autonomous, free or moral. Utilitarians often like to believe that they can predict consequences but, perhaps fortunately, they often cannot. If they could, then utilitarianism would be without choice too – another morality for puppets. This is a grim lesson for the business ethicist who believes, like Bowie, that ethics pays. Your intentions cannot really be good if you know (with any certainty) that you will be rewarded for your actions. Now we can see the awful depth of Kant's claim that goodness can only be good if it is done for the sake of goodness, and for no other reason.

CONCLUSION

The implications of this become even more apparent if we realise that although there is some sort of relationship between virtue and happiness, we should by no means believe that the prospect of happiness should be the main motivation for acting virtuously. In this sense, Kant certainly questions a neat relationship between being good and being happy. He does not provide us with some sort of 'seven steps to smiling' advice or guaranteed pathways to pleasure. Indeed, the very idea that there could be such a relationship merely shows a lack of real insight into the limitations of our knowledge. But if this is the case, why should we act virtuously? Why not simply let greed be good, and hope that money makes you happy?

Kant's answer to this is quite straightforward. For Kant, 'there is not the least ground in the moral law for a necessary connection between morality and the proportionate happiness of a being belonging to the world' (1788: 240). This does not mean that we should not strive for the good. Quite the contrary. But it does mean that the good and happiness are quite different matters. Morality 'is not properly the doctrine of how we are to *make* ourselves happy but of how we are to become *worthy* of happiness' (1788: 244). Happiness is beyond moral control. You might end up being happy, or you might not. What you can try to control, however, are your good intentions. In Kant's writings, everything hinges on this insight into human limitation. There are only a few things that we, being finite and fragile creatures, can control. This, however, does not allow us to be lazy when it comes to morality. On the contrary, while we should understand that we can not have god-like powers, we have the duty to act as if we do. It is, in other words, understandable and excusable that we fail in our understanding of the world, but we really should not fail when it comes to morality. That we do often fail in daily practice, again and again, and always will, is perhaps tragic. But simply because things rarely work out according to our intentions and plans does not mean that we are somehow relieved from our duty to keep trying. Being good is not a condition, or a rule, but an endless struggle.

Business ethics has historically portrayed Kant as a philosopher who offers us rules, and many arguing for and against Kantian business ethics have, often uncritically, accepted the resulting picture. In this chapter we have sought to modify this picture somewhat, and in doing so to introduce what we consider to be a more Kantian version of Kant. In our view, Kant's primary concerns are not so much related to ethical duties as to ethical being, freedom and struggle. It is an ethics that, while acknowledging our finitude, gives central stage to human dignity. Unlike the utilitarians that we looked at in Chapter 3, Kant invites us to look inside ourselves and find our truths there. In doing so, for Kant, an appeal to the law has very little to do with ethics. On the contrary, an encounter with ethics is far more to do with a searching self-reflection which finds it very difficult, in practice, to live up to the ceaseless demands of ethics.

This Kant, far from being a historical relic, seems to us to have much to say to business ethics today. Provided, that is, that we see the importance of reading him carefully, and not simply slotting him into easy pre-existing pigeonholes. Kant is a challenging thinker, not simply because he is a complicated thinker who writes hard books. Kant is a challenge because for him, and for us, ethics is about challenges and difficulty. From this chapter we can see how business ethicists have tended to make Kant far more palatable and less challenging than he is if we read him carefully. But we propose to reclaim this more challenging version of Kant for business ethics. As we argued about utilitarianism, there is something troubling about taking ethical theories seriously, even though business ethicists have often tried to domesticate ethics by turning its theories into rules for businesses. We will find the same when we turn to the third main ethical theory that has been found in business ethics, virtue ethics, which is the subject of the next chapter.

Chapter 5

'Business ethics' III: virtues

INTRODUCTION

Bentham and Mill mostly talked about pleasure, and Kant about intentions, but what about all the other words that we use to talk about good and bad? These other words often come in pairs – courage and cowardice, honesty and deceit, cleverness and stupidity, virtue and vice. Most of the time, we would apply these judgement words to people, and specifically to the character of particular people, perhaps to explain why they had spilled a bottle of tomato sauce or burnt the toast. All these words, and many more, surely need to find their place in a theory of ethics too. The third variety of ethical theory that has had a huge influence on the domain of business ethics, and that uses these sort of words routinely, is virtue ethics. This sort of ethics takes the common sense terms that people use every day much more seriously than do ethics based on consequences or intentions. It also insists that ethical ideas are not independent of particular social contexts, and that what is regarded as good in one place might be regarded as bad in another.

Perhaps if Kant had ever left Prussia, he might have realised that not everybody shared his rather stern approach to redemption through moral struggle. The important point here is that a virtue approach replaces the individual thought experiments of utilitarian and Kantian theories with a more 'social' approach to understanding how ethical values are produced. In other words, and perhaps of particular relevance in a globalising world, we should perhaps not assume that there are any general ethical calculations or dispositions that can be successfully applied regardless of circumstances. This provides us with a very positive affirmation of the virtues of different belief systems, but also creates the alarming possibility that all beliefs are equally true. This problem is normally called relativism, the position that all beliefs are relative to each other, and that there are no timeless versions of good and bad. But if there are no 'golden rules', then what sort of ethics are we left with?

We will investigate these ideas as we move through the chapter, but let us begin with a brief description of virtue ethics. As we noted, one of the ideas that is important to virtue theorists is that of character, and most particularly the idea that particular forms of character are regarded as virtuous in different societies. Indeed, the very word 'ethics' comes to us from the ancient Greek words *ethos*, meaning character, and also meaning habits or dwelling place. So perhaps a warlike society will value courage, a scholarly society will value the intellect, and a trading society will value cunning. Aristotle, the ancient Greek philosopher who really began these discussions, was aware that what was seen as good in Athens (a democracy, for some people, some of the time) was not necessarily seen as good in Sparta (a warlike and hierarchical city state, for most of the time), let alone in Egypt or in Rome. For an example that comes from far into the future (rather than the past) remember the different societies in *Star Trek* and imagine the virtues that would matter to the Klingons, the Vulcans, the Ferengi or the Borg. If we accept that societies have particular characters that they value, then it is not a big leap to apply these ideas to the notion of organisational character. For example, think of the army, a university or a business. What sorts of character might they value?

In business ethics, the work of Robert Solomon has been crucially important in introducing these ideas to a wider public (Solomon, 1992; 1993; 1999a; 1999b; 2004). Solomon described Aristotle 'as the continuing focus of discussion' for contemporary virtue ethicists (Solomon, 1999b: 30). While we think that nobody would be in disagreement with this, it is quite remarkable that Solomon thinks that Aristotelian understandings of ethics can be so easily transposed from societies to businesses. 'Corporations,' he suggests, 'are real communities, neither ideal nor idealized, and therefore the perfect place to start understanding the nature of virtues' (1992: 325). His expectations of this approach are staggering:

> One might say that the bottom line of the virtue approach to business ethics is that we have to move away from 'bottom line' thinking and conceive of business as an essential part of a society in which living well together, rubbing along with others, and having a sense of self-respect are central, and making a profit merely a means.
>
> (1999b: 37)

These sort of statements have meant that Solomon has stirred massive interest amongst business ethicists in the virtuousness of corporations. The *Journal of Business Ethics*, for example, has published a wide variety of articles inspired by virtue ethics. One article discusses the sorts of ethical practice which are so important in Aristotelian philosophy (Brewer, 1997); another has focused on the individual moral understandings of virtue in business practices (Forsyth, 1992) and one on the issues raised by cultural relativism (Limbs and Fort, 2000). Along similar lines, Murphy (1999) has argued that the core virtues of international marketing should be integrity, fairness, trust, respect and empathy. Finally, Shanahan and Hyman (2003) have tried to develop a full-blown scale of ethical virtues which is based on Solomon's work and which purports to help researchers with understanding and judging business practices all over the world.

What are we to make of this interest in virtue? As in the last chapter with Bowie and Kant, here we will argue that the relationship between Solomon and Aristotle is rather problematic. In part, this is a question as to whether business organisations can be treated as communities, as collectives that share a particular character and set of values. We will proceed in three sections. In the first section, we will briefly discuss Solomon's most important texts on virtue ethics; in the second section, we will look more deeply into Aristotle as a source of inspiration for virtue ethics; in the third section, we will discuss whether virtue ethics is useful for business practitioners. While we are, to a certain extent at least, in agreement with the idea that many businesses are disconnected from the communities in which they operate, we will argue that Solomon's solutions for this problem are not very plausible and, like Bowie, reflect a rather naïve optimism.

VIRTUE AND BUSINESS?

When discussing common sense in Chapter 2, we saw that business is often seen as having little to do with the warm world of morality. We use all kinds of metaphors to describe these ideas. Organisations are money-machines, they operate in a jungle or in a dog-eat-dog world, they have to wage war with competitors, or are at best the mindless playthings of unshakeable economic laws. This is not the kind of world where one would expect much virtue.

Yet, there is a lot of evidence that business people are moral through and through. We may not share their particular moral outlook on the world, but perhaps this should not tempt us to think that 'their' morality is somehow thinner and less meaningful than ours is. We should not think that business is carried out in a morally indifferent or even selfish world, a world that is somehow placed beyond good and evil. In addition, we should consider that it is, to a certain extent, a shared understanding of rules and values that shapes businesses as more or less coherent forms of organisation. Furthermore, it is clear that most people who work for organisations are more than slaves or puppets: they invest emotionally in these organisations and what happens there has an impact upon them. Happiness, sadness, melancholy, love, friendship, hostility – it is all there in the soap opera of organising. Sometimes, one might even get the feeling that organisations do resemble the real world after all.

Ideas like these allow Solomon to imagine business organisations as real communities, as potentially warm places inhabited by fully human beings. These understandings are supported by a very particular understanding of the market too. Organisations can become real communities only because the market in which they operate is not as callous and unfeeling as some people think it is. If trust and values are so important for the environment of business, then the claim that business enterprises can become (and perhaps already are) real communities seems increasingly plausible. Solomon thinks of these communities in terms of 'practices', which he understands as social activities that are, while being competitive and motivated by self-interest, also characterised by mutual concern, trust and citizenship. Important here is the typically Aristotelian understanding that such social activities are based on an understanding of shared goals (Solomon, 1993: 152). This is an understanding which Solomon does not relate to profit making but to what you might refer to as 'human flourishing' in the broadest sense of the word. For Solomon, business is not a necessary evil, something that a decent human being would not want to be involved in unless they are somehow made to do so, but a civilizing force that eventually creates moral and commercial excellence (which are actually the same). These goals are in no way limited to the business itself but can spread through the rest of society. Solomon's dream is profoundly holistic: business people who want to attain excellence are also people who have substantially broadened their moral scope. They are not only interested in sound business practices but also in the well-being of all stakeholders, in the consequences of their actions for the environment, the character of their employees, and so on.

To put it more succinctly, businesses are communities that positively reward people's virtues. A lot of what Solomon has to say is dedicated to the concept of virtue. Aristotle, according to Solomon (1993: 192), argued that a virtue is a personal trait that becomes manifest in an exemplary way of getting on with other people combined with a distinct loyalty to the aims of the community. Solomon spends a lot of time defining typically Aristotelian virtues that, in his view, businesses cannot do without. Toughness, for example, is defined as 'ultimately having a vision and persevering in the long-term plans and strategies necessary to achieve that vision' (1993: 215). Loyalty is another example and is defined as 'integrity, not within oneself but rather with oneself conceived as a part of a larger self, a group, a community, an organization, or institution' (1993: 220). In a book called *A Better Way to Think About Business*, he lists and defines no less than forty-five virtues, ranging from 'ability' to 'zeal' (Solomon, 1999a). In this list, the virtues are defined in a more straightforward way, as if this would transform them into real business virtues. Toughness is now defined as 'maintaining one's position' or 'being a take-charge type of person', whereas loyalty is 'working for the well-being of an organization and one's status in it'. The change in tone in these definitions is interesting and, like the example of Bowie's use of Kant in the previous chapter, serves to illustrate the kind of work that the business ethicist must do in order to make famous philosophers palatable in the world of business.

Solomon is consistent about the all-importance of justice, which he regards as a virtue that underlies all others. In the business context, justice is very much about treating other people fairly, that is, about giving them their due. This relatively straightforward understanding of justice notwithstanding, Solomon is at pains to show how complicated it is to be 'just'. He provides his readers with the example of a manager who must split $1000 bonus money between two of his employees. If the manager wants to act justly, quite a lot of deliberation on their behalf is necessary before actually splitting the money. They should take into considerations issues such as merit, result, need, right, seniority, loyalty, equality, virtue, and so on (1993: 238–239). Solomon is well aware of the difficulties involved in this kind of decision making and argues that in these scenarios there is no one way in which one can behave in a perfectly just manner. The virtues are therefore not to be seen as criteria that allow us to judge whether a particular action can be understood as clearly right or clearly wrong. What we have here is not a rule-based ethics, such as utilitarianism, or Bowie's version of Kant. It is much more complicated

59

than that because it involves judgements about vague things like virtues, and about their appropriateness in a wide variety of contexts.

This raises the question of whether the virtues emphasised by Solomon can be put into practice at all. What sort of guidelines do they offer? Solomon maintains that these virtues can lead to some form of action provided that they are grounded in a feeling of care and concern. Any sense of what is just and good and right can only begin with a care for the world, for those whom we love and feel responsible for, and, indeed, for our-selves (1993: 241). Here, Solomon leaves us with the vague but ambitious spiritual sensibility that we referred to earlier. Indeed, we might suggest that he allows himself to get carried away by musings about empathic and nurturing communities in which people excel in such virtues as amiability ('being a friend'; 1999a: 74), caring ('caring in the corporation consists of mutual affection'; 1999a: 77) and compassion (deemed to be indispensable for 'the very life of the organization'; 1999a: 80). Generosity, kindness, humility and other business virtues are also mentioned, almost in passing, as crucial for these communities. Apparently, cunning, decisiveness and efficiency, to mention just a few virtues that seem to be pertinent to some old-style businesses, play relatively minor roles in the new-style corporate world envisaged by Solomon.

Solomon is not afraid to dream and perhaps he deserves credit for this, particularly since so much of business ethics seems to be limited to apologetic tinkering. But while we do share some of the understandings he puts forward, we think that his appro-priation of Aristotle has some problems. One may wonder whether Aristotle's understanding of the ancient Athenian community is really comparable to Solomon's understanding of contemporary business. Behind this issue, however, lurks a perhaps more important one. Is ethics something that allows for the rather spiritual framing that Solomon and many others (e.g. Murphy, 1999: 113; Shanahan and Hyman, 2003: 204) are keen to put forward? It is one thing to claim that business practices can and should be 'spiritualised' but it is something entirely different to claim that ethics can and should be. If we are to consider these questions, then we will need a detour through Aristotle's *Nichomachean Ethics*.

VIRTUE AND COMMUNITY

Aristotle did not belong to the Athenian community. He was a foreigner and spent many years of his life as an exile. Eventually, he died as such. It is difficult to understand Aristotle without taking into consideration his more or less permanent state of non-belonging to the Greek world.

Questions about the possibility of human togetherness permeate Aristotle's work, and his ethical questions can only be understood, we suggest, if one understands them against this background. Something of this has been captured by Solomon, too. The emphasis on mutual concern and care that characterises his work on business communities has, to a certain extent at least, an Aristotelian flavour. However, the qualifier 'to a certain extent' is important here for two reasons. First, we want to point out that Aristotelian communities are not only characterised by warm care and concern. Indeed, the emphasis placed by Aristotle on 'affection' (**philia**), a feature of his work that is highlighted by Solomon, is much more complicated than is suggested by the latter and should in no way be seen as an excuse for a sort of romanticism about communal life (Yack, 1999: 273). Care, concern and a shared understanding of the world are hallmarks of Aristotelian communities, but so are disorder, conflict and betrayal. There seem to be some contradictions here, so let's exlore them in a little more detail.

Almost at the end of Book IX of his *Nichomachean Ethics*, Aristotle writes:

> friendship is a partnership, and as a man is to himself, so is he to his friend; now in his own case the perception of his existence is desirable, and so therefore is that of his friend's, and the activity of this perception is produced when they live together, so that it is natural that they aim at this.
>
> (Aristotle, 1984c: 1171b32–1172a1)

Here friendship is linked to 'partnership'. The original Greek word is *koinonia* and among scholars there is quite a fuss about the adequacy of 'partnership' as a translation. Nowadays, after all, 'partnership' seems to be a word that is linked to some kind of contract between the persons involved, be it a business contract, a marriage or a military treaty. It is clear, however, that Aristotle's understanding of friendship or other forms of togetherness is not necessarily contractual. He does use the word *koinonia* for business relationships, but also for passengers on a boat, for the audience at a stadium or for those who share a household (Yack, 1999: 273). These examples imply that Aristotle's understanding of togetherness does not rule out the presence of formal laws or contracts in any 'community' or 'association'. But people who are brought together in a business, on a boat, at a stadium or in a household do not, and this is a crucial point in Aristotle's ethics, create the kind of community or association typical of the political *koinonia*, the state. In the *Politics*, Aristotle is exceptionally clear about this:

> if men dwelt at a distance from one another, but not so far off as to have no intercourse, and there were laws among them that they should not wrong each other in their exchanges, neither would this be a state. Let us suppose that one man is a carpenter, another a farmer, and another a shoemaker, and so on, and that their number is ten thousand: nevertheless, if they have nothing in common but exchange, alliance and the like, that would not constitute a state.
>
> (Aristotle, 1984d: 1280b18–23)

Essential for the association that takes the form of the state is a shared friendship, 'for to choose to live together is friendship . . . the state is the union of families and villages in a perfect and self-sufficing life, by which we mean a happy and honourable life' (Aristotle, 1984d: 1280b38–1281a2). To live well in this sense is typically not the main

61

aim of a business organisation (or of being on a boat, at a stadium, and so on). It is, however, the aim of the political community. Aristotle stresses that this sort of good life can only be attained if the life lived together is the product of affection, for 'it is our affection for others that causes us to choose to live together'. The possibility of a community that is not merely contractual is therefore based on the possibility of affection and friendship.

No doubt this sounds attractive to those who long for more communality and warmth in their working and non-working lives, but it is by no means easy to grasp what words like affection and friendship might really mean. *Philia* is a notion fraught with so many difficulties of interpretation that it makes any straightforward translation difficult. For Aristotle, friends can be anyone provided that you have affection for them: relatives, those who are in your social group, other members of your wider society and even business partners. So affection is something to do with the willingness to care for and trust the other, and with feelings of mutual and reciprocated goodwill (Aristotle, 1984c: 1156a3–5). Above all, this is also an understanding that the other is someone with whom you might develop the same kind of relationship as you have with yourself. This involves a certain care for the self, it is not only an emotion directed towards others.

Contemporary definitions of friendship do not really seem to capture this Aristotelian understanding of it. Friendship is not only a somewhat warm emotion combined with a vague sense of loyalty, or merely what two or more persons are engaged in when they have 'shared ideas or tastes or skills or interests' (Saul, 1994: 140). For Aristotle, real friendship and community are actually rather dangerous relationships. Friendship is always an ambition, a desire, and desire necessarily involves activity, tension, risk and intensity (see 1984c: 1166b34–36). So friendship in the Athenian city was not a permanent condition enjoyed by happy citizens, but a way of living together perme-ated by trial and error, risk and uncertainty (see also Derrida, 1997: 20, 29), by gossip and slander (Kingwell, 1998: 323–326) and by distrust and betrayal (Yack, 1999: 285–287). To recap in Aristotle's words: 'Those who quickly show the marks of friendship to each other wish to be friends, but are not friends unless they both are lovable and know the fact; for a wish for friendship may arise quickly, but friendship does not' (1984c: 1156b30–33). Friendship needs to be worked at.

Perfect friendship, in which both friends trust each other unconditionally and in which one treats the other as you would treat yourself, is in Aristotle's opinion very rare and difficult. It should therefore not be seen as a set of characteristics of a relationship but rather as an ambition of the good citizen in the political community. Aristotle points out that perfect friendly relationships can never be entertained with many different people, if only because very few people are going to have the sort of character that you will see as 'good' (1984c: 1158a11–14). It is for such reasons that Aristotle contrasts the perfect kind of friendship to more down-to-earth varieties of it, that is, to friendships based on pleasure and utility – a casual lover, work colleague or member of the same sport team, for example. These instrumental friendships are unlikely to be free from tensions either, but they at least allow for the possibility that we can entertain civil relations with many people, for 'with a view to utility or pleasure it is possible that many people should please one, for many people are useful or pleasant, and these services take little time' (1984c: 1158a16–18).

In contrast to the perfect type of friendship, these less than perfect friendships do not take much time and investment, which is why they actually promise pleasure and utility fairly quickly. Like the utilitarian versions of stakeholder theory, this is really a description of a network of mutual support, of all those others that we need in order to occupy the position that we do. This is perfectly normal behaviour anyway, because Aristotle believes that it is only after one has satisfied these more instrumental needs that one starts to desire the perfect type of friendship. In the case of pleasure this seems to be pretty obvious for hedonistic young people who are living fast; in the case of utility this seems to be obvious for calculating business people who are always thinking about the bottom line. For both groups, musings about businesses as friendly communities would just be an instance of wishful thinking that has little relevance for their more immediate desires.

In the *Nichomachean Ethics*, when he focuses on utility-based friendship, Aristotle makes a similar distinction between legal and moral friendship (1984c: 1162b23), arguing that the former is bound by explicitly specified conditions whereas the latter is not. This means that moral friendship is always shaped by conflict and insecurity because a gift to your friend (such as a book like this one) might raise particular expectations that may or may not be fulfilled. But even under conditions of legal friendship, conflict and insecurity cannot be ruled out either. There is, as Aristotle points out, always reason for complaint, especially in business relationships. Suppose that a person has a contractual obligation to pay their debts to someone else. According to Aristotle, the creditor will always be inclined to take the contract as literally as possible, whereas the other party will inevitably try to stretch the terms of the contract. Some differences in interpretations are part and parcel of utility-based friendships because laws and rules are always ambiguous and capable of different readings. As Aristotle argues in the *Politics*, all people cling to justice, 'but their conceptions are imperfect and they do not express the whole idea', and therefore people in a dispute will often disagree because 'they are passing judgement on themselves, and most people are bad judges in their own case' (1984d: 1280a10–16).

All these ideas about conflict, ambiguity and insecurity suggest that in Aristotelian communities debate and argument are rife. This may be inconvenient for those who would like to believe that good laws will rule out ambiguity, or for those who would claim that warm feelings will in the end dissolve all problems (Yack, 1999: 287), but Aristotle's point is that this inconvenience is an intrinsic feature of morality. Right at the start of his *Nichomachean Ethics*, Aristotle alerts us to the difficulties involved when discussing morality or ethics (1984c: 1094b13–27). Differences of opinion and lack of precision, he argues, are always the case in political communities. It would therefore be foolish to expect in a treatise on ethics the kind of precision or agreement that can

63

be found, for example, among mathematicians. Human beings and their communities cannot be reduced to rules and laws.

When he speaks about virtues this becomes particularly clear. For Aristotle, the virtue is not so much an innate property of a person, but more the fulfilment of a task and the realisation of specific capabilities or possibilities. As such, virtue can be ascribed to both human and non-human entities. An instrument that works well is, in this sense at least, virtuous and so is a beast of burden that performs well. Thus we would speak of a 'good' hammer, or a 'good' book. Human excellence, on the other hand, should always be grounded in the character of the person, that is to say, not in 'nature' but in the combination of attitudes and behaviours that determine who one is (1984c: 1103a: 17–20; see also 1984a: 1220a37–1220b3). To say a person is 'good' is a judgement made about their habits of thought and action. This implies that virtue is only attainable if it is embedded in a particular formation of habits that allow the person to frequently engage in practical deliberation as well as a constant attempt to tame the less rational parts of the soul and create a certain moral robustness.

What is crucial is that Aristotle suggests that there is a necessary relationship between virtuousness and its social context. In discussing specific Aristotelian virtues, one will always have to take into consideration that Aristotle emphasises social or interpersonal virtues and thinks that morality requires the proper social setting. A person is, he stresses over and over again, a political creature, that is, a creature that belongs to the community. Quite simply, 'man is sociable by nature' (Aristotle, 1984c: 1097b11). A person without a community would be like a fish out of water, a stranger, so imagining ethics without community is an impossibility. The virtues put forward by Aristotle are typically communitarian, concerned with sharing and seeing the point of view of the other.

Almost at the end of his *Nichomachean Ethics*, Aristotle is at pains to explain that the independence necessary for a happy philosopher's life – a life which is not available to more practical people – should not be understood in terms of a total disengagement with the daily goings on of the community. While it is undoubtedly true that busyness and bustle can stand in the way of a contemplative life, the philosopher should never forget the fact of being a human being, living together with other human beings, and hence should try to put into practice whatever good characteristics they may have (see 1984c: 1178b5–7). Indeed, in order to immerse the self in the contemplative life, one must have taken care of one's daily affairs in a proper way. Good deeds can only be done in relationship to others. In our business transactions with shopkeepers and employees and students we will have to take care – and care is to be understood here as an emotion – that they will get what they are entitled to (1984c: 1178a11–13). Only gods, Aristotle alerts us, can evade this implacable law for they do not have the complex feelings that human beings have towards each other. Rather like Kant, Aristotle simply recognises the finitude of human existence and the fact that we are not carefree gods. As human beings we may aspire to become like them, but philosophical happiness is the best that we can get. In fact this is the very answer to the initial question that guides Aristotle's entire ethical system: what constitutes a happy life?

This question is not the same as the sort of ethical question that we have addressed in the previous two chapters: 'How are we to live?' Aristotle is very clear that excellence or virtuousness as such cannot be the goal of life:

> But even this appears too incomplete; for possession of excellence seems actually compatible with being asleep, or with lifelong inactivity, and, further, with the greatest sufferings and misfortunes; but a man who was living so, no one would call happy.
>
> (1984c: 1095b30–1096a1)

In other words, being unhappy in order to be virtuous is pointless, and suffering is unlikely to be good for its own sake. For Aristotle, virtuousness is a community oriented form of practical action, not the sort of rational calculation favoured by utilitarians, or the stern self-discipline that Kant imagined. But if Kant emphasised the struggle needed for a moral disposition, then perhaps Aristotle seems rather keen on showing off one's virtues in rather a smug way. Indeed, virtuous action as it is envisaged by Aristotle is perhaps a little bit too conspicuous, being characterised by contentment, self-sufficiency and also, to a certain degree, conceitedness. For almost all the Greek philosophers, virtuousness is not a private affair but something that is very visible in the community. A virtuousness that does not show off, that is not public, is simply unimaginable (and rather pointless). Frankly, this may have been the only ancient lesson that has been taken to heart by contemporary business ethics.

The conceitedness of the virtuous person, however, also serves to show that there is always something contentious about ethics. For Aristotle a virtue is always a path between two extremes, a continual balancing act, a **golden mean**. Too much courage is recklessness, and too little is cowardice. Too much confidence is conceitedness, too little is shyness. It is very tempting to reduce his ethics to a system that makes this into a form of balanced accounting, but the idea of the mean was never intended to arithmetically determine the right point between a deficit and an excess. Virtue ethics is not really about golden rules. Aristotle famously warns the reader that one should not aspire to more precision than is necessary for a particular topic (1984c: 1094b13) and ethics is a case in point. A broad outline rather than a very systematic and accurate account will be quite enough, because simple rules can never be applied in all circumstances. Aristotle adds that with ethics the proof of any idea always lies in practice, that is to say, in particular actions done in specific circumstances. What we need in such circumstances is practical wisdom, not rule-like generalisations.

BUSINESS COMMUNITIES?

Practical wisdom undoubtedly sounds like a good thing for business people, but to what extent can Aristotelian virtue ethics be 'applied' in the way that Solomon wants them to be? There seem to be two difficulties here, one related to the problem of whether we can treat organisations as communities, the other concerning the sort of advice that Aristotle appears to be giving us.

Firstly, Aristotle's understanding of community is certainly not warm and cuddly. He sees real communities as being confused and contradictory places that manifest all sorts of political tensions. So far so good, organisations manifest all sorts of tensions, and are certainly political places too, so perhaps virtue ethics could apply quite easily. However, when Aristotle is writing about community, he is encouraging us not to assume that business relationships are the same as friendships. In a sense, he is suggesting that friendship and community are not simply states of affairs that we can start and stop easily, in the same way that we might begin work at 9.00am, or leave a job at the end of the week. In part, this is a matter of common experience, because we rarely care about work in the same intense way that we might care about family and friends. We do care about people at work, but most of us wouldn't carry on going to work if they stopped paying us. In addition, the aim of businesses is really just to make money, whilst the aim of friendship and community is happiness and living a good life. The aim of real friendship is the friendship itself, and we could almost never say this about businesses. So when Solomon draws upon Aristotle, he is doing so in rather a limited way. For Aristotle, there is no particular reason why we should not try to live well and virtuously at work, but these sort of practices will only be a pale shadow of the really complex and difficult virtue that is needed amongst our friends and community.

The contemporary virtue theorist Alasdair MacIntyre (1981) has argued that the figure of the manager, as a contemporary character, is incapable of virtue in a genuinely Aristotelian sense. Because the manager is a manipulator, and because their aim is efficiency, and not human flourishing, their friendships will always be legal, and not moral. Whilst MacIntyre may be very pessimistic about business, it seems to us that his understanding is closer to Aristotle's than is Solomon's. There is a more general point that is also worth making before we close this chapter. Solomon is making a really important plea here. He is asking that business organisations be like families, or communities or some other form of warm human caring association. He wants organisations to be fully moral places, places where humanity and empathy can inform decisions. The reason that this sort of claim has been so often welcomed is precisely because these are *not* usually the sort of characteristics that business organisations are generally believed to possess. Quite the opposite. When we think about business, we are more likely to think about characteristics like ruthlessness, self-interest and hypocrisy. People often believe that business executives are like the greedy, plotting Mr Burns, from *The Simpsons*, and not heroic characters who really do care about their employees and customers. The vast majority of popular portrayals of managers are as calculating megalomaniacs or smug hypocrites. They might say that they care, but only in the sense that you are one of their 'stakeholders', or worse, one of their objects of calculation. Indeed, and as we outlined in Chapter 2, if we thought that businesses were already ethical, we would have no need for business ethics anyway.

This is not a comment on what businesses are 'really like'. No doubt there are good people and bad people in every business, but it is to stress that any account of businesses that imagines them as shared cultures, or happy communities, or associations of equal citizens is engaged in some form of wishful thinking (Parker, 2000). Solomon and other virtue ethicists are being extraordinarily optimistic if they think that their version of Aristotelian virtues is going to make much difference in large organisations that have managerial organisational structures and operate in capitalist markets. Being optimistic is not a bad thing, but what leads Solomon to believe that his words might change the way that businesses operate?

The power of virtue ethics is precisely that it begins by recognising that social context shapes everyday morality. It does not apply abstract golden rules, but attempts to understand what counts as good in different places and at different times. It seems ironic then that the business ethicists who wish to spread virtue theory seem to have neglected this central insight. Their sort of virtue ethics ends up being curiously de-socialised, a sermonising about goodness in business that fails to take the context of business seriously. Because of this deficit, we will be doing this sort of work in Chapters 7 and 8, when we look at bureaucracy and capitalism respectively, and also (like Aristotle) begin to dismantle the boundaries between ethics and politics.

'How can I live a good life?' is not a question that can be answered with a code that applies here or there, or indeed a question that can ever be answered once and for all. Yet it is this very specificity of virtue ethics that raises a final question for this chapter. The comforting thing about golden rules is that we might think that we have found the answer to ethics, and all textbooks should contain answers. Shouldn't they? The problem is that virtue ethics suggests that different textbooks, written by Athenians or Spartans, Klingons or Vulcans, will contain different answers. And all these answers will be right, because different virtues and characters matter in different societies. This is the problem of **relativism** that we mentioned at the start of this chapter. But what if we disagree, perhaps fundamentally, with the morality that matters somewhere else? Of course this is a problem that we encounter often enough, when we travel and come into contact with the food tastes, laws or assumptions about gender that apply some-where else. We might well not agree with what other people believe, but being sensitive to such issues is part of being a cosmopolitan and sophisticated person. But using this same logic, it then becomes quite difficult to understand how any other form of virtue might be criticised. When in Rome, do as the Romans do, and don't presume that you know better.

If ethics is a purely relative social matter, then perhaps we have reached the end of talking about ethics. If we treat business as a different culture to the one that people live in, then perhaps we should not rush in demanding that they change what they do just because we say so. That would be a terribly arrogant position, and one that would be unlikely to change business very much. Perhaps philosophy has nothing to say to business people. If the practice of business has different virtues than those that apply in universities, and perhaps in everyday life, then on what grounds can business ethicists (let alone 'critical' ones) speak about business? All of Solomon's preaching about certain values, Bowie's version of Kant and the many versions of utilitarianism and stakeholder theory, together with all our re-readings of this work might be just so much hot air. Different opinions, formed in different places. That's all.

But of course that is not all. You are only half way through this book, and we did tell you at the start that we wanted to introduce some new thinking into business ethics, as well as re-thinking some of the old thinking. So, in the next chapter, we want to ask a more fundamental question. It seems to us that much of the thought that we have covered so far has simply assumed 'ethics'. It has largely been thinking that assumes that we know what ethics is, and merely need to name it (using concepts like pleasure, or intention, or virtue) and order it (by applying the utilitarian calculus, or categorical imperative, or golden mean). But we can give something a name, and arrange it neatly, without understanding what it means. So what does 'ethics' mean?

Chapter 6

The meaning of ethics

INTRODUCTION: THE CHARM OF BUSINESS ETHICS

In 1938 Gaston Bachelard, the French philosopher of science, published a charming little book with the title *The Psychoanalysis of Fire*. In this book he discusses the way that scientists have, through the course of history, treated fire as an object of inquiry. Bachelard begins from quite a simple observation:

> When, as I have done on many occasions, one asks educated persons and even eminent scientists, 'What is fire?', one receives vague or tautological answers which unconsciously repeat the most ancient and fanciful philosophical theories.
>
> (1938: 2–3)

Rather than letting this rest, Bachelard enquires into how this situation could have come about. Obviously the discovery and manipulation of fire was central to the evolution of the human species. And for thousands of years people have talked about fire and have created stories about its origins and powers. But to science, fire has always remained somewhat enigmatic, partly due to the fact that the concept of oxygen is a very recent invention, usually attributed to the English chemist Joseph Priestley (or the French founder of chemistry, Antoine Lavoisier), who posited the existence of oxygen in 1774. One might have thought that the discovery of oxygen would have cleared things up, given that one can make a pretty simple explanation of what makes fire when listing the ingredients: heat, fuel, oxygen.

With this kind of recipe for fire, which explains what one needs to make a fire, one might be excused for thinking that chemistry would have finally straightened out the question of fire. But quite the opposite. At the very moment when an explanation of fire became available due to the discovery of oxygen, fire disappeared as an object from scientific discourse. As Bachelard notes:

> In the course of time the chapters on fire in chemistry textbooks have become shorter and shorter. There are, indeed, a good many modern books on chemistry in which it is impossible to find any mention of flame or fire.
>
> (1938: 2)

In his book, Bachelard sets himself the task of understanding the inability, or unwillingness, of modern science, or the modern science of his day, to discuss fire, and in doing so provides us with concepts that we can apply to a number of other objects. What he does is to identify what he calls the 'epistemological obstacles' (1938: 59) that stand in the way of understanding fire. In particular, he pays attention to the nature of fire as an object, and the way that it presents itself to our consciousness. That is, he is concerned to think about the way that we perceive the phenomenon of fire. He discusses, amongst many other experiences of fire, the way that people will sit and gaze at fire, around a campfire or at an open fireplace in a home. And as one sits and watches fire, the fire tends to produce a hypnotic and calming, pleasurable effect. Not only does a fire bring warmth, but its presence weaves a certain magic, a certain charm on those that view it. Bachelard relates the inability of scientists to treat fire directly to the peculiar way that the object of fire presents itself to consciousness. With fire, the scientist encounters an object that is charming and attractive, mysterious and entrancing. And it is very difficult for anyone, let alone a scientist, to break away from the charm of the phenomenon and then treat it 'objectively'.

Interesting enough, but how is this relevant for a book about business ethics? This example is important for us because Bachelard's explanation of the way that scientists treat fire, and some of his concepts such as the idea of epistemological obstacles, can be used in explaining the way that scientists and others approach their object. Most directly, for the purposes of our argument in this book, it seems to us that 'business ethics' is an object very much like fire. After all who, in their right mind, could question ethics? Who could be against business ethics? Business ethics is a charming and attractive idea, seemingly irresistible to many. But what Bachelard's story about the fire reminds us of is that sometimes charming objects can hold us spellbound and prevent us from reflecting on their meaning, their significance and their potential danger. It is as if the warmth of these objects immerses us in a feeling that somehow renders critical distance impossible.

So it is with ethics. What we have done so far is to provide you with an overview of ethical theories ranging from an ethics of consequences to an ethics of intentions and an ethics of virtue. We have established links between these theories and business ethics and we have tried to take issue with some of the ways in which business ethicists discuss these theories. But let us inquire more deeply into ethics itself. What is its nature? What is its meaning?

MEANING

Early in the twentieth century, a subtle and apparently small shift took place in philosophical circles. A philosopher by the name of Edmund Husserl (1859–1938) was teaching and writing in what appeared to be a traditional way. He asked a basic question, a question that philosophers have been asking at least since the time of the ancient Greeks.

This question, to put it simply, is: what is the meaning of this or that phenomenon? Husserl was not the first to raise this question. His so-called **phenomenology** should be related to a tradition of German philosophy that goes back at least to the philosopher, physicist and mathematician Johan Heinrich Lambert (1728–1777) who is credited with having invented the term. For Lambert, 'phenomenology' was a 'doctrine of appearances', that is to say, a theory about various forms of pseudo-knowledge and about ways to combat their illusions. For philosophers such as Kant and, importantly, Georg Wilhelm Friedrich Hegel (1770–1831), phenomenology would lose its association with illusion or false knowledge and rather refer to the various forms of consciousness that appear to the mind. Kant and Hegel set out to describe in great detail these 'appearances' and they also suggested that these appearances were subject to a kind of developmental process. What appears to the mind of a child is not what appears to the mind of an adult or, as Hegel was keen to point out, what appears to an individual is not what appears to the 'mind' of a collective. Different kinds of minds are 'directed' to the world in different ways and hence experience different kind of phenomena. Edmund Husserl (1859–1938) pushed phenomenology into novel directions when he started to ask about the meaning of these phenomena. He wondered what *sense* they make.

Now, Husserl was by no means the only philosopher to ask this question. But what makes him a key figure in the history of philosophy is *how* he approached it. When we think about the meaning of things, we sometimes think that meaning resides in objects themselves. So, for example, the meaning of a film can be found from watching it, or the meaning of a book from reading it. But the problem with this theory of meaning should be quite clear – if meaning simply resided in things, then different observers would almost always come up with the same meaning, providing they looked hard enough. But observers disagree with each other. Some of you probably hate this book, others might love it, others might not understand it, others disagree with it, and so on. Because of this problem, some have been inclined to think that meaning does not reside in the objects that we observe, but in the human subjects that do the observing. After all, a film with no one watching it, or a book with no-one reading it, would not 'mean' very much, would it?

While Husserl has often been accused of endorsing a subjectivist theory of meaning – meaning does not reside in a thing but is related to the person who 'makes' meaning – he was in fact very critical of *both* the theory of meaning that privileges things and the theory of meaning that privileges people. The first assumes that the object is all that matters, and the second that it is only subjects that matter. Instead Husserl argued that meaning is a result of a complex interplay of an object and an observing subject. It is at the meeting of the subject with a phenomenon that meaning takes place. He therefore set out to construct a phenomenology that would take account of the relations between the object of enquiry and the enquiring subject, and in doing so create a new understanding of meaning.

But Husserl did more than this. Husserl took up the insights of earlier thinkers such as Kant, who argued in his *Critique of Pure Reason* (1781) that perception is always influenced by previous ideas, and by a vast array of assumptions and prejudices. The first task of Husserl's phenomenology, therefore, was to clear away these prior ideas, and get, if possible, 'to the thing in itself'. Husserl certainly did not think that this would be an easy task, and he sometimes implied that hardly anyone has been able to ever achieve this in the past. But despite the difficulty, it is an essentially important task, and perhaps the only task of philosophy: to clear away the barriers that stand in the way of understanding, which involves clarifying and demystifying the phenomenon that we have in front of us. Otherwise we stand hypnotised by the objects of perception, as in the case of the flickering flames of the fire. Husserl saw it as his task to get beyond this hypnosis, even if this would entail asking apparently silly questions that defy common sense.

This way of thinking about meaning has had a profound impact on twentieth century thought. It has made its way into how we think about society, culture, literature, art, poetry and ethics (though we may wonder what influence it has had on business ethics so far). However, it is perhaps best known not through Husserl directly, but through another German philosopher who is widely considered to be Husserl's best and most inventive student, Martin Heidegger (1889–1976). Heidegger was one of the most brilliant thinkers of the twentieth century, but many people think his writings are obscure and even confused. Others believe that there is something very important at stake in Heidegger's work. In his most famous book, *Being and Time* (1927), he boldly condemned the entire tradition of Western philosophy for having forgotten how to ask the question of the meaning of basic things, such as 'Being'. Think about this for a moment, and you will realise just what a difficult question this is. What does it mean to exist and what does it mean to be? For Heidegger, though being is the most universal of things, 'this cannot mean that it is the one which is clearest or that it needs no further discussion. It is rather the darkest of all' (1927: 4).

So Heidegger chastises the philosophers not only with an inability to answer the question of the meaning of Being, but with actually forgetting that this is a question at all. The implication is that philosophers, who have been charged with thinking since the Greeks, have not really been thinking very thoroughly, if at all. And science does not fare any better. He infamously claimed that '[s]cience does not think' (1978: 373). Modern knowledge has been overcome by technology, by an instrumental way of getting things done, and as a result we have lost our ability to imagine, to speculate and to think. This relates not only to the way that we ask questions, but to the questions that we are able to ask in the first place.

While Heidegger might appear to be a little pessimistic, some see in his work a hopefulness and a desire for the renewal of thought. His thought has also been subjected to critical scrutiny across the board, as a range of thinkers have tried to extract from Heidegger what is valuable and profound while being careful of what is extravagant, poorly-argued or outright dangerous. After all, admiring a thinker does not mean that you have to agree with everything that they say. And it is perhaps in these critical responses to Heidegger that some of the most productive thinking of recent years has emerged. In response to his insistence on thinking as well as to his scathing judgement about science, many commentators have taken up the challenge and have formulated new ideas about the meaning of phenomena. From Husserl and Heidegger we have learned the importance of a sustained and profound thinking of the meaning of things, from the most everyday to the most abstract.

THE MEANING OF ETHICS

In relation to ethics it is perhaps not Husserl and Heidegger themselves but Emmanuel Levinas (1906–1995), a student of both, who offers us much to learn about the meaning of ethics. Husserl and Heidegger were working in the early and mid twentieth century but most of Levinas's work was written after the Second World War. His transformation of phenomenology, and in particular his efforts to emphasise ethics in phenomenology in particular and in philosophy in general, are important for what we have to say in this book.

While we do not wish to provide you with an introduction to Levinas, we would like to alert you to how he turned his 'phenomenological' gaze towards ethics. At its simplest this involves asking the kind of questions that Bachelard asked about fire, but turning these to ethics. These are basic questions, such as: 'What is ethics?' 'Is ethics a thing?' 'How does ethics relate to other concepts, such as science and politics?' and, perhaps most importantly, 'What do we mean when we use the word ethics'?

Levinas is very suspicious of the seeming ease with which even great philosophers such as Aristotle and Kant have taken on these questions. Ethics, they have argued, is about consequences, virtues, duties and intentions. But is it? Or more precisely, is this all there is to say about the possible meaning of ethics? Levinas asks about the meaning of ethics not in order to establish a new or alternative system of ethics but in order to understand the meaning of sentences about ethics. As he himself put it: 'My task does not consist in constructing ethics; I only try to find its meaning' (Levinas, 1985: 90).

Trying to find the meaning of ethics might seem pretty straightforward. We could look it up in the dictionary, in the glossary of this book, or in other books on ethics or on business ethics. But the problem is that the meaning of ethics is far from clear, and definitions tend to push us in the directions of other words (such as 'good' and 'bad') which are themselves also open to contestation. Dictionary definitions are often circular. For 'ethics', see 'good'. For 'good', see 'ethics'. Indeed, as we saw in the first half of this book, the various ethical theories that have dominated business ethics (utilitarianism, deontology and virtue ethics) have tended to simply assume the meaning of ethics. It is also important to note that they have all assumed that ethics means something different. This is just what we would expect if, as Husserl suggested, the meaning of objects does not lie solely within the object, but also has something to do with the subject who observes it. People disagree about ethics.

The problem with an **essentialist** approach to ethics is the basic fact that ethics can be conceived in a number of different ways. Because of this, Levinas could be said to take an *anti-essentialist* position in relation to ethics. This means that he does not set out to find the essence of ethics, as if it might be hiding under a rock waiting to be found. Levinas is also anti-essentialist in that he does not think that a study of ethics will result in a clear or coherent closed system of rules or procedures as to how to behave. He resists the notion that ethics could form a 'totality' which would be enclosed and finite. This would be like the sort of ethical code that businesses sometimes produce, one in which good and bad are defined by laws. For him ethics is not about such closure, but about openness and the infinite. Ethics cannot be finished with, or solved, by a technocratic procedure. For this reason he speaks of his work as involving an 'ethics without ethical system' (Levinas, 2001: 81).

To understand what is meant by anti-essentialist ethics, we could consider the example that Levinas himself offers. It comes from the well-known children's story *The Little Prince* (Saint-Exupéry, 1999). In this short story, the narrator tells of meeting with a very special young boy, the 'little prince'. As a child, the narrator, who had always wanted to be an artist, had been forced to learn mathematics, geography and history. With these skills the narrator became a pilot and all was well until one day he crashed in the Sahara desert. There he first meets the little prince, who insists that he draws a picture of a sheep. The pilot tries to draw a sheep, but is unable to draw one that satisfies the little prince. Finally, after the little prince rejects all of his attempts, the pilot draws a small box. The pilot explains: this is a box with little holes in it and the sheep that you want is inside. The little prince is delighted but does not disturb the sheep, as it is sleeping.

Levinas draws an analogy between this story of the little prince and the way that he has tried to approach ethics. Rather than drawing ethics, which will be rejected by all the little princes and princesses who think they know what it is, he tries to draw the box in which ethics might be sleeping. This suggests that ethics is not something that we can approach directly or something that is easy to represent, but neither should we deny that it is important, or give up because minor royalty are confidently telling us what is in the box. Levinas explains:

> I do not know how to draw the solution to insoluble problems. It is still sleeping in the bottom of a box; but a box over which persons who have drawn close to each other keep watch. I have no idea other than the idea of the idea that one should have. The abstract drawing of the parallelogram – cradle of our hopes. I have the idea of a possibility in which the impossible may be sleeping.
>
> (1999: 89)

OTHERS AND THE OTHER

Given his anti-essentialism, which causes him to call into question well-entrenched understandings of ethics, Levinas might appear to be rather pessimistic or even nihilistic.

Can we say anything meaningful about ethics at all? Is Levinas's contribution not entirely negative?

Our answer is no. We, and many other commentators, believe that there is also a positive side to his work. Levinas has been an important figure in a now vast movement in European philosophy that has sought to both re-emphasise the importance of ethics and also to transform the meaning of ethics. Levinas's work has been an important motivation for many authors in this rethinking of ethics, and even if many have disagreed with some of his ideas, others have joined in his project of rethinking ethics. Here we want to sketch some of the basic ideas of Levinas's reconstruction of ethics.

Central to the work of Levinas and the work of Levinasian thinkers is the idea of '**the Other**'. This is often written with a capital 'O', which is not a mistake or something merely done to appear clever. It is done to indicate the specific meaning that Levinas gives to 'the Other', and to distinguish this from 'the other'. This distinction relates to the two different French words, *autre* and *autrui*, which are translated as 'other' and 'Other' (see Levinas, 1961: 24). These words refer to two different registers of otherness, to two different ways in which someone or something could be considered to display alterity or otherness. 'Autre' ('other') simply refers to other people in general, to the vast mass of other people. 'Autrui' ('Other'), however, refers to someone who is so close as to open up his or her radical difference to me. 'Autrui' is not just another person, but displays radical otherness.

This is an all-important distinction for Levinas. His ethical thought is all about the relation with the Other. Of course, this is not entirely unusual, because ethics has almost always been about the way that one relates to others. Utilitarianism, deontology and virtue ethics all emphasise the way that one relates to others, in terms of the greatest good, of intentions and of the virtues that one should display in the community of human beings. In fact, it would be hard to imagine what ethics would mean if it did not involve a relation with others of some sort. And this is why Levinas takes the relation to others as the starting point of his reflection on ethics. Even if we subject everything else to scrutiny, if we doubt all the common sense that congeals around 'ethics', the idea that ethics is about a relation to the Other is one of the things that remains.

But Levinas is suspicious of the way that relations with others have been treated in Western philosophy. He is deeply concerned with the way that people in modern societies see others. And this is why it is important to distinguish between the other (without a capital) and the Other (with a capital) – because, Levinas argues, Western thought has often denied real Otherness, and has converted it into this smaller or reduced version of the other. Levinas shows the way that relations with others often reduce otherness to the category of the same. For example, when I see someone else, do I not often have the inclination to treat this person as someone who shares, at least to a certain extent, the same characteristics or desires as me? But what if everybody else is not just a mirror-image of me? What if they have really different ideas and needs? How can I treat them ethically if I do not recognise this difference? So otherness, for it to be Otherness, must break with this reduction of the other to the same. Otherness which is not radically different should not be considered otherness at all. In short: 'The absolutely other is the Other' (Levinas, 1961: 39).

We encounter other people all of the time. Human life is social. There are basically four ways of treating these people: (1) we can treat them as objects; (2) we can treat them as the Same; (3) we can treat them as others; (4) we can treat them as an Other. For Levinas, it is only in the relation with the Other, the radically other, that we find ethics. Here we see that Levinas's anti-essentialism is not total. For him the essence of ethics, if there is such a thing, is a matter of the relation with the Other. That is to say, ethics involves an opening up of the subject, a willingness to allow oneself to be changed by experiencing the difference of the Other.

Imagine some tourists visiting exotic places and meeting strange people. Imagine them treating these places and these people as a set of photo-opportunities. They will probably not be changed by their experiences. On the other hand, imagine a traveller who is affected by what Levinas refers to as the Other. What would they experience? As they eat the local food, try to learn some language and get lost in the backstreets, they will undergo a radical change. Even when they have left the place where the Other lives, they take some of it with them, because they have been transformed (Jack and Phipps, 2005). As is the case with travel, so it is, if we are to believe Levinas, with ethics. It is only by allowing the existence of otherness to change us that we can be said to have a truly ethical relationship. That which is outside us, and that which we acknowledge as strange, takes us beyond ourselves. Beyond our common sense. The Other transforms the one who sees the Other.

Levinas explains the encounter with the Other through an extended discussion of what he calls 'the face'. As he puts it, we encounter the Other through the vision of the face, through the face-to-face encounter. When he speaks of 'the face', however, he is not speaking of any old face, the kind you might see when you raise your eyes from this book, for example. The face is not an empirical face. It is much more mysterious than that, for in it the manifestation of otherness becomes most apparent. The face of the Other 'is neither seen nor touched – for in vision or tactile sensation the identity of the I envelops the alterity of the object. The alterity of the Other does not depend on any quality that would distinguish him from me' (Levinas, 1961: 194). What Levinas is pointing to here is something that lies behind the physical objectivity of the face, which he calls the 'plastic form' of the face. This outward face is otherness, but beyond this is the experience of an Other, an Other that calls on me to respond, that calls me towards the ethical.

Levinas insists that ethics is not a matter of theory or word play but is part of the most practical everyday experience. What this might mean is illustrated by one of the stories that Levinas tells from his own experience. During the Second World War Levinas, a Jew, was captured by German soldiers. Because of his official rank in the French army they did not kill him immediately but rather sent him to a prison camp, where he spent the remainder of the war. Levinas tells a story of how, when at the camp, the prisoners met a dog who befriended them. From the story it emerges that the dog displayed an openness to the prisoners that was of a higher ethical order than the German townspeople who treated the Jewish prisoners as dirty sub-humans. As he tells the story:

> A little dog associated himself with us prisoners one day as we were going to the workplace; the guard did not protest; the dog would install himself in the commando and let us go to work alone. But when we used to come back from work, very relieved, he welcomed us, jumping up and down. In this corner of Germany, where walking through the village we would be looked at by the villagers as *Juden* [Jews], this dog evidently took us for human beings. The villagers certainly did not injure us or do us any harm, but their expressions were clear. We were the condemned and the contaminated carriers of germs. And this little dog welcomed us at the entrance of the camp, barking happily and jumping up and down amicably around us.
>
> (Levinas, 2001: 41)

Could a dog be more ethical than a person? If the dog displayed more openness to the Other, Levinas would suggest that this might be the case. There is a further implication too. If we follow the general principles of virtue ethics, then German soldiers and villagers no doubt might reason that what they were doing was quite right. The soldiers of the German army had 'God with Us' written on their belt-buckles. They probably did not believe that they were doing wrong. Yet, for Levinas, whatever these soldiers and villagers thought they were doing, they were denying the fundamental ethical relation with the Other. They did not even treat Jewish people as merely other human beings, but flatly denied them any personhood at all. In other words, these subjects were treated as objects – as objects with which one should not entertain any ethical relationship. Indeed, with respect to these sub-humans, the very notion of ethics and responsibility became devoid of any meaning whatsoever.

THE OTHER AND CRITIQUE

One might think that Levinas's image of ethics verges on the unrealistic. For him it involves an infinite openness to the Other, one in which my very own sense of selfhood is called into question. When we try to apply this to our own lives, we might be able to remember life-changing situations in which this has happened, but experiences of fragility in the face of the Other seem to be rare. Meeting a future partner, or reading a life-changing book, or being moved to tears by seeing a homeless person begging – perhaps these are the sort of things that Levinas means, but they are not common.

We should not take this to be a limitation or a problem with Levinas, but rather the very thing that he is so good at drawing our attention to. That is to say, Levinas offers us a way of thinking critically about how and why it is that we experience an openness to the Other so infrequently. If we agree with Levinas that ethics is something about openness to the Other, then the lives that we live – both in business and in our homes – do not seem to measure up very well. We seem to be insulated from Otherness, doing our tourism from hotels, seeing the starving via the TV, reading books about how to be good. This is the limitation that Levinas shows us. But the ethical relation to the Other calls us to an alterity in another and less obvious sense.

Levinas realises that, in the modern world, we do not display anything like the openness to the Other that he understands as ethics. Instead, we mostly live a pale narrow version of ethics, an ethics of codes and rules, an ethics that is useful for our business. In his works he makes some moves towards explaining why this is the case, although we believe that he does not make this quite as clear as he could. Therefore, in the next two chapters of this book we will look at what we think are two of the most important social forms that restrict the responsibilities that we display towards others. In Chapter 7 we discuss the way that responsibilities towards Others can be denied by bureaucratic organisational structures that dampen any sense of responsibility for the Other. In Chapter 8 we look at the way in which, in capitalist societies, we tend to treat others as objects that are available for economic manipulation and gain. In these two chapters we will therefore move towards an understanding of the two parts of what one of us has elsewhere called 'market managerialism' (see Parker, 2002a). In Chapter 7 we discuss management and bureaucracy and in Chapter 8 we discuss the market and capitalism, both being essential components of the contemporary business landscape, and both being routinely ignored or treated uncritically by most people who write about business ethics.

We are trying both to supplement and to extend Levinas's analysis of ethics as relation to the Other. At the same time we will be drawing attention to the way that Levinas always recalls us to an ethics that is *critical* of the way things are, that displays a suspicion of common sense. By analysing bureaucracy and capitalism we will be taking on two of the central figures of modern organised business and also of business ethics. Following commentators like Bauman (1989; 1993), we claim that they can, in specific ways, delimit responsibilities to the Other. In doing so we wish to gauge the extent to which, and the ways in which, bureaucracy and capitalism are significant forces that press against anything that could be called ethics in the Levinasian sense. Of course, Levinas is by no means the only source of ethical criticism. But his relentless probing for the meaning of ethics seems to be particularly useful if we want to understand how bureaucracy and capitalism (that is to say, business) might have actually changed the meaning of ethics today.

As we continue this journey, we are also taking up the idea that ethics calls us to imagine other worlds and other social formations that might look inconceivable to us at the moment. Put simply, this is a call towards the willingness to be critical of the current order of things. My responsibility to the Other is not just something that happens in a space in which everything remains stable. I could assume that everything is already in its right place, and that what I want is no surprises, but that would be to deny the Other from the very beginning. If I am afraid to leave my hotel, I will learn little about this new place. If I already think that the world that I live in is the best of all possible worlds, then I have no need for a book on ethics. The Other calls me to responsibility in a *different* way, both in the sense that my relation to the Other will be different and that I will be different. And in such a context, the very world that you and we inhabit might be a radically different one too.

Levinas's ideas might guide us in our endeavours to imagine a different world. Like a few other philosophers he has looked into the fire of ethics. And as Bachelard might also point out, if you get too close to the fire, you may get burned.

Chapter 7

Denying ethics I: bureaucracy

INTRODUCTION

If what we understand to be 'ethics' is shaped by social context, then business ethicists need to try to understand that context. That is, unless they believe that God or reason will eventually deliver some eternal rules that will make equal sense in any place or time. However, as we have seen in the book so far, this prospect doesn't look that likely at the moment. So what would it mean to understand social context? Business ethicists have certainly spent quite a lot of time writing about the things that managers should do, and a certain amount of time considering the relationship between their businesses and the states and societies that they are a part of. However, there is very little evidence that business ethicists have considered the opposite, the way in which social context has shaped business. Other philosophers, such as Aristotle, who we came across in Chapter 5, emphasised the close relationship between individual ethical action (*ethos*) and social political action (*polis*), but this isn't something that has preoccupied business ethicists too much. In the next chapter we will look at the economic context of capitalism for some answers. In this chapter we will open out the question of the relationship between individual ethical action and social context, by looking at context in terms of business organisations themselves.

It is easy for us to believe that we have always lived in a society of organisations. Nowadays, in much of the world, we are born in hospitals, taught in schools, work in organisations, and are buried by funeral directors in cemeteries maintained by local councils or facilities companies. Our money is held in banks; our food, entertainment, houses and transport are provided by corporations; and our clothing is marketed with the name of the organisation that made it. This book was brought to you by an organisation, Routledge, now part of Taylor & Francis. The Taylor & Francis Group has offices in London, Brighton, Basingstoke and Abingdon in the UK, New York and Philadelphia in the USA, and in Singapore and Sydney. It publishes more than 800 journals and around 2,300 new books each year, and has a backlist in excess of 20,000 specialist titles. It is a big organisation. You might like to think about the universities that employ the authors of this book; the ink and paper manufacturers; the printers; the distribution company that moved the book from the printers; the (real or internet) bookshop that sold you this book; or the library that you borrowed it from. In the modern world, citizens live suspended in a web of organisations. This is not to suggest that nowadays all people are living in this web. Against such a suggestion, critics might point out that the majority of people on this planet are still living in conditions of disorganisation and lawlessness and they argue that liberal-capitalism can be blamed for this. That we live in a web of organisations should not tempt us to think that there is nothing outside of this web.

There have been large 'organisations' in human history. Think of the armies, monasteries, churches and states that fill history books. But the large 'business' organisation, or corporation, is a relatively new invention (Bakan, 2004; Korten, 1995; Micklethwait and Wooldridge, 2003). Corporations are fictional entities, legally constructed non-humans that are exempted from many of the laws of a particular state. Like similar words – company, organisation, association – this is a word that refers to the collective activity of a group of individuals, usually (but not always) those engaged in some form of commercial business. The first English corporations were charitable institutions – hospitals, schools and churches – that used incorporation to avoid taxes, death duties, and so on. Having a license from the Crown meant that, in certain defined circumstances (which did not initially include profit making) they would be treated as different in kind from the people who inhabited them. When, in the sixteenth century, similar charters were awarded to trade associations, this gradually led to the construction of large profit-making companies of shareholders such as the Company of Merchant Adventurers (1505), the Russia Company (1553) and the Levant Company (1581). Perhaps the best known was the East India Company which conquered a subcontinent, ruled over 250 million people, raised and supported the largest standing army in the world, deployed 43 warships and employed its own bishops. It was, in a very real sense, a global corporation. As you will remember, it also employed J. S. Mill.

The construction and legitimation of large business organisations has raised all sorts of questions about the morality of those people who work within them. Let us pause a minute here, because we might want to wonder why this is the case. Even though the rise of the business corporation has been unstoppable, our society has always harboured ambivalent feelings about this, and has never been able to suppress certain suspicions with respect to the motives and means used by business people to get what they want. Before the rise of big business, this was generally aimed at the moral qualities of individual merchants: in the plays of Shakespeare or Molière you find many examples of this suspicion towards business people. Even Adam Smith, the so-called father of capitalism, suggested in 1776 that 'People of the same trade seldom meet together, even for merriment and diversion, but the conversation ends in a conspiracy against the public, or in some contrivance to raise prices' (Smith, 1776: 55). The point here is that merchants, 'sharpers' and 'userers' were people of questionable morality. But this was largely a judgement about individuals. Perhaps it might be assumed that certain sorts of people would be attracted into this sort of trade: greedy, clever and calculating people. The sort of people who you would not trust because their character did not seem to include a conscience. And if they were challenged about over-charging, or mixing wood shavings with the flour they used to make bread, they might apologise (and not mean it) or smile like a crocodile at being found out (but not feel guilty).

THE BANALITY OF EVIL

Now consider a very different story. When living in Argentina in 1960, the Nazi officer Adolf Eichmann was kidnapped and smuggled to Israel, where he was put on trial for crimes against humanity. The *New Yorker* magazine sent Hannah Arendt to cover the trial. In her book *Eichmann in Jerusalem* (1963) she considers how a dull little man such as Eichmann could have been responsible for transporting countless Jews to concentration camps. The facts of Eichmann's case had been established before the trial and were never disputed. Far from being evil, as the prosecution painted Eichmann, Arendt suggests that he was an average person, a petty bureaucrat interested primarily in furthering his career. As she writes, 'everybody could see that this man was not a "monster", but it was difficult indeed not to suspect that he was a clown' (1963: 54). What he had done relied upon the organisational power of a totalitarian state, a conformist adherence to the Nazi cause and a considerable capacity for self-deception. Indeed, Eichmann's only defence during the trial was 'I was just following orders'. The point being that breaking an order itself constitutes an immorality of its own kind. Arendt's suggestion is a disturbing one. We would like to think that anyone who could perpetrate such horror must be different from us, and that such atrocities are exceptions in our world – but was Eichmann even aware that his actions were wrong? A huge number of ordinary Germans were involved in the **holocaust**, but did they all know that they were acting unethically? Such judgements, Arendt seems to suggest, should not only involve condemnations of individual character, as is the case in the examples that you may find in the works of Shakespeare or Molière, but must consider the social contexts within which certain ideas about 'good' and 'bad' were constructed. Indeed, Arendt suggests that, 'under the conditions of the Third Reich only "exceptions" could be expected to react "normally" '(1963: 26–27). From the viewpoint of our moment in history, disobeying orders and breaking with the 'morality' of the time would be a testament to strength of character, and behaving abnormally would be normal.

The idea of 'rule following' is an idea of major importance in an organised society. One of the definitional characteristics of any formal organisation is that it has formal rules. If an organisation didn't have rules concerning what different members should do, how much they get paid, who has authority and so on, then it wouldn't really be an organisation in the modern sense of the word. When Eichmann defended himself by saying that he was merely following orders, he was actually pointing to a common way that people in organisations still account for themselves nowadays. It is almost as if organisations allow people to disclaim personal responsibility for things that they have done. This is an argument that has some force. If your lecturer sent you an email which said that copying essays from the internet would be fine, then, despite what your university's plagiarism policy (and perhaps your conscience) suggests, you would have a reasonable defence for doing just that. Not necessarily a watertight argument, but certainly the beginnings of some sympathy from others and comfort for yourself.

Partly because of the questions raised by the holocaust, much social research in the 1950s and 1960s was concerned to investigate the sociology and psychology of rule following. Rather alarmingly, much of it suggested that ordinary people would follow orders if they were given by someone who claimed legitimate authority. In experiments conducted at Yale University by the social psychologist Stanley Milgram during 1961 and 1962, people were led to believe that they were inflicting pain on someone behind a screen through electric shocks (Milgram, 1974). As the shocks grew greater, so did the screams. Much of the time, people seemed to obey orders to continue because the instructor was wearing a white coat and pretending to be conducting a scientific experiment. So why didn't people just refuse to follow these orders?

Already in 1940, the American sociologist Robert Merton had argued that bureaucratic organisations value conformity not innovation, and that this leads to a situation where adherence to the letter of the rules becomes more important than their spirit. He defined a number of problems that were related to this:

1   Relationships between members of the organisation tend to become de-personalised as they respond to rules rather than to persons;
2   Rules become so important that they are seen as ends in themselves rather than as means to an end;
3   Moral decision making becomes a technical matter: people only check whether they have abided by the rules (Merton, 1940).

This rigid attitude towards rules helps to create the so-called 'bureaucratic person-ality', a conformist who wants to fit in and not rock the boat. Effectively, behaviour that might help the institution to adapt to changing circumstances is discouraged in favour of predictable routines. If Milgram showed that modern people tend to obey authority, Merton suggests that modern organisations tend to create a particular character type which is inclined to obey authority. As William Whyte noted, in his book *The Organization Man* (1956), an age of organisations is an age of 'yay-sayers', puppets following orders.

The idea that there is a connection between bureaucracy and conformity is not something new. At the start of the twentieth century, Max **Weber** had been particularly interested in how social change had altered the way that people understood what sorts of authority were considered legitimate. He suggested that there were three main ways to justify social action, which he called traditional, charismatic and rational/legal. In the modern world, Weber suggested, rules were taking the place of inspirational leaders and long-standing traditions as the basis for collective life. In doing so, rules are standing in as the grounds for ethics. Weber saw the rise of big bureaucratic organisations

83

in the public and private sectors as both a blessing and a curse. On the one hand, he lists their technical advantages:

> The fully developed bureaucratic mechanism compares with other organizations exactly as does the machine with the non-mechanical modes of production. Precision, speed, unambiguity, knowledge of the files, continuity, discretion, unity, strict subordination, reduction of friction and of material and personal costs – these are raised to the optimum point.
>
> (Weber, 1948: 214)

Yet he is also painfully aware of its consequences:

> Its specific nature, which is welcomed by capitalism, develops the more perfectly the more bureaucracy is 'dehumanised', the more completely it succeeds in eliminating from official business love, hatred and all purely personal, irrational, and emotional elements which escape calculation . . . the professional bureaucrat is chained to his activity by his entire material and ideal existence. In the great majority of cases, he is only a single cog in an ever-moving mechanism which prescribes to him an essentially fixed route of march.
>
> (Weber, 1948: 215–216, 228)

For Weber, bureaucracy is both world changing and dehumanising at the same time. He can't imagine modern life without large organisations, but at the same time he sees the human spirit becoming mechanical and slavish. Bureaucracy achieves both of these things because of a particular orientation to rules and rule following. Bureaucracy literally means rule from the desk (the *bureau*) rather than the priest's pulpit or the queen's throne. Its characteristics can be sketched as a set of rules about rules: there is a strict hierarchy of control and communication; jobs are defined by functions; appointments are made on the basis of contracts; selection is made on the basis of appropriateness to function; promotion happens on the basis of defined criteria.

These are the basics, but in any given organisation this list could be extended to include all the different rules that the organisation has constructed. Rules about plagiarism, or the correct sort of flour to be used in bread, or the criteria that you need to fulfil in order to pass your examinations. In addition, there will also be rules which are intended to cope with all the legal rules that are generated by the state, and now surround any organisation. These are called laws. The point is that obeying the rules becomes a justification for action. For the bureaucrat, acting 'without hatred or passion' is simply a way of being impartial. So, rather than letting one's own personal prejudices get in the way, the bureaucrat follows the letter of the law. This is clearly a very important way of thinking, both for the bureaucrat, and for the people who come into contact with them. If you felt that the manager of a hotel was denying you a room because of your colour or your haircut, you would have a legitimate complaint. Breaking the rule of fair treatment for whatever reason the manager invented, is simply wrong. And not breaking rules requires a certain moral courage. According to Weber, the individual member can only be persuaded of the moral virtues of rule following if they come to believe that this way of acting is in accordance with a certain legal-rational perspective on the world. Ultimately, it is the belief that this world view is fair and reasonable, that is to say, morally responsible, that infuses the bureaucrat with a will to abide by the rules.

The horror of Eichmann is therefore that there might be more substance to his excuse than we would have thought is possible. He, like many people who work in business organisations, claimed to have had some doubts about what he was being asked to do. But to disobey would have also been wrong, because obedience to legitimate authority is a higher good, and sometimes it is more morally defensible to obey than let one's scruples get in the way. Of course, here we have another example of one of the dilemmas of business organisation. Do I obey my manager, or my conscience? Though he doesn't claim to solve such problems, Weber has some more interesting things to say here. After all, if there were only three different sorts of rationality, where could he claim to be speaking from? To deal with this, Weber adds a further form of rationality to the three already mentioned. Following Kant, he evokes the idea of value-rational action, which is motivated by the striving towards some sort of goal, which might be ethical, political or even religious. The point is not whether such a goal is possible, but that it justifies all sorts of actions and judgements. This contrast also helps to clarify something about the nature of the bureaucratic, or technocratic, attitude. This he calls ends-rational action, which stresses a particular set of means to be employed and uses these means as instruments to achieve particular ends.

Imagine an engineer wants to build a bridge. The entrepreneur employs ends-rationality in terms of the best placing of the structure, the ideal materials, and so on, but has no particular interest in the economic, or aesthetic, or environmental impacts of the bridge. These latter points of view would have to be supplied by value-rationality. So, if we wanted to object to Eichmann, we would have to acknowledge that his adoption of a bureaucratic ethic was *ends*-rational, but perhaps not *value*-rational. If your goal is to kill as many Jews as you can as quickly as you can, then the trains need to run on time. But why would one have to accept the goal of genocide in the first place?

McETHICS

Weber explains the dominance of a bureaucratic legitimation by suggesting that it is based in a changing social order. But if we transpose this sociological argument to virtue ethics, then we can find a similar story in Alasdair MacIntyre's ideas about the rise of the managerial character. As we noted in Chapter 5, MacIntyre (1981) argues that we no longer have a moral language which is rooted in tradition and solidarity, and are hence living 'after virtue', as he puts it. Shared ideas about 'good' and 'bad' can only grow from a common experience, not the logic of consequentialists or Kantians. As a result, he argues, our moral landscape is populated by one-dimensional characters that provide narrow role models for behaviour. One of these characters is the manager.

This manager is a person who is efficient, even ruthless, at using human and non-human resources to achieve their aims and objectives. The only morality they observe is that of the optimum input–output ratio, or as it has also been put, the logic of 'performativity'. For MacIntyre, there is no ultimate goal in the world of the manager, no 'value-rationality' beyond the goals of the organisation. In the absence of character types who could express the virtues of community and ultimate values, we are left in a sort of moral vacuum in which any argument could be true. Since there is no yardstick with which to measure morality, then any argument will do. The more forcefully it is expressed, the more likely it is to be heard – a state of affairs that MacIntyre calls 'emotivism', the conviction that ethical judgements are based on feelings or emotions. There is no point in arguing with the emotivist, because such characters do not have the grounding and depth to engage in such a discussion. It would be meaningless to them because there is no basis on which you can appeal to a shared sense of virtue.

Although MacIntyre's thesis is a grand – and perhaps somewhat overstated – condemnation of contemporary character and morality, a more mundane example of this sort of analysis can be found in George Ritzer's *The McDonaldization of Society* (1996). This bestselling book suggested that more and more aspects of contemporary life were becoming 'McDonaldized', which is to say that they are subject to efficiency, calculability, predictability and control. So we have fast foods that are cheap and convenient, hospitals that minimise expensive interaction with patients and academic textbooks that guarantee easy success – or even ethical 'goodness' – without too much effort. None of these are in themselves bad things, but it means that foods are full of sugar and fat, patients don't feel cared for or listened to, and graduates have no idea about what they have studied. They can 'gesticulate well', but there is no life in these puppets (Kant, 1788: 258; see also Chapter 5).

The rise of McDonald's, McHospitals and McUniversities is, for Ritzer, an example of the ends-rationalisation of the world. A set of organisational principles are delineated and generalised across the globe. On a small scale, it means that everyone who serves in a McDonald's must end the customer service interaction with 'have a nice day' or 'enjoy your meal' even though they might not really mean it. It is common sense to think that insincerity is unethical, but in this case it is built into the routines of organised modernity.

On a more basic level, McDonald's could be argued to be complicit in some much more troubling practices: for example, paying low wages, being hostile to trade unions, providing robotic jobs, exploiting children through its advertising, encouraging a reliance on unhealthy foods, killing animals and being complicit in the destruction of the rain-forest (which is being cleared for cattle grazing). These were precisely the accusations that were brought against McDonald's in 1990 by five activists based in London who published a pamplet called 'What's Wrong with McDonald's?', leading to what is now known as the 'McLibel' trial (see Vidal, 1997). But whatever conclusions one reaches on such issues, whether one is 'for' or 'against' McDonald's, the point of this chapter should be quite clear, which is that the structure of organisations and the characters they produce are profound ethical and political questions.

INTENTIONS AND CONSEQUENCES

Here we might briefly return to the idea that judgements of intentions and consequences must be understood in the context of a recognition that bureaucracy is one of the basic social facts of modern society. At the time of writing, McDonald's employs over 420,000 people in more than 31,000 branches in 119 countries across the world and serves 47 million customers each day. If an employee in Mumbai doesn't wash their hands, and a customer becomes ill, we would not assume that a chief executive in the US should be punished. But what if employees in Mumbai were simply too busy to wash their hands properly? Or what if the sink had been broken for a week and no-one had come to fix it? Perhaps we would agree that the head of McDonald's in India could then be taken to court by the sick customer. Now consider a wider issue. Could we accuse McDonald's of degrading work by routinising all its practices so that they can be done by an automaton, scripting interactions with customers, paying minimum wages and making people wear stupid uniforms? Before you answer this, consider whether you would like to work in a McDonald's for a long period of time. Would Kant work in McDonald's flipping hamburgers and cleaning floors for a living? Would you?

If you decide that there is a legitimate complaint about McDonald's, you will doubtless also have realised that this complaint applies to a huge number of other business organisations. If we want to construct a sustained argument concerning a worker's right to an interesting and varied job, then we are also going to end up explicitly criticising very widespread organisational practices. In fields, factories and offices across the planet, employees are routinely subjected to deskilled and demeaning work in order to earn money. In historical terms, there has been a long-standing tendency for business organisations to do just this, fragment and deskill work, or replace workers with machines (Braverman, 1974). This is usually justified in terms of cutting down on costs and increasing control over labour processes but, whatever its justification, its consequences for workers are clear enough. You might want to say that 'this is just the way that the world is'. 'It's a shame, but there's nothing that can be done about it.' But this latter argument is precisely the sort of common sense that we discussed in Chapter 2. Why does the world have to be like this? Because when we take ethics seriously we see that ethics rests on a refusal to confuse what 'is' with what 'ought' to be. Ethics asks us exactly the question of whether the world should be as it is.

We will return to McEthics and the is/ought distinction in the next chapter, but the key point is that here we are evaluating *organisational* relationships. Most business ethicists tend to insist that ethics is about people's intentions, their character and the local consequences of their actions. But, why not suggest that business ethics could *also* deal with the intentions of organisations, the character of particular institutions and the global consequences of their actions? These are certainly big questions, but they might actually be rather important ones. When we accuse a person of having done something wrong, we usually assume that they had, and understood that they had, an alternative course of action available to them. To accuse an organisation or social context of having done something wrong is only foolish if there are no alternative choices. If it is really the case that people and things have to be organised like this, then there is no 'ethical' choice and hence no ethics. But most people would, in other contexts, like to believe that the world could be different, that things can change and that people can make a difference. How else would the Berlin Wall have fallen, or apartheid been dismantled in South Africa?

IN PRAISE OF BUREAUCRACY?

The British sociologist Paul du Gay, to whom we will return later in this chapter, has argued that bureaucratic rationality, inefficient as it may sometimes appear to be, is 'crucial to the securing of effective parliamentary democracy' (2000: 146). In this he is following Weber, who had earlier claimed that 'bureacracy inevitably accompanies modern mass democracy' (1948: 224). But du Gay makes a stronger case than Weber for the democratic status of bureaucracy. His claim is based on an understanding that it is only the moral neutrality of bureaucracies that can produce the decisions that need to be taken by democratic politics. He takes issue with various kinds of new public management initiatives which he argues have undermined, in the name of moral responsibility and customer orientation, the 'impartial responsibility' of the bureaucrat. Representative democracy cannot function without this kind of impartiality. It is therefore a danger to democracy when bureaucrats develop moral attitudes that differ from the legal-rational attitude described by Weber.

A case in point here might be the former King of Belgium, Baudoin I, who in 1990 refused, for religious reasons, to endorse a law on the legalisation of abortion. As a consequence, Belgium ran into an unprecedented constitutional crisis. The highest member of the red tape, the king himself, had brought democratic decision making to a standstill. The problem was resolved by allowing the king to abdicate from the throne for just one day.

Now, consider the ideas of the philosopher Avishai Margalit (1996), who argues that decent societies have insurmountable difficulties with bureaucracies because these institutions humiliate people. Margalit argues that decent societies are defined by their will to keep their institutions from humiliating people. He claims that bureaucracies in democratic societies pose a serious philosophical dilemma: they endanger democracy while making it possible. In other words, democracy needs bureaucratic institutions to achieve social justice while it must accept their humiliating and hence antidemocratic effects. The gist of all humiliation, Margalit believes, is dehumanisation. Bureaucracies clearly dehumanise by reducing their members to mere mechanical functionaries and by reducing customers to mere numbers.

Where du Gay argues, following Weber, that bureaucracies make democracy possible, Margalit stresses that this might eventually lead to democracy's own undoing. Where du Gay argues that we should be grateful to those who acknowledge the *ethos* of the office, Margalit believes that we should be on the alert against them. Indeed, he goes so far as to claim that a society with reprehensible rules and corrupt officials is better than a society with reprehensible rules and rule-abiding officials. That we, as democrats, are not able to escape bureaucracy, might be our most serious weakness.

What we are moving to in this chapter is the idea of an ethics *of* business, not merely an ethics *for* business. Consider the following story. In David Fincher's film *Fight Club* (1999), the character Jack works for an unnamed car company, organising recalls on defective models. However, he only arranges a recall if it costs less than the total paid to relatives of people who might have been killed or injured by the defective vehicle. This is based on a true story. The Ford Pinto was first introduced in 1971 and became the focus of a major scandal when it was discovered that its design allowed its fuel tank to be ruptured in the event of a rear end collision. Ford was aware of this design flaw and decided it would be cheaper to pay off possible lawsuits for resulting deaths than to redesign the car. A cost-benefit analysis prepared by Ford concluded that it would cost $11 per car to correct the flaws. Benefits derived from spending this amount of money were estimated to be $49.5 million. This assumed that each death which could be avoided would be worth $200,000, that each major burn injury which could have been avoided would be worth $67,000 and that an average repair cost of $700 per car would also be avoided. It further assumed that there would be 2,100 burned vehicles, 180 serious burn injuries and 180 burn deaths during the lifetime of the car. When the unit cost was spread out over the number of cars and light trucks which would be affected by the design change, at a cost of $11 per vehicle, the cost was calculated to be $137 million, much greater than the $49.5 million benefit. It was hence perfectly rational, according to this instrumental logic, to decide that 360 people should be burnt or die rather than Ford pay out an extra $87 million.

Set aside moral outrage for a minute. What we have here is a story about the use of ends-rationality within an organisation, and this kind of rationality is widely in use in modern corporations today. It certainly has echoes of the Eichmann story that we have already discussed, but is not an extraordinary historical event of the same order as the holocaust. We would be unlikely to suggest that this was an act of great evil. Neglectful, stupid and naïve perhaps, a collective failure of imagination and sympathy – an everyday story of the ways in which businesses manage to produce bureaucratic personalities.

MORAL DISTANCE

In his book *Modernity and the Holocaust* (1989), Zygmunt Bauman suggests that this was exactly how the holocaust happened. Countless small acts of administration and bureaucracy that allowed trains to run with specified numbers of passengers, exact quantities of gas to be manufactured, and death camps to be designed on a system of flow production. People came in at one end, smoke and piles of ash left at the other and in between – an efficient bureaucracy. The interesting question is how bureaucratic organisations managed to allow ordinary moral people to behave in what would be generally regarded as immoral ways.

The key issue, for Bauman, is the creation of moral distance. How is an organisation member encouraged not to care about the Other? Bauman suggests a few strategies, all of which make it easier to forget, or never see, the face of those one might be hurting. One such strategy is to stretch the distance between an action and its consequences. In other words, if the person who gave the order never sees the person who the order ultimately affects, then they will find it harder to care. This was horrifically expressed by Marshal McLuhan:

> It is obviously true that most bomber pilots are no better and no worse than other men. The majority of them, given a can of petrol and told to pour it over a child of three and ignite it, would probably disobey the order. Yet put that decent man in an aeroplane a few hundred feet above a village and he will, without compunction, drop high explosives and napalm and inflict appalling pain and injury on men, women and children.
>
> (cited in Desmond, 1998: 179)

This suggests that a long chain of organisational relationships can efface the relations that make them possible. When the chief executive of Nike asks for a training shoe that can be sold for a 1000 per cent profit, they are attempting to attend to the bottom line and please nameless shareholders. Similarly, when you buy a cheap T-shirt, you might have no idea about the sweatshop labour that went into making it, or the wages that are being paid to the person who is selling it to you. Neither you nor the chief executive directly *intend* any harm. You are both behaving as rational members of your society, but harm will be caused nonetheless. Big decisions are effectively made through the addition of small decisions. The manufacturing of an attack helicopter which destroys a school in a country far away is also a story about metal being efficiently welded, about computers being programmed, about production schedules and sales charts. Distance, particularly in an age of giant businesses and global production and consumption, is a good strategy for disposing of care. But distance doesn't need to only be thought of as a geographical issue. Organisational hierarchies produce distance too. If the order comes from 'on high' (because both chief executives and gods presumably live up there), then it must be obeyed. It is hard to argue with someone if you never meet them.

But even if you do meet them, there are other ways in which organisations can create moral distance. In war today, victims are routinely described as objects. Terms like 'targets', 'casualties' and 'collateral damage' depersonalise victims and allow them to be aggregated into charts and graphs by generals and statisticians who can then calculate the number of dollars spent per kill. Business organisations use similar language when referring to 'customers', 'employees', 'market segments', and so on. Indeed, using such terms is almost inevitable when you are dealing with large numbers of people, whether killing them or selling them soap. But the consequence of such terms is that named collectives can be (at least partially) treated as different from ordinary individuals towards whom we feel a responsibility to behave morally. Large numbers of people can be subjected to an essentially utilitarian calculation concerning the best means available to meet a particular end. People become a set of problems to be solved, objects framed within organisational language in terms of competitive advantage and sales figures. For university teachers and administrators, individual students with particular needs and abilities become units of resource to be processed with as little input as possible. (Which might be why so many lecturers rely on textbooks.) This is not to say that using such language, or using ends-rational logic, is in itself a bad thing, but it certainly makes it easier for members of organisations to use Eichmann's excuse, if they feel that they need to.

Lurking behind the language of the objectified collective is another issue, the division of human beings into functional parts, with specific requirements that go with them. Eichmann and his administrators were using their employees to transport bodies, and then to dispose of different sorts of waste. So too are contemporary managers using functional elements of people within their organisations, and targeting other parts outside their organisations. Different employees are used because of their particular skills – for mental, emotional or physical labour – and the purses of customers are opened by selling to their stomachs, eyes, ears, and so on. Think about how McDonald's sells its hamburgers. The people who work there could be seen as the 'hands' and the people who eat there are the 'mouth'. There are few other ways in which employee and customer are meant to interact. Indeed, you could argue that the business would be much more efficient if people did not have to service the parts of the body which are surplus to the matter at hand.

> The production of the Model T Ford required 7882 distinct work operations, but Ford noted, only 12% of these tasks – only 949 operations – required strong, able bodied, and practically physically perfect men. Of the remainder . . . we found that 670 could be filled by legless men, 2,637 by one-legged men, two by armless men, 715 by one-armed men and ten by blind men.
>
> (Seltzer, 1992: 157)

If you divide people into sets of competencies, or desires waiting to be fulfilled, then you are less likely to see them as complete persons. They become merely a $200,000

91

expense, and nothing more. Interestingly, when General Motors was making similar calculations about the legal costs of fatalities in the early 1970s, they also used the figure of $200,000 per death (see Bakan, 2004: 62–63). Such expenses represent a faceless object, not the mother of children who enjoys gardening and collecting models of cats. So moral neutrality is achieved, through physical and hierarchical distance; aggregation into categories; and the focus on selected attributes. In such ways is the face of the Other made to disappear.

MODERN BUSINESS

In *Modernity and the Holocaust*, Bauman is not saying that all organisations are evil, or that they are places that always produce inhumanity. However, he is suggesting that the ruthless efficiency of the holocaust was only possible because of bureaucratic reason and ends-rationality. So, before we dismiss Eichmann's excuse, or indeed the calculation performed by the Ford recall engineers, we might want to think about what sorts of people are being constructed by the organised society that we live in. In Chapter 5 we noted that one of the axioms that Kant derived from the categorical imperative was to treat people as ends and not as means. Don't use people as mere tools, but attend to their needs. Strictly speaking, such an injunction would rule out the possibility of formal organisation altogether. The employment relationship itself is an example of treating people as a means to an end. Furthermore, for most employees, the end is usually determined before the employee even signs the contract. But let's not be too hard on Kant, because we can also use this as an opportunity to see the power of his thought. Quite simply, he can be understood as pointing to the ways in which some forms of contract change our relationship to other human beings. To some extent, these changes are inevitable in complex societies, but this does not mean that we should take them for granted. From Kant's time onwards, and as the large organisation grows, 'business' becomes a problem for 'ethics', and 'ethics' becomes a problem for 'business'.

One common story that claims to solve this tension is the 'end of bureaucracy', and the growth of more humanised public and private sector organisations with caring management and transformational leaders. Indeed, much of conventional business ethics is very much part of this story, and its rise is often used to legitimate ideas about ethical progress in work organisations. Many management gurus argue that the globalising and chaotic world we live in nowadays has no time for bureaucratic red tape, so a new form of organisation is required. This is organisation (and its management) which is functionally flexible, and held together by shared beliefs, values and culture. In some ways these 'new management' ideas echo the criticisms put forward by Weber, MacIntyre, Ritzer and Bauman, that bureaucracy is dehumanising because its dull procedural rationality causes human beings to become morally encrusted and incapable of passion. So perhaps we should be welcoming these moves against bureaucracy? A good place to start thinking about these arguments is with Paul du Gay's book, *In Praise of*

Bureaucracy (2000). Du Gay takes issue with the idea that the organised world is one that produces ethical distancing and argues that bureaucracy should not be disposed of so easily. In doing so, he injects some pragmatism into the breathless rhetoric of change, and takes the critics of bureaucracy to task for, as he says, a certain 'unworldliness' about what human beings are and do.

At the heart of his argument is a return to Weber's writing on rationalisation. Du Gay suggests that Weber was primarily interested in the different moral qualities of different social roles. Perhaps social roles are (in an important sense) different worlds with different ethics which are not reducible to each other in some search for the authenticity of the morally whole person. That is to say, we vary our actions depending on the context we find ourselves in, and we should judge others in the same way. This is particularly important since some sense of pluralism and tolerance is at the heart of du Gay's reassessment. Democracy, in the form that it exists in administered societies, should involve mediation and compromise between conflicting interests. It is a programme of checks and balances, and is always unfinished in the sense that conflicts can never be finally resolved. This is precisely why the bureaucratic character is such an important figure, because it embodies the spirit of careful impartiality that is vital to state administration.

Putting it crudely, would anti-bureaucrats complain if lesbians were given different treatment at their library? Would Max Weber feel aggrieved if his election vote was discounted on the grounds that he had expressed suspicion of people who acted without hatred or passion? Of course he would, and this is du Gay's central point. The procedural impartiality that characterises liberal democratic administration is a vital aspect of its functioning. In many contexts, we expect that we will be treated without regard for who we are, and assume that some formalistic Kantian spirit of doing as you would be done to is necessary to prevent the arbitrary use of power by organisational functionaries. But, du Gay insists, this does not mean that bureaucrats are morally deficient, rather that they have cultivated an *ethos* of impartiality in their public lives that attempts to guarantee relative freedom in other areas. In other words, and echoing Carr's (1968) treatment of the bluffer at poker, we have different standards of conduct in different roles or, as it is often put, we 'wear different hats'. This is not only an empirically sensible description of ordinary people, but a politically necessary separation for other reasons too. Politicians, who come and go with spinning rapidity, are likely to let their particular obsessions and desire for re-election drive demands for policy formulation. However, these policies must be implemented in more detailed and careful ways by people who actually know something about education, welfare benefits, asylum seekers, and so on. Hence a degree of separation between the two groups provides a certain amount of friction on the enthusiasms of sound bite politics, and ensures that ministers are held responsible for policy directions whilst administrators translate them into workable procedures.

Du Gay's argument is a vital corrective for anyone who thinks that the public sector can be run like a corporation. The seemingly uncritical assumption that what is good for a business is good for a state simply disregards the possibility that we might want a different ethic in our governmental bureaucracies. But in making the case for the public sector bureaucracy so strongly, du Gay runs the danger of presenting an almost nostalgic picture of its functions. Or, to put that more precisely, he elevates the character of the bureaucrat to a level of ethical perfection and altruistic service that seems rather unlikely. Such an idealised picture leaves him open to easy criticism since bureaucrats can also use their unelected powers to kick new policies into the long grass, to insist on rules of precedent that are pointlessly ritualistic, and to disavow their responsibilities in the name of procedure.

Perhaps on either side of this argument we have some rather over-drawn positions. MacIntyre (1981) and Bauman (1989) characterise management and bureaucracy as being machinically utilitarian. For different reasons, both these authors end up arguing that the calculating human needs to be replaced by the feeling human. Du Gay is quite right to treat much of their argument as being rather un-worldly. For example, he does a particularly good job in arguing (against Bauman) that the National Socialist party actually disassembled Weimar bureaucracy as a precondition for the holocaust, and not the other way round. But neither is Bauman suggesting that all bureaucrats are always morally impoverished. Both MacIntyre and Bauman are taking aim at instrumental forms of reason which efface the possibility of asking more general questions about ethics – precisely the sort of questions which were opened up in the previous chapter. If du Gay is insistent on defending the separation of different roles and spheres, then MacIntyre and Bauman wish to ask questions about the legitimacy of the boundary between personal convictions and administrative duty. The former stresses the need for a communal agreement on the ends of human activity, the latter comes down in favour of an un-conditional responsibility for the Other which is borrowed from Levinas. Either way, their question is 'what does it mean to be moral?' Du Gay's faith in separate lifeworlds, as MacIntyre understood, means that this question becomes almost nonsensical.

Now this might be a good thing. Perhaps this endless agonising about an unified theory for ethics, about the different merits of utilitarianism, or deontology, or certain virtues, should be subordinated to more practical matters for people who need to get things done by the next day. But these rather obscure debates are only really possible because this defence of bureaucracy is grounded in public sector management. When we turn to the character of the manager in the private sector, in business, it is much more diffi-cult to claim that the bureaucracy is defensible with reference to a certain conception of impartiality and service. Of course it could be argued that the bureaucratic character, in du Gay's sense, is not found in the private sector at all, so any comparison is futile. Yet this would be to re-define what bureaucracy, as a structural description of large organisations, has meant for most of the past century, and certainly what it meant for Weber. So, if it is admitted that businesses can be termed bureaucracies too, then we can begin to discuss whether the social roles that we find there are morally justifiable. For managers to insist that their shareholders are the only stakeholders that they respond to, or that the market is the ultimate umpire, is to practise an art of separation too. Yet most of us would probably deem this separation to be problematic if a company discharged toxic waste, or bribed public officials, or costed a human life at $200,000.

So du Gay's defence of the bureaucratic character starts to look a little weak when it runs up against the contested boundaries of action. When, in other words, the bureaucrat refuses to follow an order or the manager insists on due process despite the imperatives of getting it done by Friday. These are precisely the issues that Arendt, Weber and Bauman are opening and that, despite du Gay's argument, have not gone away. Ethics is not only found in defined arenas bound with red tape, but also urgently occupies these gaps between social roles and the moments when they are breached and undecidable decisions need to be made. This sort of understanding also presses a question upon us. If ethics is shaped by social context, then how do people manage to 'step outside' such context into the 'gaps' or 'breaches' in order to disobey? If we modern persons are bureaucratic characters with narrow senses of moral connectedness, then how can things ever change? The answer to this is simply that we have only discussed one dimension of ethical context – organisational structure. As yet, we have only briefly touched on another way to describe the modern world – in terms of capitalism. And that will be the topic of the next chapter.

Chapter 8

Denying ethics II: global capital

WTO KILLS FARMERS

On 10 September 2003, a 56-year-old rice farmer from South Korea stabbed himself in the heart in a dramatic protest against the World Trade Organisation (WTO) during a meeting in Cancún, Mexico. In this action, Kyung-Hae Lee symbolised so much of the growing global despair over the spread of the 'free market' and the institutions such as the WTO that represent the interests of global capital. Lee, former president of the Korean Advanced Farmers Federation, was protesting against policies of the WTO which would reduce government subsidies to South Korean farmers and institute the 'laws' of the free market. For Lee and his supporters, these policies would make farming economically impossible and would drive farmers in South Korea and many other poorer countries into poverty: hence the slogan: 'WTO Kills Farmers' and his protest against the WTO.

It is reported that the last words Lee spoke to his fellow Korean farmers were, 'Don't worry about me, just struggle your hardest'. His suicide is indicative of a widespread sentiment which has been expressed in recent years against the actions and policies of global capital. Since the protests against the WTO in Seattle in 1999, a series of protests throughout the world have expressed a similar anger at neoliberal economic policies, which assume that unregulated markets will bring prosperity to all. As to so many others in the developing world, this neoliberal story of the benefits of free markets was to Lee a façade disguising the economic interest of large capitalist corporations, which are overwhelmingly dominated by the pursuit of profit. Writing shortly before his death, Lee expressed his concerns, in a global language that was not his own:

> My warning goes out to the all citizens that human beings are in an endangered situation that uncontrolled multinational corporations and a small number of bit WTO members officials are leading an undesirable globalization of inhuman, environment-distorting, farmer-killing, and undemocratic. It should be stopped immediately otherwise the false logic of the neo-liberalism will perish the diversities of agriculture and disastrously to all human being.
>
> (Lee, in Mittal, 2003)

This broken language, the anger at global capital and the despair of an individual suicide in the name of others might give us pause to reflect. So much of the content of business ethics takes its starting point from the position of the powerful, imagining that we are in the position of the executive who decides on the fate of others. But here we see the face of an Other, an ordinary representative of the principal form of labour on the planet. The fate of these others can be decided in convention centres in hotels in Cancún or Davos, but these decisions are today contested, and the idea that these decisions are made in the interests of everyone is rather unconvincing. We therefore turn, in this chapter, to the ethics of global capital.

THE SOCIAL RESPONSIBILITY OF BUSINESS

In business ethics, discussions of interests and responsibilities of business typically begin with a discussion of an argument between Milton **Friedman**, on the one hand, and defenders of stakeholder theory, on the other. Usually what we find in these discussions is the idea that Friedman, a renowned Nobel prize-winning economist, claims that the only responsibility of a business is to increase its profits, and that nothing else really matters. If businesses act in their self-interest then the results for all will be best, as if action were, as Adam Smith (1776: 194) famously claimed, led by an invisible hand. Against this, stakeholder theory (as well as other ethical positions) claims that businesses have responsibilities not only to shareholders but also to employees, customers, the environment, and so on.

Typically this debate ends up reinforcing rather predictable positions, in that it mirrors political divides between those for and against free, unrestrained capitalism. But we want to argue, in a fashion similar to what we have argued above with regard to other theorists cherished by business ethicists, that there is more to this debate around social responsibility than meets the eye. We will suggest that Friedman's arguments would have to be twisted to turn them into an unconditional defence of capitalism. Also, we will suggest that there is something profoundly undemocratic and strangely pro-capitalist in arguments for stakeholder theory. In doing so we will, once again, seek to upset the set up of this debate in business ethics. In the second half of this chapter we will then offer some different ways of thinking about global capitalism by looking at some other parts of the tradition of critique of global capital.

Friedman's famous contribution to business ethics was signalled by an essay published in 1970 with the title 'The social responsibility of business is to increase its profits' which reworked an argument he had made in his earlier book, *Capitalism and Freedom* (1962). Friedman is analysing what takes place in a 'free', which he understands as capitalist, economy. It is worth quoting this section at length, because one phrase is typically dragged out of the context in which it is written. Friedman writes:

> The view has been gaining widespread acceptance that corporate officials and labor leaders have a 'social responsibility' that goes beyond serving the interest of their

stockholders or their members. This view shows a fundamental misconception of the character and nature of a free economy. In such an economy, there is one and only one social responsibility of business – to use its resources and engage in activities designed to increase its profits so long as it stays within the rules of the game, which is to say, engages in open and free competition, without deception or fraud. Similarly, the 'social responsibility' of labor leaders is to serve the interests of the members of their unions.

(1962: 133)

The standard reading is to assume that Friedman simply thinks that capitalist economies without regulation will work out well for everyone and will be relatively free from conflict. This reading is plausible as long as we only cite the title of his 1970 article, or the sentence in which he argues that 'there is one and only one social responsibility of business – to use its resources and engage in activities designed to increase its profits'. But as soon as we read this fuller section we see that this understanding of capitalism is far more idealised and conflict-free than what we find Friedman talking about. This is so for three reasons.

First, Friedman explicitly recognises that capitalism is marked by a conflict of interest, and in the section cited here this conflict of interest is clearly expressed between business and labour. Labour leaders form unions and for Friedman these unions should have one interest, which is to serve the interests of their members. These interests are typically expressed in terms of wages, working conditions and so forth. Friedman is not so dreamy-eyed as to think that business and labour would all agree that increasing profits is the goal of all involved. Rather, the way he puts it is that increasing profit is the responsibility of business, and protecting the interests of labour is the responsibility of labour leaders. Between these two groups there is an unassailable conflict of interest which is a matter of politics, and this cannot be wished away by economists or business ethicists.

Second, Friedman does not simply think that the state is a bad thing that should be done away with, as if capitalism could continue without the state. The role of the state is to maintain the rules of the game and to protect against law breaking. But the state also has the function of redistribution of wealth, and functions such as the alleviation of poverty, something which is, we should note, the subject of the penulti-mate chapter of *Capitalism and Freedom*. Indeed, one of the reasons that Friedman is concerned about business people exercising functions of 'social responsibility' is that these businesspeople have not been democratically elected for the purposes of repre-senting the community at large, and are therefore unlikely to represent the broader interest. Hence, he writes:

If businessmen have a social responsibility other than making maximum profits for stockholders, how are they to know what it is? Can self-selected private individuals decide what the social interest is? Can they decide how great a burden they are justified in placing on themselves or their stockholder to serve that social interest? Is it tolerable that these public functions of taxation, expenditure, and control be exercised by the people who happen at the moment to be in charge of particular enterprises, chosen for those posts by strictly private groups?

(Friedman, 1962: 133–134)

Third, Friedman is often taken to argue against any ethical principles, or to assume that ethics is irrelevant to business. In his later essay Friedman expands on the earlier notion that business can engage in competition 'so long as it stays within the rules of the game' (1962: 133), writing that the desire of business will be to make as much money as possible 'while conforming to the basic rules of society, both those embodied in law and those embodied in ethical custom' (1970: 33).

In many discussions of the social responsibilities of business and of corporate social responsibility we find the suggestion that there are several levels of social responsibility, including for example economic, then legal and then ethical responsibilities (for classic statements, see Carroll, 1979; 1991; 1998). In Friedman we also have these levels of responsibility recognised in practice, but he will not have the legal and ethical responsibilities taken on by business. However, this is not because he thinks that they are not important. Rather, he suggests that it is because business is caught up in the context in which it operates. That context – civil society and the political institutions it generates and ethical expectations it produces – is not and *should* not be a matter of corporate control or governance. It must be part of a properly democratic politics, and this cannot take place if businesses take over the functions of the operation of democracy.

Perhaps we have given too generous a reading of Friedman, and perhaps we have overstated our case so as to invert the usual way that the debate is set up between shareholder and stakeholder notions of responsibility. We should admit that there is quite a lot that is deeply objectionable in many of Friedman's arguments and we have been silent on these here. But what we are clear about is that there is more to Friedman than an idealised and trouble-free notion of managerial responsibility to shareholders. Yet again, the version of theory that we inherit from the business ethics literature seems to be rather deficient, and a more careful reading begins to open up some interesting questions. There is more conflict in Friedman's view of the economic world than most commentators note. There is a conflict between capital and labour, and between capital and legal and ethical expectations. Yet Friedman is himself not able to adequately theorise these conflicts, and neither have most of those who have followed him.

NEOLIBERALISM

Having suggested that there is more to Friedman than meets the eye, we should remember that he has been used – by economists, by sociologists and by business ethicists – as an exemplar in the defence of global capital. Even if this is a partial reading of

Friedman, which ignores much in his work, Friedman does, on a number of occasions, suggest that capitalism is a pretty good thing. He has been used, alongside an earlier economist, Friedrich Hayek, as a defender of a certain type of argument for capitalism. This set of economic claims is often known as 'neoliberalism'. Neoliberalism represents a set of ideas that caught on from the mid to late 1970s, and are famously associated with the economic policies introduced by Margaret Thatcher in the United Kingdom and Ronald Reagan in the United States following their elections in 1979 and 1981. The 'neo' part of neoliberalism indicates that there is something new about it, suggesting that it is an updated version of older ideas about 'liberal economics' which has long argued that markets should be free from intervention by the state. In its simplest version, it reads: markets good, government bad.

Now, this is a strange idea, for a number of reasons. As you will have already noted, Friedman himself sees a certain place for the government, and one of his major problems with corporations acting on 'social responsibility' is that they would be interfering with the proper actions undertaken by democratically elected governments. In any case, neoliberalism is something which is introduced, and marketed by, well, governments. For its critics, this is one of the basic distortions of defenders of neoliberalism. They claim that markets should be free from state intervention, but actual neoliberal economies are heavily defended and promoted by governments. To go back to the example we started this chapter with, farming, the countries which are officially in support of neoliberal economic principles actually make enormous efforts to protect their markets, and they do that by providing subsidies to farmers and restricting imports by charging tariffs. So American and European governments go around telling all of the developing countries to deregulate their economies, which means to open them to the forces of the capitalist market, but at the same time do not want to open up their markets for things such as food.

Because of this discrepancy, a number of critics of neoliberalism suggest that there is a basic hypocrisy in the economic policy of Western governments. This came clear in arguments that have taken place since the November 2001 meeting of the WTO in Doha, flared up (as we saw above) at the meeting in Cancún in September 2003, and then calmed a little at the meeting in Geneva in July 2004. At these meetings a group of poorer countries – Brazil, India and some African states – turned the neoliberal economic policies of the WTO against the powerful rich countries. These countries, which had been repeatedly told by institutions such as the WTO that they should liberalise their economies, have for years been unable to compete with Europe and the USA, where farmers receive government support.

For critics of neoliberalism, what becomes clear from examples like farm subsidies is the way that neoliberals use arguments for the market in rather selective, and politically motivated, ways. If the market will help them, they argue for it; if the market will damage them, they quietly introduce protection – which suggests that neoliberals actually know, at a certain level, that capitalism (rather like fire) is a fascinating but dangerous thing, and that if it isn't controlled, it can wreak havoc.

100

Globally, this is something which is becoming increasingly apparent. If we look at the past 30 years, in which capitalism has been 'set free' throughout the world to do its work, we see something that neoliberals have trouble explaining. And this is the other funny thing about neoliberalism. Neoliberalism is often defended by economists, who take a lot of pride in their scientific and objective status. With mathematics and abstract theoretical modelling, they seem intent on proving the merits of free markets. But at the same time, these scientists seem entirely uninterested in looking at the actual impact of free market policies in the world. In this context, it was interesting to see how Joseph Stiglitz, who had previously been the chief economist at the World Bank and won the 2001 Nobel Prize in Economics, recently came out against institutions such as the World Bank, IMF and WTO. From a position of experience working with these institutions, he claimed that decisions in these organisations 'were made on the basis of what seemed a curious blend of ideology and bad economics, dogma that sometimes seemed to be thinly veiled special interests' (Stiglitz, 2002: xiii).

Critics of neoliberalism have therefore looked at the evidence that documents the results of this great experiment of the past 30 years, in which many markets have been set free. Looking at the evidence, we can see that the total amount of global trade has increased significantly, but that global poverty has increased, with more today living in abject poverty than before neoliberalism. Almost all environmental indicators suggest massive environmental degradation over the past quarter of a century. The experiment with neoliberalism, which has involved systematic but selective deregulation of the global economy, has been a massive failure from the point of view of the natural environment and the economic and working conditions of the majority of the planet. It has destroyed species and traditional ways of life, and has increased inequality.

STRIKING BACK

Given this situation, it is perhaps not surprising that organisations such as the WTO are now on the back foot, being forced into making concessions to the poor countries it had previously advised on policy. And perhaps not surprisingly, we also find that the World Bank, which had previously been criticised for having one solution to all problems – liberalisation, that is to say, removing governments and making way for capital – is seriously moderating its position. In 2004, we found the World Bank arguing *against* the position that 'government should give up and leave everything to the private sector', forcefully asserting that such a position 'would be wrong' (World Bank, 2004: 10). Equally, and perhaps in direct response to critics such as Stiglitz, the World Bank now stresses that 'no single solution fits all services in all countries' and, more poetically, that 'there is no silver bullet' (2004: 12, 17). Emphasising the need for institutions to govern global capital, it now concludes that, 'What is needed is a set of institutional arrangements that will give policymakers, providers and citizens the incentives to adopt the solution and adapt it to local conditions' (World Bank, 2004: 11–12).

From this we can see that there are possibilities of change in these global institutions, for challenging the rule of global capital and developing what David Held (2004) calls a new 'global covenant' based on notions of 'global social democracy'. This involves changing the goals and purposes of these institutions or, probably more accurately, recognising that these institutions are already changing. Institutions such as the IMF, WTO and World Bank should not be thought of as a single homogeneous block all based on the same blind faith in global capital. These institutions all have different histories and are currently moving in different directions. And it is possible that in the future such institutions could be a formidable tool against global capital.

Other critics of global capital are not, however, so optimistic about the chances of reforming these institutions. They insist that these institutions are so fundamentally co-opted that there is not much chance for reform. For example, Kevin Danaher argues that, in respect of questions such as how capital should be invested:

> The World Bank and the IMF are fundamentally incapable of addressing these questions in a democratic manner. They have shown time and again that they cannot open themselves up to public participation and allow the poor majority to control how capital gets invested. They share so many interests with banks, corporations, and the ruling élites, that no amount of tinkering with their rules and policies will convert them into democratic institutions. These, and other global capitalist institutions such as the World Trade Organization, need to be scrapped and replaced with a democratic process that includes representatives of the poor at all stages of planning and rule-making.
>
> (2001: 88–89)

Some who propose abolishing these institutions of global capital do not see any need for any other global institution to replace them. But amongst those who propose alternatives, some of the most interesting are emerging at the World Social Forum. The World Social Forum was first held in January 2001, in direct response to the meeting of the World Economic Forum, which has been meeting since 1971. The World Economic Forum is a private corporation set up in order to support the interests of global capital by promoting a neoliberal agenda of free trade, but the World Social Forum sets itself against such a project. Hence, in its statement of purpose:

> As a forum for debate, the World Social Forum is a movement of ideas that prompts reflection, and the transparent circulation of the results of that reflection, on the mechanisms and instruments of domination by capital, on the means and actions to resist and overcome that domination, and on the alternatives proposed to solve the problems of exclusion and social inequality that the process of capitalist globalization with its racist, sexist and environmentally destructive dimensions is creating internationally and within countries.
>
> (World Social Forum, 2001: §11)

Although there are obviously disagreements about this statement, the World Social Forum is one of the key focal points, and an annual meeting point, for thinking about different possibilities, based on its popular slogan: 'Another World is Possible'. In doing so it has become a central point in the protests that have been described as anti-corporate and anti-capitalist, which are opposed to global capital. But one of the things that is clearly emerging in this movement is a recognition that such movements are not purely negative or oppositional. Instead, even if they are opposed to neoliberalism and global capital, they are not merely reactive but are ultimately affirmative. And what is being affirmed? Often, it is things such as democracy, freedom and humanity. Turning back to the discipline of business ethics again, we might ask what this all means for business ethics? It is certainly surprising that business ethics has failed to respond in a sustained or serious way to this movement, which claims so much about justice and ethics.

CAPITALISM, COMMODITIES AND ETHICS

In the first half of this chapter we have looked at what might appear to be 'big picture' arguments: arguments for and against capitalism, and discussion of broad, sweeping change in the global political economy. In the remainder of this chapter, we want to move away from this 'macro' level focus to what could be the 'micro' level of economic activity. From the structures of global capital to the most basic and obvious feature of capitalist economies – the commodity.

The commodity is the point at which Karl **Marx** begins his three-volume work, *Capital*, and we need to look at some of the arguments he makes there. But in the same way that we have found, throughout this book, that careful reading of original sources often makes those sources look somewhat different than we might assume, in this chapter we will find that Marx is more insightful, sophisticated and, dare we say it, philosophical than he is often made out to be. We also want to suggest that Marx has some important things to say about business ethics today, not in terms of a moral dispute with capitalism as such, but with offering concepts that can explain those microscopic practices that we go through when we buy and sell things. This goes right down to basic phenomena such as why it is that so many people take the price stickers off things when they get them home from the shop. A renewed understanding of Marx and insights into everyday business can be found, we suggest, in Marx's discussion of **commodity fetishism**.

Marx's discussion of commodity fetishism can be found in the final section of Chapter One, Volume One of *Capital*, titled 'The Fetishism of the Commodity and its Secret' (Marx, 1867: 163–177). Having noted that, quite obviously, in capitalist societies wealth appears in the form of a monstrous collection of things, Marx seeks to understand the dynamics of commodities. He writes, famously, 'A commodity appears at first sight an extremely obvious, trivial thing. But its analysis brings out that it is a very strange thing, abounding in metaphysical subtleties and theological niceties' (Marx, 1867: 163). When something begins to be traded on the market – which is, after all, what it means to say that something is a commodity – it takes on a character all of its own. An apple that we buy at the market takes on a quite different form from an apple that we grow ourselves, on a tree that we have tended.

Marx is particularly intrigued by the way that, in the process of becoming a commodity, a thing will tend to become 'abstracted' from the conditions in which it was produced. From the purely physical characteristics of the apple, it is hard to know anything about the conditions under which it was grown and brought to market. Marx uses examples such as the following: 'From the taste of wheat it is not possible to tell who produced it, a Russian serf, a French peasant or an English capitalist' (Marx, 1859: 28). Or to take another example: 'The taste of porridge does not tell us who grew the oats and . . . does not reveal the conditions under which it takes place, whether it is happening under the slave-owners brutal lash or the anxious eye of the capitalist' (1867: 290).

What Marx draws attention to with these examples is a phenomenon of profound philosophical and, we will argue, ethical significance. It is something important about the way that objects present themselves when they become commodities. The point being that commodities are made by real individual human beings, in fields, factories and offices. Commodities are the product of a specific set of human relationships. But when the commodity arrives on the market, instead of seeing those human relationships we see only an object. As Marx puts it, the mysterious character of the commodity consists 'in the fact that the commodity reflects characteristics of men's own labour as objective characteristics of the products of labour themselves' (1867: 164–165). Hence commodity fetishism 'is nothing but the definite social relation between men themselves which assumes here, for them, the fantastic form of a relation between things' (1867: 165).

Thinkers who have written about Marx and ethics such as, for example, Steven Lukes (1985) have tended to ignore Marx's analysis of commodity fetishism. This is unfortunate, we think, because there is a lot that can be taken out of Marx's discussion of commodity fetishism for thinking about ethics, especially if we think of ethics in Levinasian terms. As we noted in Chapter 6, for Levinas, ethics is a matter of a relation to the Other. If capitalist societies are marked by the omnipresence of commodities, and commodities turn relations between people into relations between things, then this says something powerful about the relations to the Other which are part and parcel of consuming a commodity.

The consequences of this are particularly clear when we consider the way that many commodities today pass along very long supply chains. Today, many of the things that we consume are produced in such far off locations, and with techniques we are not familiar with, that it is very hard to see the commodity as anything other than a simple thing. But the critique of commodity fetishism shows that when we are consuming the most basic commodity, it has been produced by another person, and hence we are, in a very real sense, engaging in a relation with another person even as we appear to be engaging with a mere thing. This is quite a radical insight, and it changes the very taste of the food in our mouths when we realise that we are not simply eating a banana, but are consuming a set of relations with others – those others that planted, grew, tended, picked, packed, shipped, unpacked and stacked those bananas on the supermarket shelf.

As we saw in the last chapter, it is easier to do horrible things to others when we can't see their face, or if we excuse ourselves by saying that we are just following the rules. If we tell ourselves 'this is just a banana, and nothing more', or if we tell ourselves 'everyone else drives a car, so it must be okay', then we are denying the way that, in even the most basic act of consumption, we are involved in relations with others. In eating the banana we become complicit with the conditions in which bananas are produced, and in choosing to drive a car we are implicated in the environmental and military catastrophes with which oil and cars are fundamentally involved.

Reading Marx's critique of commodity fetishism with Levinas's ethics of the Other, we can now see a number of things about consumption and commodity relations that we cannot see with traditional models of ethics such as utilitarianism, deontology and virtue ethics. It draws attention to a vast space of action which has significant 'ethical' consequences, but which is not typically seen to involve ethics at all. By stressing that ethics is a matter of specific relations with others, and that all commodity exchange involves relations with other people, we are called to a responsibility for our place in the world and our acts of consumption. This might appear to be a far more demanding ethics than that which we typically find in business ethics. It demands us to consider and reconsider all of our economic activities, even the most basic purchases of food and drink. Because this ethics is so demanding, you might quickly dismiss it as unrealistic or as mean-minded. After all, in such a globally interconnected world, who could be responsible for all of their relations with all others? But then, if we avoid this hasty dismissal we will find that there are, in numerous places today, already a variety of efforts to challenge commodity fetishism. This is not to say that exchange or commodities are always immoral, but to recognise the social relations that are embodied in exchange and to think critically about those relations.

CHALLENGING COMMODITY FETISHISM

One of the things that theory does is to offer us new things to think about, proposing alternatives and possibilities that we might have never thought of otherwise. But theory can also clarify and illuminate existing practices, giving them different meanings and depths. The concept of commodity fetishism can show us new things, and we hope that it already has. But it can also clarify and explain some 'obvious' things that might otherwise remain mysterious about contemporary practices. In this second respect, the critique of commodity fetishism can shed light on a range of recent consumer actions, branding practices and retailers' responses to them.

Perhaps the most best known examples of what we have in mind are the recent challenges put to sportswear manufacturers such as Nike, and the wave of protests at US university campuses about clothing with university logos. In both cases, for some years, consumers in the West had purchased clothing that, it was later discovered, had been produced in sweatshops around the world, but particularly in South East Asia. Upon discovering the conditions in which this clothing was produced, many people made public declarations exposing the appalling conditions under which the clothing was made: low pay, hot and cramped working conditions, lack of union representation, long hours, few breaks and instances of verbal and physical abuse. We shouldn't need to point out that these are conditions against which most workers in the West are protected by law.

Given what we have said above about commodity fetishism, what is interesting in these cases is that there was a pressure against commodity fetishism, and an insistence that the object consumed also includes the social relations that went into its production. So the shoes or college sweatshirt came to be seen not merely as a thing but as the embodiment of the social relations through which it was produced. In having a relation with that commodity, it was realised, you would also be having a relation with other people. And the ethical bite of this realisation is that those relations with others are not the kind of relations that many could consider to be ethical or just.

Defences of the companies in question were made, of course. They claimed that they were doing good for local third world economies, and that the charges levelled against them were false or overstated. Forms of stakeholder theory, and of a generalised utilitarianism, were very often used to back up such claims. But the evidence for concern for local economies is rather weak, and compared to the empirical evidence now appears to be little more than the abstract assumption of economists. Some suggested that they were simply 'doing business', and that the only responsibility of a business is to make a profit. Against this, many in the West simply rejected these companies, insisting that these relations with others are unacceptable, and that these Western companies must change their practices. Whether they have changed or not, and whether they will change or not, remain open questions. Many companies have produced 'ethical codes' that outline their responsibilities to the communities in which they operate. While some of this is obviously little more than marketing a sort of strategic ethics, consumer pressure has recently raised the stakes in debates over global capital. It has also done something to disrupt commodity fetishism and to expose the social relations that are involved in any exchange.

We can see other examples of challenges to commodity fetishism in relation to recent developments in product labelling and in movements around organic, genetically modified and fair trade foods. Although each of these cases has different dynamics, what we see in all of these is that there has been an increasing recognition on the part of Western consumers that there is more than meets the mouth when it comes to the food we eat. Food is produced under specific conditions, and is increasingly produced with intensive industrial agricultural techniques, and often with genetically modified organisms. As a result, many farmers, of whom the French farmer José Bové has received the most media coverage, have stressed that this intensive farming and processing of food is bad for our health, bad for the environment and bad for the animals reared in such conditions (see Bové and Dufour, 2001; Lawrence, 2004; Schlosser, 2002).

There are many different arguments involved here, and there are many very different developments in relation to food. But what is often common to these arguments is an effort to expose the relations with others that are involved in a simple act of consuming food. Things are complicated here, and some of these developments, such as organic foods, can be reduced to nothing but market segmentation strategies in which the most well-off pay a premium to have food that is produced in more acceptable conditions. One might well ask why, if organic foods are better for us and for the planet, governments don't legislate more strictly on organic standards for food production. Companies and supermarkets, which are terrifyingly powerful in most Western countries, typically resist these moves, promising that they are working to the strictest ethical standards (even as at the same time they market a section of their products as, implicitly or explicitly, 'more ethical' than others).

There are also interesting and complex debates around labelling. At what levels and according to what criteria can something be considered to be 'organic' or 'fair trade', given the competing standards that define these things in different ways? The United States government has, notoriously, argued that US companies should not have to indicate on the labels of foods whether or not they include genetically modified organisms, while the European Union insists that the genetic make-up of foods is part of the food and should therefore be signalled. In doing so the EU seems to be making an argument against treating food as a mere thing, and arguing that food, like all other commodities, involves complex social relations through which they are produced, and that these relations should (at least partially) be indicated on the package.

To close our discussion of commodity fetishism, let us consider briefly the suggestion that, today, because so much of business trades in services rather than material goods, the critique of commodity fetishism might no longer apply. If a commodity is a set of relations with others that assumes, under fetishism, the fantastic form of a thing, then what happens when we consume services? In such cases, it seems obvious that I am having a relation with an other person, and the ethics of the situation are much clearer. If we are now in, or moving into, a 'service economy' or a 'knowledge economy', then perhaps commodity fetishism no longer holds sway.

The first response is that arguments for service and knowledge economies tend to vastly overstate the extent to which people today trade and work in services rather than things. Think about some of the things you have bought in the past month, and you will notice that we still consume goods as well as services. But second, we need to think carefully about how the service economy works. We should remember that an enormous amount of service work includes very dull and deskilled labour. The prototype of this is the telephone call centre, which is perhaps the model of the service-factory of the post-industrial age. In these kinds of 'bright satanic mills' there is, ironically, an overwhelming pressure to reduce the social elements of contact. Call centre workers and retail assistants work from scripts, and are encouraged not to see their callers as people but as 'cases' (Knights and McCabe, 1998). Likewise, call centre operators are turned into mere objects both by customers (providing information or fulfilling other functions) and by human resource managers (who simply want results, best expressed in numbers if possible).

It is perhaps because of this very dehumanisation of service work that people typically hate calling call centres, and also why call centre workers routinely resist management policies and introduce a social element into their work and their conversations. Thus, even though there is a tendency to commodity fetishism in capitalist economies, there is also a strong pressure against it. It is almost as if, no matter how much global capital, businesses, economists and global institutions such as the WTO try to turn every-thing into commodities, there is an enduring pressure against such a project. This is a tendency to see the face of the Other in the coffee I am drinking, to recognise the labour of the worker who stitched my shirt, perhaps even to wonder where this book was printed, and who was paid how much to sell it to you? Which is perhaps to suggest that global capital has not quite won the game yet.

CAN WRONG LIFE BE LIVED RIGHTLY?

Let us conclude this chapter with discussion of one more aspect of the critique of global capital, which relates to the critique of commodity fetishism but also to the critique of the politics of global capital. This is stated clearly by one of the key figures in a group known as the Frankfurt School of **Critical Theory** (sometimes simply called 'the Frankfurt School' or 'Critical Theory' with capital letters). In his lectures on moral philosophy and in his dissection of modern immorality, *Minima Moralia*, Theodor Adorno presented the stark thesis: 'Wrong life cannot be lived rightly' (1974: 39; 2000: 1). In the final part of this chapter we will try to understand what he means by this.

To begin with, it is important to realise that Adorno is clear that life, as it is at present, is not right. Organised modernity, and in particular the twentieth century, is, for Adorno, pretty much a disaster. Modernity is the time of the greatest number of deaths by war, the greatest violent atrocities, and an era of the commodification of all life and the reduction of humanity to little more than automated functionaries filling factories and offices. As he once famously put it, despite the fact that the enlightenment which accompanies modernity promises to set people free, 'the fully enlightened earth radiates disaster triumphant' (Adorno and Horkheimer, 1969: 3).

Rather than simply discarding this kind of thinking as unnecessarily grumpy or as something to do with Adorno's somehow messed-up personality, let us try to understand what he is concerned about. In addition to the obvious disasters of modernity, of which the Nazi holocaust and the Stalinist gulag are probably the clearest examples, Adorno is equally concerned with the impoverishment of life in those societies that claim to be democratic. Having fled from Germany to the United States shortly before the Second World War, he found a world equally degraded and degrading as the disaster overrunning Europe at that time. Hence the diagnosis that the countries of industrial modernity share a tendency towards commodification and total control, regardless of their stated political goals. In this world, which is wrong, a 'right life' is impossible.

To understand what is meant by commodification, we need to go back to Marx again. Marx gives this explanation, almost a fairy story (with a sad ending, however) of the progressive commodification of the world:

> Exchange has a history of its own. It has passed through different phases. There was a time, as in the Middle Ages, when only the superfluity, the excess of production over consumption, was exchanged. There was again a time, when not only the superfluity, but all products, all industrial existence, had passed into commerce, when the whole of production depended on exchange. . . . Finally, there came a time when everything that men had considered as inalienable became an object of exchange, of traffic and could be alienated. This is the time when the very things which till then had been communicated, but never exchanged; given, but never sold; acquired, but never bought – virtue, love, conviction, knowledge, conscience, etc. – when everything, in short, passed into commerce. It is the time of general corruption, of universal venality, or, to speak in terms of political economy, the time when everything, moral or physical, having become a marketable value, is brought to the market to be assessed at its truest value.
>
> (1847: 30)

Marx's use of the word 'truest' is, of course, ironic, and he certainly doesn't think that the value something has on the market is the only way something could be valued. The point we can take from this is that, in capitalist societies, the value of all things tends to become nothing more than what one pays for them. And even things that we used to think could not be sold come to be given a cash value. Think, for example, of the way that today human genes are 'owned' by pharmaceutical companies. The very stuff that, apparently, makes us human, is brought to the market and sold to the highest bidder.

Adorno would presumably be dismayed if he saw the things that are often said about business ethics and corporate social responsibility. One might imagine him asking how it is even possible to think that things such as ethics and responsibility could be for sale, perhaps in books with titles like this one. For Adorno, these are fundamental human characteristics, not something available for global capital to market and sell more toothpaste, bananas, or petrol.

You will perhaps be starting to get a sense now of what Adorno means when he speaks of modernity as an era of 'wrong life'. When life becomes a commodity, and when humanity becomes something for sale, as workers and buyers (or, as it is more nobly put, employees and consumers), all that used to be life becomes something else. And in these conditions, talk of the 'right life' – which is, as we recall from Chapter 1, the classic project of ethics – becomes nothing more than idle chatter. Which is why, for Adorno, wrong life cannot be lived rightly.

109

Now, we do not want to give the impression that Adorno is purely negative, that he has no hope at all or that all talk of ethics should be abandoned. People have said such things about Adorno, but we think that they are wrong. This is because Adorno is a dialectical thinker, which means that he seeks to see how something can emerge out of its opposite. In this case, how the wrong life and denial of ethics by organised modernity and global capital can make way for talk of a good life, one which transcends and breaks open wrong life. In this sense, while Adorno's diagnosis is pessimistic, his prognosis is optimistic. How is this?

The first thing to note is that for Adorno ethics, as consideration of the good life, is always a matter of critique. Thinking about the good life involves thinking about how life could be different, and better, than the life we have now. To simply reassure ourselves that our life today is good is not the game of ethics. Hence, as Adorno puts it, 'the reflection on moral questions stands in something of a contradiction to the object of its own reflections' (2000: 9). Ethics is therefore almost by definition a critique of the wrongs of the world, combined with an optimism of the will. As we have seen, or will see as soon as we leave our studies, the wrongs of the world are many. It will perhaps now make more sense when we find Adorno suggesting that nowadays:

> life itself is so deformed and distorted that no one is able to live the good life in it or to fulfil his destiny as a human being. Indeed, I would almost go so far as to say that, given the way the world is organized, even the simplest demand for integrity and decency must necessarily lead almost everyone to protest. I believe that only by making this situation a matter of consciousness – rather than covering it up with sticking plaster – will it be possible to create the conditions in which we can properly formulate questions about how we should lead our lives today. The only thing that can perhaps be said is that the good life today would consist in resistance to the forms of the bad life that have been seen through and critically dissected by the most progressive minds. Other than this negative prescription no guidance can really be envisaged.
>
> (2000: 167–168)

This may be a miserable and even contradictory position, but Adorno closes his lectures on moral philosophy with this affirmation and call for resistance. He is clear that ethics is not a plan, and he has no intention to provide an 'ethical system' (Adorno, 2000: 20). On the contrary, ethics is not something useful or functional to the administered society of global capital, but is the very thing that endangers the wrong life sponsored by corporate capital. Because the search for the right life involves resistance to wrong life, Adorno argues (and as we saw in Aristotle in Chapter 5) that ethics is fundamentally a matter of politics. 'In short, anything that we can call morality today merges into the question of the organization of the world. We might even say that the quest for the good life is the quest for the right form of politics' (Adorno, 2000: 176).

110

What we see here is that ethics is no longer merely a matter of living the right life within a predefined definition of what 'life' is, but is a matter of challenging the political organisation of life. As we have argued elsewhere, bringing politics into ethics and calling politics into question cause all sorts of problems for traditional business ethics, which has typically left politics either out of the picture or unquestioned (see Parker, 2003b). Insofar as business ethics does not demand of itself a critical understanding of politics, it seems to assume existing definitions of the good life, or, to put it more directly, a lot of business ethics, by leaving politics out of the picture, is complicit with the reproduction of what Adorno, and others, would diagnose as the wrong life.

If we consider the way that business ethicists have typically responded to the protest movements we have discussed in this chapter, we find business ethics lacking again. Typically, these are seen not as a radical attempt to build a world in which life was organised differently. Movements against global capital are often seen as something to be 'managed' or to be marketed towards, in the sense that business as usual can proceed, but 'taking into account' and 'responding to' these new 'stakeholders'. Following Adorno, these kinds of response are a matter of sticking plaster, and are nothing to do with ethics. Ethics is one of the things that the movement against global capital is calling for. This is not more marketing or codes of responsibility, but would involve creating a different world.

We might start to see, then, that ethics is far more dangerous than business ethicists normally let on. They clean it up and make it into something useful. In this sense most business ethicists are not interested in ethics at all, insofar as ethics is about other worlds. At least Milton Friedman was clear enough on this point, preferring to be honest about what businesses can (and should not) do, rather than sugar coating them with talk of corporate social responsibility. For him, business can only be about business as usual. And we find that much that Adorno has to say about ethics resounds clearly with the movement against global capital. One of the slogans of the anti-corporate movement is: 'another world is possible'. There is no prescription about exactly what that world would look like, but an insistence that another world is possible. And as this movement grows in strength it has little interest in being placated by businesses that market themselves as ethical but continue business as usual. As the movement grows, there is an increasing sense of possibility, of changing the very way in which we define the good life. Reflective of this confidence, we often find the movement saying, on banners and on walls at protests, that 'We are Winning'. As Arundhati Roy, one of the representatives of the movement against global capital and for global justice, puts it: 'Another world is not only possible, she is on her way. On a quiet day, I can hear her breathing' (2004: 246).

Chapter 9

Business ethics today

INTRODUCTION: FASHION AND UTOPIA IN BUSINESS ETHICS

This is the second to last chapter in the book, and we are now beginning to move towards something that looks like a conclusion. In terms of the structure of the book, in this chapter we will look at some of the most fashionable issues in business ethics today, and in the next chapter explain what exactly we are 'for'. But before we do this we need to clarify a bit of terminology.

Throughout this book we have been pointing out some of the ways that words get used in all kinds of peculiar ways. If you have looked at the glossary you will see that even the key words relating to business ethics are subject to a great deal of debate and disagreement. In fact, one of the major arguments in this book is that the word 'ethics' is far more slippery than business ethicists tend to admit. This is not to say that words mean any old thing that we want them to. To think such a thing (which is sometimes called **relativism**) would be to stop thinking altogether. And that is the last thing we want.

Now, given that this book was written by three people, and people use words in different ways, it is hardly surprising that we, the authors, have in the past used the same words in ways that are inconsistent. We do not always agree with each other, and we sometimes disagree with things that we thought or wrote in the past. This is important because in this chapter we are going to discuss **fashion** and in the next chapter we are doing to discuss **utopia**. All three of us have thought and written about such things. But if you read what we have written in the past you will find us in disagreement with each other. Sometimes, you will find us actually arguing almost the opposite position regarding fashion and utopia. Let us try, therefore, to clear this up. In doing so, you might reflect on what scholarly work is for. We think that, in part, it is a matter of clarifying for ourselves and for others why and how we disagree with each other. After all, this is a book for us, as well as for you. It was not written because we knew all the answers, but because we thought we might have some interesting questions.

On one reading, Martin Parker's concluding essay in his edited collection *Utopia and Organization* is a brazen statement for utopia and for utopianism. Against those intellectuals and politicians who are not interested in the possibility of radical alternatives,

Parker insists that what is required today is an admission that 'we are unhappy with the present state of affairs and prepared to acknowledge that there are always alternatives. History has not ended' (2002b: 218). Against the hegemony of market managerialism, together with the idea that there is no alternative, Parker and many others have been insisting that there *are* alternatives, and that a different future *is* possible (see also Fournier, 2002; Godfrey et al., 2004; Jones, 2004; Jones and Böhm, 2003; Parker, 2002b; Parker et al., forthcoming).

Given that Parker and Jones might be read as outright advocates of utopianism, a reader might be a little confused to find ten Bos making a case against utopia, which is exactly what we find in his book, *Fashion and Utopia in Management Thinking* (2000). Here, he could not be more explicit: 'I do not want to live in Utopia or to work for a "utopian" organization' (ten Bos, 2000: 20).

This might be the kind of thing that some people would gleefully expose as a contradiction. Parker and Jones are for utopia, but ten Bos is against it. How could they ever write a coherent book together, let alone make a coherent argument? But we think that this conclusion is wrong. We have perhaps not been clear enough in the past, and we have not specified exactly which version of utopia we are for, and which we are against. We have not adequately distinguished between two very different concepts of utopia.

On the one hand, there is what might be called a 'closed utopia', or simply Utopia with a capital letter. This is an idea of what the perfect future looks like, in which everything is planned out in advance, and then all that is needed is to move towards that Utopia. We know where we are going, we have the map and we just need to get there. We might run into complications on the way, people might resist us, but we will persevere and reach our target, whatever the cost. In the name of the good end we might have to break a few eggs, but this is a price worth paying for a perfect omelette in a perfect world. However, as you can hopefully see, this **hygienic** conception of Utopia is potentially a very dangerous one, and some have argued that this kind of idea of Utopia is behind some of the greatest mistakes of the twentieth century, many of which we have complained about in Chapters 7 and 8. It is this concept of Utopia with which all three of us have some serious problems.

On the other hand, there is what might be called an 'open utopia', or utopia with a lower case 'u'. On this understanding, utopia is a movement away from the present state of affairs, away from the present place, or as it is put in Greek, the *topos*. On this view Utopia is not really utopia at all, because the idea of Utopia already has a place, a *topos* in mind. By contrast, an open utopia, or we might even say an unrestricted utopia, is not about moving towards another location with a destination known in advance. It is more like the kind of thing that Jacques **Derrida** calls the 'to-come', without knowing exactly what it is that will come. This open utopia is almost little more than saying that the future is possible, and there is no absolute reason that tomorrow must look like today. This is the kind of utopia defended by many in the contemporary anti-capitalist movement, who argue that 'another world is possible', but don't know in advance what that world will be. This is space in which there is 'one no, many yeses' (Kingsnorth, 2003) or as it is put by Subcommandante Marcos 'in the world we want, many worlds fit' (1996: 250). For this movement of an open utopia, the place is not known in advance.

As will become clear in the next chapter, at the same time as we are critical of Utopianism, we insist absolutely on utopianism. Without it, we are effectively saying that this world is the 'best of all possible worlds'. Without a notion of a different place, a utopia, we are saying that all of the suffering in the world today is unavoidable. We might as well say that this world is okay, the best of all possible worlds. But we think that this would not be something that most of the people on this planet would agree with.

We will consider the place of Utopia and utopia in business ethics in the next chapter, but let us also clarify what we mean by fashion. Business ethics is clearly a fashionable thing today, and some are suspicious of business ethics exactly because of its fashion-ability. But we want to argue, as ten Bos argued in *Fashion and Utopia in Management Thinking*, that the problem with business ethics is not that it is fashionable but rather that 'management fashion is not fashionable all the way down' (ten Bos, 2000: 175). This is to say, fashionable ideas about management are often not actually in touch with the present, let alone the future, and hence the problem is that 'management fashions are not fashionable enough!' (ten Bos, 2000: 21).

We saw in the first half of this book that most of the philosophical sources that business ethicists draw on are very traditional, and are based on traditional and often partial readings of the classics. We tried to bring them up to date, but without losing the critical tension at the heart of great thinking. In this chapter we propose to look at some of the most fashionable issues at the cutting edge of business ethics today. In turn we will discuss the ideas of: (1) community, (2) trust, (3) whistleblowing, (4) responsibility, and (5) cynicism. With each of these ideas we will argue that business ethicists have almost always treated them in a way that blunts their sharp edges and makes them less dangerous. So we propose to renew these topics by taking their fashionability seriously. Indeed, if business ethics were not so stuck in a rather conservative past, then these fashionable issues might well effectively radicalise business and business ethics as they are usually understood.

Our treatment of these five topics might be thought of as a statement of position in relation to business ethics, in which we try to show what a radicalised business ethics, the kind of business ethics we want to defend, would look like. We conclude the chapter by arguing that if business ethics has any merit at all then it is going to be in this renewed form, which would be 'more fashionable than fashion'. We imagine a community of business ethicists who would write books on these fashionable topics, and many many others, but in doing so would go beyond the reductive and **technocratic** way in which these fashions have been treated so far. (This community might also do other things than write books, because politics cannot be confined to armchairs.) This community would start from the ground that the problem with business ethics is not that it is fashionable, but that it is not fashionable enough. It would perhaps also agree that the problem with business ethics is not that it is Utopian, but that it is not utopian enough.

COMMUNITY

As we already saw in Chapter 5, one of the issues that has permeated the field of business ethics for a long time is the question of community. Morality, it is often assumed, cannot come without a sense of belongingness. If it is to function at all, it should be embedded in a culture that provides the moral person with a proper frame of reference. We do not live in a moral vacuum. In other words, whatever moral inclinations you may have, they will inevitably erode when there is nobody who recognises or perhaps even endorses them. It is therefore hard to see how business ethics can ever be fruitful if it neglects the issue of community.

Already half a century ago, the American sociologist William Whyte (1956: 34) warned that debates about the organisational community were totally dominated by a scientific approach which aims to engineer the perfect form of belongingness and togetherness. He refers to this phenomenon as 'scientism' and he claims that it 'appears in many forms – pedagogy, aptitude tests, that monstrous nonentity called "mass communication" – and there are few readers who have not had a personal collision with it' (1956: 34–35).

We do not think that Whyte's insights are obsolete. On the contrary, since the publication of *The Organization Man* we have witnessed a proliferation of self-help texts (Garsten and Grey, 1997), business audits (Power, 1998), and many more soft and hard technologies that are supposed to create efficient communities. Nowadays, even the human qualities that seem to belong to the private domain – kindness or mental health are examples that spring to our mind – are considered to be extremely important in the creation of the efficient community.

The danger of this widespread scientism, Whyte claims, is that it has a profound impact on our values and that we therefore tend to surrender uncritically or perhaps cynically to its workings and its promise. A basic assumption of the social engineers pervading our organisations – often cloaked as management trainers or consultants – is that we should always treat different individuals in organisations not as the individuals they are but as members of the group to which they belong. Whyte argues that this assumption is based on what he refers to as the fallacy of false collectivisation: 'We are confusing an abstraction with a reality. Just because a collection of individuals can be called a group does not mean it functions as a group or that it should' (1956: 51).

The point is not that groups or communities are bad or repressive. The point is rather that in organisations people tend to become morally judged as group members rather than as individuals. And this, of course, influences the kind of values and ethical goals that are assumed to be important in the organisation: loyalty, accuracy, communicativeness, trustworthiness, diligence, trust, obedience and other traits that generate group coherence and consent (Willmott, 1998: 85). Inevitably, part of what might be considered as more individualised values – creativity, intuition, aimless thinking, and the ability to ask unpractical questions are some examples mentioned by Whyte – tend to become neglected in organisations. Leaders and managers stress the importance of belongingness and togetherness. They do not usually tell people to ignore them. But, as Whyte astutely points out, '[p]eople very rarely *think* in groups; they talk together, they exchange information, they adjudicate, they make compromises. But they do not think; they do not create' (1956: 52).

It is senseless to deny the importance of community for ethics and morality, but that should not tempt us to think that the very idea of engineering perfect forms of belongingness and togetherness will somehow hand us moral excellence on a silver platter. Even if it were possible to organise perfect Utopian communities, something about which we are very doubtful, it is by no means certain that it will bring us moral improvement. The point with morality is always that the good never comes without the bad. It is exactly this paradoxical nature of morality that resists organisation or planning.

However, for business ethics the good is something that can only be achieved in communities, in businesses. Therefore, it offers us a plethora of techniques – varying from mission statements to integrity audits, rules of conduct, ethical codes and stakeholder analyses – that might help to bring about the good community or, as business ethicists themselves prefer to express it, 'businesses of excellence' (see Solomon in Chapter 5). There is little joy in all of these rules, and actually rather a lot of fear of losing control. Most importantly, though, these are all techniques that aim to have the individual employee surrender to the overarching organisational values. If *you* want to be good, become one of *us*.

As it is currently practised, business ethics is just one more branch of the bewildering varieties of 'scientism' with which Whyte took issue. Much of what we have to say in this book is actually in defence of precisely the kind of values that this early commentator already considered to be pivotal for morality: doubt, intuition, paradox, improvisation, thought, creativity, aimlessness, or even uselessness or idleness. Perhaps these are not the values with which you can forge a coherent community, let alone a 'strong' culture (Peters and Waterman, 1982), but we do believe that organisations that paid attention to these values would not necessarily be worse places than organisations that did not.

However, we also believe that most business ethicists do not share our interest in these values, partly because these values defy social engineering. How on earth are you to engineer idleness or aimlessness? This is also because the focus is on the good organisation that is constituted by ranks of identically good individuals. Idleness and aimlessness may on occasion spur individual creativity, but can the organisation afford them? What sort of organisation would be created if all the employees were thinking all the time; or were encouraged to loudly express public doubts about what they were doing? These are ideas that would probably be dismissed by business ethicists and their patrons as unrealistic or useless. This should be a book about business, and all this undisciplined thinking about the virtues of joyful laziness entirely misses the point. Business communities are hard nosed ones, and you do not have to like them (or be liked by them) in order to be successful. And if you don't like that, you can always leave, perhaps to join a community of people more like you. But this means you will no longer be one of us, and you will not be welcome here any more because we will not trust you.

TRUST

One of the bestselling management books in the Netherlands of the last couple of years has been a text with the title *The Way of the Rat: A Survival Guide to Office Politics*. The author of this text, Joep Schrijvers (2004), advocates a form of Machiavellian behaviour in organisations, claiming that it is the sole key to survival and success. Lying, cheating, repression, anything goes, as long as it safeguards or even reinforces your own position in the organisation as well as the position of the organisation itself. As was to be expected, the author has been accused of cynicism, most notably by management consultants and business ethicists. But we would argue that the popularity of this text is probably related to an understanding among many of its readers that the author has probably drawn a quite accurate picture of organisations. Most people know from harsh experience that organisations are probably not the kind of places where you can trust anybody.

It is hardly a surprise that trust is an all-important issue in business ethics, but its predominance is, we would suggest, also related to an obsession with the possibility of treason (Sievers, 2003). The more we read about trust initiatives, the more we know that something has gone sadly wrong in organisations. Scandals in international business life are a perfect illustration of the treacherous character that organisations and their inhabitants can assume. Fraud and corporate misconduct, it is argued, undermine the trust we put in corporate leaders; indeed, are bad not only for the organisations involved but for the business community as a whole. Therefore, nothing seems to be more obvious than launching a new set of ethical programmes and techniques that will, if carried through with enough persistence, tackle the problem. But will it? There are, we suggest, at least two reasons why we should be suspicious.

First of all, we often find that people who have unconditionally surrendered to the dictates of capitalism are not to be trusted. Economists who have studied the 'laws' that govern the capitalist economy have often assumed that human beings are inveterate egoists who are always keen on increasing their own profit. The *homo economicus* that we discussed in the chapter on utilitarianism is, as far as we can see, not the type of person that we would want to unconditionally trust. There has been a furious debate among economists concerning whether this perspective on human beings is adequate, but by and large this has not led them to abandon the assumption that 'people will act as self-interested individuals often enough for the "laws" of economics to be a useful guide for making predictions and formulating public policy' (Fukuyama, 1995: 21). It is therefore no surprise that in many economic models trust or, perhaps better, the crisis of trust, plays a crucial role.

You only need to glance at textbooks on microeconomics, or in the many popular and academic books on contemporary management, and you will see that there is a pervasive concern with trust. After all, any economic or social transaction between two or more human beings seems to presuppose a kernel of trust. You will not buy a car if you do not trust the car-dealer of the company that has produced the car. Chrysler once decided to move its production plants to Mexico, a low wage economy. No doubt Chrysler executives thought that this was a sound strategy for lowering costs and maximising profits, but the American consumer responded by not buying Chrysler cars. Mexicans, it seems, are not to be trusted when it comes to the manufacturing of cars, and neither were the Chrysler managers who were exporting jobs out of the USA. That the 'Mexican' cars were later sufficiently vindicated in tests carried out by the best experts did not help either the company or the Mexicans working there. The relationship of trust was, for various 'irrational' reasons, irredeemably violated.

The solution that is often offered for the crisis of trust in textbooks on economy is a particular form of institutionalisation – organisation and hierarchy. We only trust people – after all, most of them are strangers – if we are able to make them responsible for their acts, that is, if we are able to *formally* issue a complaint about their behaviour and eventually to gain some sort of redress. But trust may have its informal qualities in the sense that it is also a matter of inspiration, affiliation, or intuition, but economics insists on more concrete matters. But trust can only function if it is somehow backed up by the possibility of formal sanctions. As one shrewd commentator has put it: 'the point is that I do not need to like or care about [the person with whom I interact] to deal confidently and reliably with him' (Seabright, 2004: 64). In other words, we may all be rats, but our 'ratness' can be mitigated if we construct reliable institutions which channel our behaviours. A balance of cheese and small electric shocks is usually sufficient to make rats do the right thing.

The second reason for being suspicious about efforts to create more trust is related to the fascination that we all feel for treason and for traitors, that is to say, for people who cannot be trusted. Jean Genet, the famous and notorious French novelist, once argued that the person who has never experienced the ecstasy of treason is deemed to be fully unaware of what ecstasy is all about. This may be an exaggeration, but the sense of excitement that comes with being a traitor is, from a psychological perspective, quite understandable. Traitors generally do make a difference, whereas the loyal and subservient do not. Trust is boring, whilst treachery is exciting.

Part of our curious fascination with treason is no doubt related to an understanding that the traitor, in being a danger to the community of which we might be a member, also opens up a perspective to what is outside this community, perhaps even to new and more inspiring communities (Sloterdijk, 1998). Hence, we might see the traitor as a human being standing on the threshold of a new world that simultaneously beckons to us and abhors us. Who are these people? They are, we would like to suggest, 'rats'. We may think of these creatures as critical minds, wayward individuals or rebels who occasionally come to the fore in teams or groups. However we think about them, their actions spur in us the ambivalence that we sense when we talk about treason. Nowhere does this become more evident than with the so-called whistleblower, the type of traitor who is the pre-eminent specialist in ratting-on and who has therefore attracted by far the most attention in the business ethics literature.

WHISTLEBLOWING

Blowing the whistle suggests the metaphor of a referee in a sports match. The attentive individual spots an infringement of the rules, and draws everyone's attention to it. If their decision goes against the home team, they draw the outraged abuse of the fans. Against the visiting team and we will see nods of approval and applause. So what is it that allows a referee to ignore the crowd, and blow the whistle?

The reason it is worth asking this question is because, as virtue ethics teaches us, we are all part of crowds. We seem to be creatures that gain our ideas about good and bad from social context, from the times and places we find ourselves in. Most of us, most of the time, follow the crowd. But don't get the idea that this is simply a bad thing, or that it reflects a lack of willpower. If we didn't try to 'fit in', and copy those around us, we would never learn to become members of the social groups that surround us. Imagine someone who always refused to be part of a crowd, who insisted on having their own values, ethics, and even language. Such a person would be beyond good and evil, a sociopath who was outside any commonsensical understanding of what it might mean to be a moral being. So the referee, in order to blow the whistle, is not ignoring the crowd in some self-assured gesture of defiance. They are actually attempting to apply a set of abstract rules, without hatred or passion, on behalf of another agency. The referee is trying to be a good referee, according to the standards of refereeing set by the rules of the game and their professional association. They can, more or less, ignore the crowd because of the legitimacy granted by the social identity of being a referee. Or, to put it another way, they can ignore the crowd in the stadium because they are already a member of another crowd outside the stadium.

It is important to understand this, because one of the curious things about whistleblowing as it is represented in much conventional business ethics, is that it is suggested to be a heroic form of resistance to collective evil – an exemplary individualistic Kantian act in many ways, one that requires a certain moral fibre and determination. Another curious thing is that it is acknowledged to be very rare, and that (sadly) most people don't blow the whistle often enough on the various disreputable, illegal or immoral practices of their organisations. This seems to lead us to the conclusion, usually unacknowledged, that most people, most of the time, turn a blind eye. As Punch (1996) concludes, based on his substantial study of corporate misconduct, very few people actually act on the forms of reasoning which business ethicists suggest that they should. Most of them shrug their shoulders, claim it is someone else's responsibility, or think about their mortgages and their summer holidays. Most powerfully of all, they can also claim Eichmann's excuse – that they were 'only following orders'. Employees have a duty to follow orders, and employees who don't follow orders are not reliable employees.

119

They are not team players, they are not loyal, they are not trustworthy. Which takes us back to trust of course, because people who blow the whistle are traitors. They have broken the rules of their community, and exclusion will inevitably follow.

So organisations tend to encourage conformity, and they brand difference as a sort of treachery. Not being like 'us' means that you won't get promotion and that you will eat your lunch on your own. Such anticipated responses are (of course) painful, and they encourage people to use the sorts of excuse we discussed in Chapter 7 in order to rationalise their conduct: 'I didn't say anything because it wasn't my responsibility.' But there is another aspect to this too. Many market managerial organisations are pushing the boundaries of what is illegal and what is immoral in order to meet ever more demanding short-term returns to shareholders, or performance targets from senior managers, or both. Everything must be done faster, cheaper, with fewer people in far away places. Not only are such situations 'criminogenic' (a criminological term for something that encourages crime), they also mean that the consequences of whistle-blowing can be disastrous for the entire organisation. Customers will be disappointed. Other organisations will gain market share. Careers might be ruined. People might lose their jobs. Criticising your organisation is not some abstract matter, but will inevitably involve suggesting that you do this and do that. And if someone loses their job or is moved to another office in another town, their dependents will suffer too. These are utilitarian calculations that have many undesirable consequences. No wonder whistleblowers end up eating lunch on their own, or eating lunch somewhere else, forever.

So, back to the question then. What is it that allows the referee to ignore the baying of the crowd? How can they do what they do, even though a few thousand people are questioning their parentage, eyesight and understanding of the rules of the game? It might be a version of Kantian freedom, or a careful calculation of the consequences of corporate immorality, or the exemplification of wider virtues that have somehow been erased within a particular organisation. All of these are credible ways of accounting for whistleblowing, but none of them addresses how such treachery can be encouraged. How might it be made easier for employees to speak out? There are certainly negative answers to this question, such as the British 'Public Interest Disclosure Act' which was passed in 1998 and is framed as legal protection for whistleblowers if they satisfy certain conditions (Fisher and Lovell, 2003: 199). Though the conditions are reasonable – such as that there should be a real possibility of harm to the public, all internal procedures should have been exhausted, and so on – they do not, and cannot, deal with the personal issues mentioned above. Legal protections, for employers and employees, are certainly important, but it should never be forgotten that the fundamental issue is how to provide a legitimate – if dangerous – social identity for the person who speaks fearlessly.

In order to blow the whistle, you must have enough breath and nerve. Fear of reprisals, of personal acrimony or humiliation, can make you breathless and nervous. At times in ancient Greece, Foucault (2001) suggests, the place of the truth teller, the person who engages in *parrhesia*, is contrasted with the place of the person who merely tries to persuade by using *rhetoric*. In some sense, then, the art of speaking to crowds in public is different to telling the truth to anyone, as you see it. Becoming a *rhetor* is a technique that you can learn, whilst becoming a *parrhesiastes* is a way of life. Being the kind of person who speaks truth to power, regardless of the consequences, involves a certain way of thinking about yourself, of living with yourself. To put it in more modern terms, the truth teller is someone who needs to be able to look at themselves in the mirror in the morning; someone with a low tolerance for hypocrisy and a high expectation of consistency, for themselves and for others. However, these should not be thought of as heroic personal qualities that exist outside crowds, because they are also social identities that can be encouraged or discouraged. The truth needs to be expected by others, to make it easier to expect it from yourself. Perhaps you will find it easier to be a *parrhesiastes* if there are others like you too, easier to be a referee if you can appeal beyond the crowd to another sense of who you are and why it matters to be a truth teller. Whistleblowing is only possible if there are people to hear the whistle being blown.

But this is not simply about some abstract version of truth. To go back to the example of the referee, the correctness of a decision depends on who you want to win the game. For some, whistleblowers will always be traitors. For others, they will always be heroes. It depends on who benefits from a particular act of fearless speech. There are no timeless mechanisms that could decide such matters. We can never say, for once and for all, that this act was good and that act was bad. Sometimes it might be better to bluff, or lie, or be silent. Sometimes it might be better to tell the truth. All might sometimes be difficult, but the latter is more likely to be dangerous. This is because whistleblowing does not happen in a vacuum (which is literally as well as metaphorically true). It often involves speaking against the powerful and on behalf of the powerless. It might also involve breaking trust, and leaving community. Perhaps the best we might do is to consider who or what we are serving in making a decision to speak, or not to speak. Who is being spoken for, and who is being left silent? Such questions might be thought of as questions of responsibility.

RESPONSIBILITY

It is hard to think of a concept that has attracted more attention from business ethicists than the notion of 'responsibility'. This usually appears in the form of something called Corporate Social Responsibility, which is almost always written with capital letters and is often abbreviated to just plain CSR. There are books, journals, conferences, research centres and professors dealing with CSR, and very few organisations of a certain size fail to have a published CSR policy. Many have officially appointed CSR managers and some even have a CSR department. (These CSR departments are usually subsections of a marketing or public relations department, which is interesting, but more on that soon.)

From the point of view of the kind of business ethics we are arguing for in this book, a lot of this CSR talk seems to have got ahead of itself and has rushed far too quickly to solutions. It seems particularly concerned to measure how well CSR works while not stopping to ask those basic questions that anyone concerned with thinking would ask themselves. So, bearing in mind that our task is to do some ground clearing work for the field of business ethics, we might go back and ask some questions about the meaning of responsibility. After all, it is an attractive-sounding word, and it is hard to imagine anyone who could be against responsibility. But then, what does 'responsibility' mean? We suggest that there are several different meanings to the word, and that the weaker, or conditional, senses of responsibility might be dispensable.

If we look at what is done in the name of CSR today, again what we almost always find is something like a code or some other set of written principles or guidelines. These codes demarcate the rules that should be followed by members of that organisation in order for responsibility to take place. This responsibility often goes beyond what is merely required by the law, and in this respect is quite worthy of celebration. But on the other hand, when responsibility is made into a set of rules and procedures, it seems to run against the common sense in which responsibility is understood as an 'ability to act independently and make decisions' (*Oxford English Dictionary*). If responsibility is enshrined in a rule book, then where is your choice to take it or not?

Responding to this kind of difficulty, in recent years Jacques Derrida has embarked on a critical rethinking of the meaning of responsibility. Derrida notes that responsibility always involves a *response* to an other person, and the idea of a responsibility without a relation to an other makes little sense (1995: 50). In this Derrida develops the thinking of Levinas, who we discussed in Chapter 6, who defined ethics as a relation of openness to the Other. Set up in this way, responsibility is a concept which is certainly related to ethics, and involves a consideration of how and to whom one responds. Both at the level of the individual and at the level of the organisation, one can think of various ways of responding to others.

If we think about how organisations have used CSR to respond to others, we find often what might be called a *strategic* or *marketing* approach. In this, the other is treated as someone who is useful to the organisation. The most obvious example is the way that CSR is used in relation to customers. As is well known, in recent years wealthier consumers in the West have expressed preferences for purchasing products from companies perceived to be ethical, and in response to this pressure many companies have marketed themselves in a way so as to appear responsible. We care about the other because the other is useful for us. This way of constructing responsibility has been beautifully described by John Roberts as an 'ethics of Narcissus' (2001; 2003). Following the Greek myth of Narcissus, the boy who was captivated by his own image and spent days staring at his reflection in a pool, Roberts argues that CSR has a tendency to narcissism. Organisations care about others, but only because they need the other to tell them how beautiful they are. Like the foolish Narcissus, they care for nothing but the surface impression that the other has of them. The other is not an Other in the full sense, but a tool to be exploited. Or, as Kant suggested (see Chapter 4), a means rather than an end.

A second approach to CSR might be described as the *stakeholder* approach, following on from ideas we discussed in the last chapter, as well as in Chapter 3 on utilitarianism. In this approach there is more of a concern for the other, who is now not just a tool to be used, but a set of interests that need to be understood, and where possible protected or managed. So CSR becomes a matter of observing social and political trends, and 'moving with the times'. This is not pure narcissism, and often recognises that parties such as employees, customers, government and environmental groups can and do exert real pressure on organisations. But the stakeholder approach to CSR still retains a strategic element, in that the goals and objectives of the organisation are the central focus, and stakeholders are a nuisance or opportunity that has to be managed. So, for example, in Africa a number of oil companies have built public amenities, villages and schools for local communities. If we look closely at the practice of these CSR projects, however, they appear to be little more than gimmicks to allow them to achieve their goals while appeasing a community that would otherwise be hostile to them. These companies do not *respond* to these stakeholders; instead they distract (or placate) them in order to continue with business as usual.

The strategic and stakeholder approaches to CSR should therefore probably be described as conditional responsibility at best. This is a responsibility that trades on the positive connotations of the word, but only loosely engages in anything that could be called responsibility in a stronger sense. As Derrida makes clear, responsibility always bears some relation to secrecy (1995: Chapter 1). Being fully responsible means that you cannot know in advance how to respond, and which Other to respond to. Responsibility, if it is to involve a genuine response to the Other, involves at least a certain element of not knowing who to respond to, not knowing how to respond and not knowing if your actions have been responsible. In this sense, responsibility is not something that could be conditioned or controlled, let alone marketed or managed. Responsibility calls into question all conditions, and demands that one responds to the Other, without knowing how.

As we have tried to explain elsewhere, this is not to explode responsibility, or to say that responsibility means anything that you want it to (Jones, 2003a; 2004). Rather, when we see responsibility as an unconditional openness in response to the other, there is no goal other than the response to the Other itself. And we do not know in advance which Other to respond to, or how to respond to them. When companies with CSR policies respond to others, they typically respond to the others most useful to them, those who can be drawn into the utilitarian calculus. This, Derrida stresses, is not responsibility. Responsibility draws us towards a welcoming of the Other, and a hospitality that invites the Other to share our table. Today, those companies that speak most loudly of their concern for responsibility are often the least concerned for others. Like someone who loudly claims they are good, we have reason to doubt why they want to persuade everyone of their virtue. Think, for example, of the pharmaceutical companies that refuse to provide anti-retroviral drugs to Africa, where many thousands are dying of AIDS, while they publish glossy brochures and slick websites promoting their corporate social responsibility. Or, even worse, these companies later celebrate that which they were shamed into doing by campaigners as an example of their own philanthropy. 'We eventually did some of what you suggested we should. Look how good we are!' What kind of responsibility is this?

CYNICISM

Perhaps it is because of the kind of thing that companies do with words such as 'responsibility' that there is a widespread negative view about any talk of business ethics today. If companies propose that responsibility is something that can be marketed and managed, then we should not be too surprised when people laugh at any talk of business ethics, or claim it is a contradiction in terms. However, if we think about it, there is more than one way to laugh at something.

In his magnificent book, with the simple title *Critique of Cynical Reason*, the German philosopher Peter Sloterdijk has exposed much about a particular way of laughing that is particularly common today, and particularly amongst business people. Sloterdijk diagnoses our age as being characterised by what he calls 'cynicism'. By this he is not referring to the belly laugh that comes when one sees something absolutely improbable. Contemporary cynics have already seen the twentieth century and all of its special effects disasters. We know what marketing is for and we know what managers do to us. We have seen through all of this and feel powerless to do anything about it, so we shrug our shoulders, pass a small chuckle, but continue with our lives as they were before. This is an educated age, Sloterdijk reminds us, and today cynics have been perfectly enlightened about the evils of the world on our television sets. The cynic knows that business ethics is a sham, that CSR is marketing, and that behind such noble talk is massive suffering and environmental degradation. The world of cynicism is a world in which everyone knows that the phrase 'business ethics' is a contradiction in terms. You, dear reader, may be one of these cynics too.

Being a critical philosopher, Sloterdijk does not only describe this world, but wants to understand it and to change it. So he doesn't simply describe the cynical worldview, but intervenes. In considerable detail he describes how cynicism emerged in its modern form, and why distancing ourselves from the action we are participating in has a significant psychological and ideological function today. Elaborating on Sloterdijk's critique of cynical reason, Slavoj Žižek explains the functioning of cynical ideology at the present time. As he writes:

> The cynical subject is quite aware of the distance between the ideological mask and the social reality, but he none the less still insists upon the mask. The formula, as proposed by Sloterdijk, would then be: 'they know very well what they are doing,

but still, they are doing it'. Cynical reason is no longer naïve, but is a paradox of an enlightened false consciousness: one knows the falsehood very well . . . but still one does not renounce it.

(Žižek, 1989: 29)

This kind of description seems almost perfect to describe many of the responses to business ethics and corporate social responsibility. It is kind of like a collective charade that everyone, or almost everyone, goes along with, even though we know it is a game. Importantly, Žižek argues, this kind of ideology 'is no longer meant, even by its authors, to be taken seriously' (1989: 30), an insight which could equally apply to business ethics and corporate social responsibility.

Sloterdijk is clear about the way that cynical ideology cannot be corrected by providing more knowledge. More facts about the ills of the world do not cure cynicism, which is already well enlightened about the facts. What is required is a different kind of relationship to the way we tell the truth; a different subjective experience of 'the facts', which breaks from cynical laughter. Sloterdijk does not propose an all-too-serious relapse into science; he wants us to carry on laughing, but differently. This different laughter is embodied in what he calls 'kynicism', with a 'k' rather than a 'c'.

While the cynic laughs at the world but leaves the world pretty much as it is, the laugh of the kynic is a laughter that makes the world stammer and stutter. 'When the cynic smiles melancholically-contemptuously, from the illusionless heights of power, it is characteristic of the kynic to laugh so loudly and unabashedly that refined people shake their heads. Kynical laughter comes from the intestines; it is grounded at the animal level and lets itself go without restraint' (Sloterdijk, 1988: 143). Most of all, this laughter must happen in public. Sloterdijk's exemplar of kynical laughter appears in the figure of Diogenes, the famous 'dog-philosopher' who lived in a barrel and whose laughter was crucial in his critique of ancient Athenians. Explaining the operation of Diogenes' kynical laughter, Sloterdijk tells the following well-known story:

> Legend has it that the young Alexander of Macedonia one day sought out Diogenes, whose fame had made him curious. He found him taking a sunbath, lying lazily on his back, perhaps close to an Athenian sportsfield; others say he was gluing books. The young sovereign, in an effort to prove his generosity, granted the philosopher a wish. Diogenes' answer is supposed to have been: 'Stop blocking my sun!'
>
> (1988: 160)

This is the kind of response that is being made to corporations by whistleblowers, anti-corporate protestors, comedians, musicians and film makers. These are perhaps the best examples today of kynical responses to the ethics of business. Inside and outside of organisations, these figures do not want to be granted the kind of wishes that corporations are offering. Not content with being silenced, and not being able to laugh cynically, they are intervening directly, not on the terms of the corporations but on their own terms (see Kingsnorth, 2003; Klein, 2000). And often with a response that evokes a form of laughter which is dangerous enough to cut through cynical ideology.

We might also consider the way that these issues manifest themselves in everyday situations more familiar to business ethicists. In business ethics, the closest we get to a recognition of the problem of cynicism comes in work such as Bird's (1996) on the problem of 'moral silence'. This refers to the way in which, very often today, people in business can see moral or ethical problems, but do not say anything about these things. It is as if they know that there is a moral problem, but act as if it was not there. 'Although they possess moral concerns, many businesspeople do not actively and forthrightly voice these convictions in relation to their work' (Bird, 1996: vii). Moral silence is different from hypocrisy. A hypocrite claims to have noble ideals, such as responsibility for others, but acts in contradiction with those ideals. By contrast, the morally silent manager does not even let their moral ideals surface. On moral matters, they prefer to remain silent, and even in the face of issues that cry out for voice, they say nothing.

Bird's argument is important, particularly in the attention he draws to the practice of ethics being in significant ways a matter of talk and communication. And he connects moral silence with the related tendencies of moral blindness and moral deafness, where others do not see or hear moral issues when they are raised. His arguments are also important in the way that he draws attention to the social and communicative action that takes place in dealing with moral issues. In this, he makes an important gesture by drawing on the work of Jürgen Habermas.

A lot has been said about Habermas, and we do not want to go into details of all of his large body of work here. But we do want to introduce some of his ideas on ethics, in particular because they offer a lot to thinking about business ethics. Of particular importance is his writing on communicative action, discourse ethics and the trans-formation of the public sphere (Habermas, 1990; 1992; 1993; 1998). What is important for us in this context is the emphasis that Habermas puts on the social and on the linguistic nature of ethics. Habermas emphasises the way that discussions about ethics are precisely that – discussions. They involve what he calls 'communicative action' or simply 'discourse'. For there to be a shared notion of what is right and wrong for a community, this must rest on a community talking about, discussing and arguing about what the norms of a good life should be. Conversation, Habermas believes, rests on some notion of equality, on the idea that you might learn something from the other.

What is particularly important about this is that conditions of communicative action do not rest solely with any one individual. Communicative action is a shared social practice. It requires individuals, for sure, but goes beyond individuals in significant ways. By stressing the social nature of communicative action, and hence of morality, Habermas usefully draws attention to the social context in which something like cynicism comes about. He emphasises, as does Bird, that moral silence will take place in a context in which moral deafness is common. It is hardly surprising that ethical concerns are not raised, when no one is willing to listen to them. More forcefully, in a community that has no space for discussion of the meaning of the good life, cynicism and moral silence will become quite normal.

Along with this emphasis on the social and communicative nature of ethics, Habermas usefully draws attention to the spaces in which public discussion about the good life can take place. He sets this in the context of a discussion of what he calls 'the structural transformation of the public sphere' (Habermas, 1992). The 'public sphere' refers to those spaces in which public discussion can take place about values and life. We think of the Athenian *agora* where Socrates encouraged people to think about the good life or, in the modern context, the government and the university, in which preferences concerning the good life are debated. Of particular concern to Habermas, and to contemporary protest movements, is the way in which the public sphere is always endangered by pressures to selectively represent not the whole of the public, but a particular private interest. The arguments against the IMF, WTO and World Bank are often that while they could be instruments in which a public discussion of the good takes place, these institutions have a very partial notion of what is good, and impose this on everybody. Or, to take another example, the World Social Forum has emerged specifically as a response to the World Economic Forum, arguing that the good life is not reducible to good economics. To be sure, both institutions have Utopian tendencies, but only the World Social Forum can also embrace utopia, and hence banish cynicism and have a laugh while doing it.

BUSINESS ETHICS, THE VERY IDEA

In this chapter, we have looked at a set of current issues in business ethics: trust, community, whistleblowing, responsibility and cynicism. In each of these cases we have found that, lurking beneath the surface of these concepts, there is a whole other world waiting to be explored. This is one of the points of this book.

Business ethics presents us with some of the most wonderful, puzzling and troubling aspects of contemporary life, and promises to investigate and understand them. But if you look at much of the literature which claims to represent business ethics, then the truly interesting ideas are ignored, or are made so uninteresting that they might as well have been left out altogether. We have seen, for example, the way that a radical idea such as responsibility has been reduced to marketing. We have seen that any discussion of trust presupposes a concept of treason. Given the way that business ethics texts tend to gloss over these issues, and either ignore or treat as a nuisance things such as the con- temporary protest movement, one might wonder why we want, in this book, to defend business ethics. Given that it is so compromised, wouldn't we be better off forgetting about business ethics?

Considering this possibility, we might be well advised to consult the work of Friedrich **Nietzsche,** a philosopher who subjected Western morality to one of its most searching and vicious critiques. Nietzsche did not disguise his disdain for what was called morality in his time, the late nineteenth century. Nothing was immune to his sharp tongue, which cut through so many forms of common sense. In his important book *The Genealogy of Morals*, for example, he attacks the way that things have been labelled 'good' and 'bad'. He writes:

> The judgement *good* does not originate with those to whom the good has been done. Rather it was the 'good' themselves, that is to say the noble, mighty, highly placed and high-minded who decreed themselves and their actions to be good.
>
> (Nietzsche, 1887: 160)

And he continues:

> The origin of the opposites *good* and *bad* is to be found in the pathos of nobility and distance, representing the dominant temper of a higher, ruling class in relation to a lower, dependent one.
>
> (Nietzsche, 1887: 160)

One might even think that Nietzsche is speaking of business ethicists and corporate social responsibility when he says this, even though he was writing more than a century ago. But even if he had a slightly different target in his sights, his conclusion is important for us. Even though he argued that the morality that he described was fundamentally corrupt, this should not turn us away from talking about what might be moral. Far from abandoning problems of morality, Nietzsche insists, echoing Socrates, that 'nothing under the sun is more rewarding to take seriously' (1887: 156).

We cannot avoid holding values, or valuing things in one way or another. But we can change what we value, and hence Nietzsche, devastating critic of our modernity, calls on us to join in a 'transvaluation of all values'. His claim: 'we need a critique of all moral values; the intrinsic worth of these values must, first of all, be called into question' (Nietzsche, 1887: 155). We find a similar sentiment in Adorno, one of the thinkers that we discussed in the last chapter. Adorno stresses that one of the central tasks of moral philosophy consists in 'the attempt to make conscious the critique of moral philosophy' (2000: 167). If thinking is an attempt to understand what makes a concept or value possible or worthwhile, then a thinking business ethics would negate and reconstruct itself. It must not *assume* what is already there, but should take its common sense apart, and try to understand how it works.

Our overall argument about business ethics is now perhaps becoming clearer. We see business ethics as one of the most promising possibilities, but as something also fundamentally compromised. And we have therefore, in the first half of this book, subjected some of the familiar terrain to criticism, finding that there is much more that is radical than business ethics would typically admit. And from Chapter 6 on, we have set out reconstructing a new, philosophically critical but affirmative business ethics. We are suggesting that this business ethics is already there, in the world, and in many of the texts that speak of business ethics. But we need to recover this business ethics, and help it to grow.

Nonetheless, while we ultimately want to argue for business ethics, we should never forget the possibility that business ethics is corrupt and should be done away with. There is an old joke about politicians, in which one suggests that the desire to be a politician should ban one for life from ever actually becoming one. Perhaps we are suggesting something similar with business ethics: that those who speak of business ethics without the slightest hesitation are not those we could ever support. But paradoxically, those who display the greatest concern and difficulty with business ethics, well, they are the ones who are truly *for* business ethics.

Chapter 10

Conclusion: for business ethics

INTRODUCTION

Often, academic work seems to be detached from everyday life, but sometimes it seems to reflect a genuine social concern. Since the early 1980s business ethics has grown in importance, and in that sense, has become fashionable. There has been a steady increase in press coverage, journals, conferences, consultancies and books that relate in various ways to business ethics. But is all this chatter about responsibility, codes of conduct or business communities just an upsurge that will dwindle soon enough? The common sense answer is that there has been an increasing perception of some kind of crisis of trust in business life, and perhaps in public life more generally. Cynicism, and some kynicism, is all around us nowadays. Collectively, we are finding it increasingly difficult to believe in politicians, religious leaders, journalists and artists. And if we can't believe in those kind of people, then what chance do business organisations have?

So perhaps there is an increasing suspicion of big companies, and a disillusion with 'market' mechanisms for regulating social and economic affairs. Stories about insider trading, stealing from pension funds, false accounting, pollution, breaches of health and safety legislation, sweatshop labour, 'fat cat' pay deals and general profiteering are common enough. In popular terms, these images of organisations are neatly summed up in films like *Wall Street*, *Fight Club* and even *Spiderman*. These films and many others present images of greedy, amoral or immoral executives with their eye on the corner office or world domination. From Mr Burns (and his grovelling assistant Smithers) in *The Simpsons* to David Brent in *The Office*, it seems we are surrounded by cynicism, and kynicism, concerning the motivations, character and consequences of the busy-ness of business people.

But, as we saw in Chapter 8, these fictional images reflect some very real politics too – the anti-corporate protest movement, green consumption, consumer boycotts, shareholder protests, increasing questioning of the relationship between states and the World Bank, WTO and IMF. Indeed, popular assumptions about management and corporations seem to be increasingly negative – accountants are 'creative', marketers offensive and manipulative, stakeholder rights are being violated, corporate governance needs addressing, global investment is resulting in third world exploitation, and so on.

Now it does not really matter whether these concerns are new or not. As we suggested in Chapter 2, the nostalgia that suggests that business used to be much kinder and nicer is not necessary in order to acknowledge the importance of contemporary worries. The problems of the present are no less pressing just because the past had problems too. Nonetheless, these ethical and political concerns seem to have become more visible in the capitalist world during an era of monetarism and marketisation that began in the late 1970s. If money is all that matters, then where do people fit in? If profit is the only goal, then why worry about good and bad? If branding is the only difference between people and things, then why bother to tell the truth? For many people, from both the right and the left, there is a sharpening perception that something needs fixing, and business ethics is a possible candidate to do some of that fixing. Which takes us back to the question of why it is that business ethics might have ever popped up. Why have business ethics?

One way to begin to answer this question is to consider some of the deeper reasons why there might be a sense of crisis, and a general lack of faith in the possibility of change which opens the door for business ethics. For many years sociologists have talked about secularisation – the decline of religious and spiritual beliefs in advanced capitalist countries. Both Max Weber and Emile Durkheim had put forward a version of this theory around a century ago. In the most general of terms it is possible to argue that, in pre-modern societies, traditional or spiritual prescriptions regulated the conduct of economic and social life. Customs, narratives and holy texts often contained various instructions for the regulation of economic behaviour – partly because no clear distinction was really possible between economic life, spiritual life, domestic life, and so on. It is now common to argue that the industrial revolution saw the beginning of the end for this way of life. Urbanisation, the division of labour and the growth of large organisations meant an increasing division between economic life and other spheres.

Nowadays, we tend to assume that work, business and management are somehow governed by different codes than the rest of our lives. We assume that bluffing and a certain pragmatism are acceptable at work, even though they would not be allowed at home. So the general argument would be that religion used to regulate public moral-ity but is now banned to the private realm. However, we need to be careful about generalising here because there is no reason to think that religion beats a retreat in our world as a whole – indeed, there are serious indications that secularisation is a very exceptional and local event mostly confined to North-West Europe. Yet, while we do acknowledge that on a global scale religion still fills the hearts of many people, it is increasingly powerless when it comes to the regulation of business and politics. And as far as the world of commerce is concerned, the fanfare about business ethics might be explained as a search for a new moral code, a new belief system that is needed to bridge the moral vacuum that is the result of the gap between business on the one hand and religious morality on the other.

Of course there are some people who claim that their businesses are inspired by religious faith, but you may wonder what has happened to a religion in which God or

Allah seem to be reduced to an instrument that might help the self to achieve its more secular goals? Are business people who claim to be inspired by the doctrine of faith not more like sport stars crossing themselves after they have scored a goal or won a race? Some people have argued that the distinction between the realm of the world and of the spirit has become blurred in our world, but is this a victory for religion or for the world? Or was the American historian Richard Hofstadter (1963: 267) right when he argued a long time ago, that both religion and a more secular outlook on the world have been supplanted 'by mental self-manipulation, by a kind of faith in magic'? And is it true, as he argued, that 'both religion and the sense of worldly reality suffer'? Is God nothing other than a twenty-four hour power station that the self only needs to plug into when it longs for inspired performances? Is religion good for business, and God on the side of business?

There is something here about the separation of spheres of life that is relevant, and which is, we suggest, very much related to the idea of the market itself. The market is, as many like to say, a jungle in which questions of morality have no force or importance. Supply and demand is the law and profit is the good. Combining the pseudo-science of economics with moralising gives you a powerful branding strategy that can incorporate anything, whether it be God or the good. In that sense, Milton Friedman was right, the social responsibility of business is to improve its profits. Nothing more, and nothing less. Let other people and institutions worry about more general senses of right and wrong, and let business do its business. But the good things about a narrow version of Friedman's argument were hidden by a much wider privatisation of social space from the 1970s onwards. For extreme market liberals, constraints on market mechanisms are imperfections that spoil the operations of Adam Smith's 'hidden hand'. Social justice will be achieved through the 'trickle down' of wealth, not through forms of taxation and public policy that penalise success and discourage enterprise – not even through holy books and ethical codes. Effectively this implies that any attempt to intervene, to construct an ethical condemnation, is almost disqualified from the start. An abstract version of market freedom and the right to manage is what matters, not trade unions, safety nets, protection of local markets, and so on. Indeed, the only partial immunity to be had in this free world seems to be one that is provided by selfishness cloaked as faith or, perhaps, by business ethics. And these two might add up to the same thing.

It seems to us that the ode on freedom leaves business ethics with broadly two places to go, to support the market managerialist project or to question it; to put it another way, to support market managerial 'freedoms' by concentrating on refining management decision making, or to argue for ethical and legislative 'constraint' by offering some alternative visions of organising. But who could be against 'freedom', and who would want to argue for 'constraints'? Is a business ethics that sets out, for example, by means of codification or regulation, to restrict the freedom of business not undermining its own market position? Perhaps business people would not like it if business ethicists engaged in what the famous philosopher Isaiah Berlin (1969) would refer to as practices of 'positive freedom', that is to say, practices of interference and intervention? Would they seriously accept ethical intervention on behalf of some 'good'? Or would they merely insist on their own 'negative freedom', that is to say, on their right or desire to be left alone? Indeed, a business ethics that violated this right or obstructed this desire would not likely be welcome in the business community (ten Bos, 2002). As a result, most business ethicists have to argue that the tension between ethical prescriptions and management autonomy can be easily resolved as no opposition at all.

In what amounts to a marvellous coincidence, you can be good and rich simultaneously. This is quite similar to people who claim to be religious and rich at the same time and can hence – like camels – pass through the eye of a needle. This is because ethics makes profits, and integrity and trust in an organisation are good business in the long run. Well, this may be true – though it seems there is little evidence to support it – but more importantly it seems to confuse marketing with ethics, and selfishness with responsibility. There are, after all, some very good self-serving reasons for corporate responsibility. At the risk of being unfair, the market segmentation strategy of the Body Shop serves to underline the point. Find a group of the slightly new age and slightly socially concerned middle classes who are not too price sensitive, and then watch the money roll in. The 'greening' of McDonald's in the early years of the new millennium also indicates rather neatly how a concern for the bottom line can be manifested as concern for free range eggs and 'low calorie' salads. Ethics is here a practical common sense brand for those organisations that position themselves in a market niche. In any case, as the marketers and strategists never tire of reminding us, successful businesses are always sensitive to what their customers want, and what other firms are doing. If customers (according to market research) want green and free range, then the business must respond. If other organisations are publishing codes of ethics in order to convince investors and employees that they are a good long-term prospect, then your firm must do it too. And this turns from strategy into ethics the moment the manager looks in the mirror and exclaims, 'look at me, look how good I am!'

Now coincidences do happen. Sometimes you get rewarded for being good. But if you are good because everyone else is telling you that you will be rewarded, then (as Kant reminds us) in what sense is your 'goodness' different to calculating self-interest and egoism? If your ethics is part of your corporate strategy then is it still ethics in any meaningful sense of that word?

So, let us consider a rather different version of what business ethics might be. Perhaps ethics should actually hurt, because it presents a radical challenge to the ways things are often done in organisations and society at large. Perhaps ethics should be a joyfully subversive thing, one where coincidences are treated with suspicion, and good people do not always get rewarded. This might mean that a combination of morally informed legislation and healthy kynical scepticism should prevent firms and individuals from doing things that would otherwise benefit them. That sort of serious laughter could be framed as the insistent voice of conscience, the worry about the consequences for an Other, the better parts of our character, or whatever. There are many ways of explaining the importance of ethical questions, but none of them exhausts the meaning of our sense of a radical business ethics. It is a form of ethics that refuses to be turned into an equation, organised and managed. Rather than being a lubricant for business, this version of ethics actively attempts to stick a spanner in the works. Clearly this is not going to be a popular interpretation. If conventional business ethics attempts to help the morally impaired employee to find ways to justify what they do, then this radicalised business ethics would refuse any such painkillers and insist on peddling a much more troubling version of what managers and organisations might become.

This almost certainly sounds like three academics trying to take the moral high ground, but it probably also (and perhaps more importantly) sounds utopian and impractical. After all, why should a manager (or a student who wants to become a manager) bother to listen to us? Put us back on the shelves where we came from, and get on with your life.

Yet there is something strangely unsatisfactory about such a response to this book. It is neat and tidy, and disposes of ethics in a box, but suggests two things. The first is that you already know what ethics is, and hence are capable of deciding that it is of little or limited use. After all, if you were not yet sure what ethics was, then the reasons for disposing of it are likely to be mere irritation, or ignorance, or even fear. How else could you dismiss it if you do not know what it is? Second, you must also assume that you already know what business is, and what it might be. In other words, that the market managerialism that we have now is the end of history and the one best way. There is no alternative, and never will be. But why should we assume that organising and coordination could not be done in ways that – to adopt some of the language of moral philosophy – treated people as ends, produced the greatest good for all, and encouraged certain common virtues? Simply opening these questions as possibilities is profoundly utopian, but requires a lot of thought about what is wrong with the present state of 'business', 'ethics' and 'business ethics'.

ETHICS AND THOUGHT

Curiously, then, it is only if you know what 'ethics' and 'business' mean that you can really decide that 'business ethics' is a waste of time. This opens the possibility that not definitively answering the question 'what is business ethics?' might actually be a very productive thing to do. At the start of this book we said that we did not like textbooks very much, and this is largely because they close things down, rather than open things up. They look like a neat and empty classroom, where all the puzzles have been solved and the exercises and answers are laid out on desks for the next class when they arrive. Jump through the hoops for teacher. But it could be that thinking about what ethics might be, in the context of what business might be, is almost an aim in itself. If it makes us think about certain topics, and makes us slow down, stop and worry occasionally, then that is a small achievement in itself. It might even stop us from doing things we would otherwise rather like to do, even though perhaps we often know that we should not.

Throughout this book, we have talked quite a lot about the importance of 'thought' and we have argued, among many other things, that business ethics as it is practised nowadays is not so very keen on thinking. But what do we mean by this charge? Not very long ago, one of us presented the chapter in this book on Kant to a European business ethics seminar. One of the responses to the paper presentation was, we would suggest, rather telling for the situation in which business ethics finds itself: 'Why bother reading Kant?' they said. Indeed, why should one bother? We do because we feel that Kant engaged in the practice of thought. Foucault, a philosopher who we have not mentioned that much but who has been with us throughout these pages, has argued that thought is:

> not what inhabits a certain conduct and gives it its meaning; rather it is what allows one to step back from this way of acting or reacting, to present it to oneself as an object of thought and to question it as to its meaning, its conditions, its goals.
>
> (1997: 117)

And he adds:

> Thought is freedom in relation to what one does, the notion by which one detaches oneself from it, establishes it as an object, and reflects on it as a problem. . . . We should permanently question the experience in which we find ourselves.
>
> (1997: 117)

The ability to do this requires a kind of freedom with respect to the rules or to the habits that we have learned to accept. As Foucault has been keen to point out, the problem is not that rules and habits constrain us and undermine our freedom but rather it is the unthinking way in which we subject ourselves to them. Freedom, therefore, is not the same as doing whatever you please to do, buying what you want in the consumer marketplace, and being a pleasure-seeking hedonist. Rather, it is the ability to distance yourself from your own ingrained habits, from your own relationship with rules and, indeed, from what you generally think and from how you generally act. Freedom is thought. Thought is freedom.

Now, in this sense, thought has generally been ignored in business ethics. And for perfectly understandable reasons, for if it had engaged in the practice of thought, in the radical sense that we are suggesting here, then it would definitely not have been welcomed by most businesses. It would have been accused of being irredeemably impractical, a point to which we will return below. It would also stand accused of being unmarketable in a world that is too busy to tolerate thought; for in a busy world, a world of busy-ness, thought can be very demoralising. Such a world prefers self-inspiration, pseudo-religion or, perhaps less hysterically, a rather dull set of ethical codes. In other words, most of the business ethics that we know, embodied in Smithers from *The Simpsons*, endorses the preoccupations of the organisational mind under capitalist circumstances and seeks to

135

deliver the kind of services and products that are required by this mind. It does not encourage questioning thought, but serves the reproduction of the same, of the common sense of the puppet.

We think that most of these products and services consist of a spurious mix of quasi-mystical ideas about leadership and teamwork on the one hand and rather straightforward techniques and recipes on the other. What strikes us most in business ethics as it is practised nowadays is indeed the curious combination of technology and naïve belief in the possibility of the good. The practice of business ethics is based on the idea that the good can be organised and ordered. Indeed, we believe that this assumption might be seen as the philosophical underpinning of business ethics. We have tried to take issue with this idea. We do not believe that the good can be organised, can be conjured up by means of technique and recipe, or that it can instantaneously be implemented after having formulated what the team or the company understands as 'good'. We do believe, however, that the good is something worth struggling for, but that this task is something that in principle can never be accomplished. The good is an ultimately unachievable goal, but this is exactly what makes it worth thinking about and orienting oneself towards. If it were merely a matter of following rules, then there would be little thinking involved, and no point in getting excited about possibility and difference.

You may wonder why this understanding of the good as something that cannot be simply planned or organised or implemented is at odds with the dictates of organisation. The reason is, of course, that organisations are goal-directed systems: almost everything that employees and managers seem to do in organisational settings is related to the realisation of particular ends. Means-end schemes permeate organisations. As members of organisations we are evaluated with respect to the goals that we are able to achieve, ideas are judged in terms of what they contribute to the overall goal of the organisation, indeed the very idea of human resource management is based on the integration of personal and organisational goals (Legge, 1995). Anybody who is hesitant with respect to the overarching means-end scheme is, when noticed, brought to heel and regarded as a source of treachery and contamination in an otherwise perfectly healthy system. The reference to pathology is intentional here: organisations can be seen as systems of immunity that attempt to block off anything that jeopardises the normal routine. As a result, emotion, impulse, love, desire, individual morality, hate, laziness, and so on are deemed to be contaminating, or in need of channelling in narrow directions (ten Bos and Willmott, 2001; ten Bos and Kaulingfreks, 2001). Employees are routinely subjected to what has been referred to as 'the game of exemplarity', that is, a set of practices in which individual persons are frequently judged against exemplars of functionality, enthusiasm and loyalty that are spelled out by leadership studies, cultural management or, indeed, business ethics (ten Bos and Rhodes, 2003). In these circumstances, there is hardly any room for what we have described as 'thought', because the necessary thinking about the goals or direction of the organisation as such has already been carried out by others. Any further thinking would thus not only be superfluous but actually detrimental to the instructions which preceded it.

136

Perhaps you think that we exaggerate, or that our view of organisation and ethics is at best one-sided and at worst ludicrous. To be sure, there is no doubt that organisations have very good reasons to act as they do. We cannot accept functionaries in departments who are constantly thwarted by their nagging conscience or by personal feelings about particular customers or about particular political decisions (du Gay, 2000). A specific kind of purity is necessary for people in organisations and for the organisations they inhabit as well. This is what the French political thinker Montesquieu once referred to as the 'pure executive': we desperately need people who are willing to carry out their functions with moral neutrality, without hatred or passion. If we do not have functionaries, in this sense of the word, not only our businesses but our entire democratic system would collapse.

However, while we recognise this, we also think that this puts the pretensions of business ethics and its corollaries, leadership studies and cultural management, into a rather sobering perspective. To put it somewhat differently, organisational 'hygiene' is crucially important, but it is not something about which business ethicists should worry greatly. A certain amount of bureaucratic hygiene is important, but in organisations people can never be completely reduced to functionaries. So we think that the fascination with hygiene has somehow got out of hand, and are concerned about the dangers of the **hygiene-machine**. Organisations do not only require decent functionaries, they also want much more: they want decent human beings who believe in the good of their organisation, who are loyal to its goals and its leadership, and who are, perhaps most importantly, thoroughly convinced that serving organisational goals can be reconciled with serving the public good. The humble and somewhat stoic functionary, who merely claims neutrality as his or her contribution to the good, is increasingly to be replaced by the manic and entrepreneurial mind who believes that his or her work will contribute to nothing less than the welfare of humanity as such. For this mind, business is not the means to life but has become a way of life, or at least a way of accounting for the meaning of a life.

Encouraged by ethical consultants, organisations have now started to organise the good and what is a more convenient starting point than the individual worker who can be much more than a morally neutral functionary? It might be thought that such a person could become a fully-fledged moral personality, and that this would be a good thing. We do not share this optimism. Actually, we think it is quite dangerous. The desire to impact upon the morality of people by means of a sophisticated ethical technology or the belief that we can tap into the unexploited moral potential that they constitute is something with which we wish to take issue. It is based on the belief that our will has a power over what individuals in organisations can become and that we can transform them into morally laudable beings by dint of a decision or an act of volition. This belief has been described by Agamben, a contemporary Italian philosopher, as 'the perpetual illusion of morality' (1999a: 254; see also ten Bos and Rhodes, 2003: 405). Encouraged by cultural management, leadership studies and business ethics, organisations have become the pre-eminent places where people have succumbed to this delusion. It is as if organisations believe they no longer stop at the boundaries of the body, but can now control your soul.

The basic fallacy is that somehow many people have grown accustomed to the idea that the good is a matter of organisation and technology. We do not claim that we know what the good is, but in this book we have tried to relate it to something that is too unstable to become neatly planned and organised. We have talked about freedom, utopia and thought and though we do not know exactly what these words mean, we do know that they are at odds with organisation and with an ethics that merely serves organisation. They are, in an important sense, disorganised and disorganising.

FOR BUSINESS ETHICS

We are, it should be crystal clear by now, pretty critical of business ethics as it currently exists. Yet despite all our endless complaints, we do not think that it is necessary to throw all talk of business ethics out of the window. If the current path of 'good sense' about ethics is that it is a good thing, then to take the other path would not achieve what we want to. Perhaps there is something of a love–hate relationship here, in that we really do have a lot of time for business ethics, even if we spend a lot of time complaining about it. Like the flame of a fire, we find it fascinating but also rather dangerous.

When we speak of the limitations of business ethics, we are clearly suggesting that there are a lot of things in the world around us that concern us, that give us some sense that there is something 'wrong', and that there are significant ways in which the source of these problems is business and businesses. Those who have a passionate interest in business ethics tend to be concerned about one or more of the terrible things that are going on in the world around us, and to charge business with responsibility. This might include anything from the lack of choice for consumers, inequalities of pay between men and women, the lack of safe and meaningful work for most people on the planet, the arms trade and wars financed by military and drug cartels, and the ecological disaster that has resulted from industrial development and now threatens to end life on the planet as we know it.

So a sensitivity to business ethics will connect with a concern over one or more of these things. And it will usually involve some sort of claim that the world that we live in could be at least a little bit better. But when we complain of the poverty of business ethics we are not only claiming that the business world is not ethical, but also that there is something wrong with business ethics, that is, with the conversations and discussions that have resulted in the academic subject area of business ethics. If you are reading this book then there is every likelihood that you will be enrolled in a course in business ethics, probably in a business school, and you might have thought that this book would be in agreement with most of what is taught around the world as business ethics. Textbooks are supposed to be about reproducing authorised knowledge, so it might seem strange that we would begin by telling you that we have some pretty serious problems with the academic languages that make up business ethics.

Here is another way of stating our problem. Traditionally, most of the people who have written on ethics have had a problem with one or more things about the world they lived in. Of course, we all have problems now and then, but the word ethics is sometimes used to refer to some kind of minor complaint, such as forgetting to buy flowers for your loved one, or lying when your conscience lets you down. Ethics, however, is also a grand word, and when we hear it we usually hear traces, however subtle, of the idea of a better world or a better life. In this sense it is possible to argue that ethics always has, in the strong sense of the word, a hopeful and critical orientation to the future. Ethics opens up into politics, and then the small things become very big indeed.

However, and for us this is a major problem, as the academic subject area of business ethics emerged over the past twenty or so years, very often this disruptive, critical and hopeful aspect has been lost. Traditionally ethics was a word that would stand against the practices of the day, and against the common sense that assumed that whatever is done must be. Ethics was, as we have seen in a variety of ways, a critique of common sense. But as it has become institutionalised in business schools, business ethics has come to generate a new common sense, and has largely forgotten the task of critique. More often than not it is thought that the role of business ethics is to add something on to present business practices, to make a minor adjustment in order to make things 'more ethical'. And as a result, the task that ethics was originally intended to achieve – a radical questioning of how it is that we should live and work – has all but disappeared from books and journals on business ethics. In the words of Foucault, it does not engage in thinking – real thinking, not just textbook thinking.

BUSINESS ETHICS AND REALITY

Some might object that the reason that business ethics has taken on this form is because of a desire to actually change things in practice, that is, to be realistic. A theory of how business should act would be of little importance if it was agreed upon by a set of very clever academics but was never put into practice. And we agree that there is no point in theory for its own sake, or for designing a Utopia that would never be put in place.

But at the same time, we insist that business ethics must always be a little bit unrealistic. The task of business ethics is not merely to confirm reality but to challenge the things that we take for granted right now. If people criticise business ethics for being unrealistic, then they have realised something important, which is that the world that we are in, the world that we call 'reality', can change. The kind of business ethics that we hope for is one that will be practical, but will also be unrealistic. It will set itself high goals, it will hope for a better future and it will call into question the merits of many of the things that we assume today to be unchallengeable.

If it is easily applicable, then it is not ethics, for ethics is about justice and about goodness and both are *always* debatable and contestable. They defy organisation and cannot be reduced to rules. But this is not to say that we can do anything we like. As Nancy points out, we all face a double imperative:

> It is necessary to measure up to what nothing in the world can measure, no established law, no inevitable process, no prediction, no calculable horizon – absolute justice, limitless quality, perfect dignity   and it is necessary to invent and create the world itself, immediately, here and now, at every moment, without reference to yesterday or tomorrow.
>
> (1997: 158)

If ethics retains something of its meaning from the ancient Greeks, then it is that ethics is something – an emotion, a feeling, an intuition, an understanding – which involves the very moment that one reflects on what the good life would be. To even begin such a reflection involves a certain impatience with the present, with the way that things are today. Discussions of ethics would be very short indeed if this world truly was the best of all possible worlds. We need discussions of ethics precisely because this is not the best of all possible worlds, and we need business ethics precisely because of the disasters that are inflicted on the planet and its citizens by market managerialism.

In this sense ethics will never live up to reality and this book has no satisfying conclusions. It will never be put into practice, once and for all. It is more like a disturbing dissatisfaction with the present, and a concern to do something about it. The classical business ethicists are perhaps right when they identify three of the most common complaints that we have about the world: many are unhappy and are suffering (utilitarianism); few today act out of a genuine moral disposition intended to good ends (intentionalism) and few play the part of virtuous characters (virtue ethics). In this sense we do not want to abandon that classical vocabulary of business ethics, but we do want to release it from its obsession with moral perfection and moral exemplarity. We want it to be infused by restless and joyful thought and kynical laughter. We want it to become both more philosophical and more practical. We want to get rid of its manic enthusiasm about the goodness of business in a world of ends –rationalised global capital. And then we can be, without reservations, *for* business ethics.

Glossary

A NOTE ON DICTIONARIES

Dictionaries are usually used to reassure. If you do not know how to spell a word, for example, or if you do not know its proper meaning, then you can consult a dictionary. There is nothing wrong with this. By no means would we wish to suggest that dictionaries are not handy tools for acquiring a particular language or for writing decent and correct prose. Sometimes we need to depend on the kind of authority that lies hidden in all dictionaries and that whispers in our ear how we should write and understand words. However, not all dictionaries have this function. So far, we have only talked about lexicological and etymological dictionaries as well as about dictionaries that tell us how to translate words from one language into the other.

In the thirteenth century monks in Italy and Germany were writing encyclopaedias that functioned as tools of power that would help the Catholic Church to convert or discipline heretics, to instruct laity, to reform morals, in short to communicate in the wider world what it saw as the only proper biblical message (Daston and Park, 1998: 44). In a certain sense, one can say that these clerical encyclopaedias were very close to the idea of the 'complete education' (*eggiklios paideia*) that underlies, at least from an etymological standpoint, the very idea of an encyclopaedia. For the religious producers of these books, the goal was nothing less than to make clear that this and nothing else could be said about the role of God in the world.

Five hundred years later a number of intellectuals, most notably in France and in England, began work on encyclopaedic dictionaries that had a different intent. The two most famous examples are probably Diderot's *Encyclopaedia* which appeared in seventeen large volumes between 1751 and 1765, and Voltaire's much less bulky *Philosophical Dictionary* which appeared in its definitive version in 1769. Diderot and Voltaire implied that the encyclopaedia or dictionary could not only be conceived as tools in the hand of authorities such as the Church but also as tools that would eventually help to undermine them. And this, indeed, is what they set out to do. Besides the scientifically adequate information that they wanted to provide as men of the Enlightenment, they also hoped that their texts would function as tools for social and political change. The *Encyclopaedia* and the *Philosophical Dictionary* were counter-propaganda directed against officially accepted dogma to which church and state so desperately clung. To prevent trouble with the powers that be, the authors of encyclopaedias and dictionaries sometimes remained anonymous. More often, however, they were using a variety of textual tricks that would help to mislead authorities: indirect or ironical language, a complex network of mutual references, a peculiar classification system that would allow the authors to treat controversial topics under a variety of different headings, and so on. Voltaire perfected these textual strategies. If one looks at his *Philosophical Dictionary*, some elements attract attention.

First, there are relatively few entries (only 118) and this is clearly not what the more conventional dictionaries mentioned above should do. Voltaire by no means aimed at a total survey of something called philosophy. Rather than striving for completion and perfection, Voltaire wanted to convey in his text a new kind of 'philosophical spirit', typically linked to the Enlightenment and primarily intended to combat religious fanaticism and stupidity but also to amuse and to be of use. When he writes, for example, about topics such as monsters, wonders, cannibalism, and so on, he frequently points out that the horror we feel for these phenomena does not say much about the phenomena themselves but more about our unwillingness to accept that sometimes conventions are inevitably violated. That this is possible is what really causes the horror we feel. Voltaire wishes to relativise our ideas about what is horrific and what is not. What he wants to convey is that a universal response to horrific incidents is simply impossible (see also Daston and Park, 1998: 213).

Second, there is a constant play with authorship and authority. Sometimes, Voltaire does not write from the perspective of the 'I' but hides his personal opinions behind pronouns such as 'he' or 'we'. He even goes so far as to communicate opinions that are not his as if they are his. What he makes clear from the outset is that dictionaries as he views them are not so much truthful as assisting in forming someone's opinions. The overall effect of this cunning masquerade is ironic and satirical. Irony and satire might be more efficient weapons in the struggle against superstition and fanaticism than boldly authoritarian claims to the truth. The reason is that they encourage the reader to think further, which is something that authoritarian speech is generally eager to exclude. Voltaire understands himself as someone who provides his intended readership with a language that might help them to develop more thought, rather than with a language that puts thought to an end. Also in this respect, such a dictionary, in spite of its obvious disregard for well-accepted histories of philosophy, can be said to be profoundly philosophical.

Third, the entries in the dictionary are much more interrelated than is generally the case in ordinary dictionaries. Subjects are not treated in isolation under a particular entry but constantly return, often under various guises. Under the apparent fragmentation of an alphabetical order lies a central idea that in Voltaire's case can be described as a willingness to combat all kinds of superstition. This is, as suggested earlier, what his entire philosophy aims to do.

After Voltaire, many authors have written 'encyclopaedic' dictionaries. Flaubert's *Dictionary of Received Ideas* (1880) and Bierce's *Devil's Dictionary* (1911) spring to mind here. But, as suggested earlier, today most producers of dictionaries have forgotten their critical and thought-provoking function. Indeed, encyclopaedias have become an item for parents who want to make serious work of their children's education and this is obviously a project that does not tolerate too much irony and satire. The questions their children have should find relatively straightforward answers and, indeed, this is what makes children's encyclopaedias so eminently successful.

A few exceptions, however, should be noted. In his self-declared 'dictionary of aggressive common sense', the Canadian political thinker John Ralston Saul has made the case that dictionaries 'should again be filled with doubt, questioning, and considerations' rather than with clear-cut answers (1994: 6). More recently, Julian Wolfreys has written or compiled dictionaries that have, we would argue, tried to reinvigorate something of the philosophical esprit Voltaire has in mind. In the introduction of his *Critical Keywords in Literary and Cultural Theory*, Wolfreys writes:

> One intention of this book is to introduce the reader to the complexity of particular words through the presentation, under each keywords heading, of a series of citations from different critics. What the reader will see, it is hoped, is that, far from being simply or easily defined, the various terms in question here share a certain semantic and conceptual slipperiness. . . . Another goal of this volume, therefore, is not to resolve instance of paradox, contradiction or ambiguity but rather to emphasise and even affirm such qualities. . . . What is termed accessibility by some, equally runs the risk of simplification and reductiveness. The writer who aims at such accessibility can do great violence to ideas. . . . Whatever goes by the name of education, in this name there never can be, nor should there be, the illusion of immediacy, transparency or accessibility in a kind of programmed rush equivalent to journalistic haste, by which or to which thinking becomes sacrificed.
>
> (2004: ix–xi)

Similar ideas underlie this dictionary or glossary that ends our little book on business ethics. As we have emphasised throughout, we consider ethics to be a slippery issue that evades simple-minded or standardised answers. Indeed, we believe that such easy answers undermine what we consider to be a central characteristic of ethics, to wit, the ability of people to cope with tension and paradox. In line with the elements that we derived from Voltaire's dictionary, we hope that the following glossary is helpful not because it provides you, the reader, with the right answers, but because it provides you with fun, food for thought, and at least our own humble opinion of what we consider ethics to be. In this spirit, we offer you the following glossary, which takes as its starting point some of the key words that appear in our book.

Anti- In an attempt to find unity in the waves of protests throughout the world since the late 1990s, we see the words anti-capitalist, anti-corporate and anti-globalisation. These protests are often given the start date of November 1999, when one of the high-profile protests against the World Trade Organisation in Seattle took place, but it is equally possible to see Seattle as part of a tendency that is much older. We could equally select the date of 1 January 1994, the date of the Zapatista uprising in protest at the North American Free Trade Agreement. Or we could remember the uprising in Venezuela in 1989 against austerity measures imposed by the International Monetary Fund. Or we could look further back in history at so many other protest movements that have resisted corporate **capitalism**.

Even if it is hard to know whether to call this movement anti-capitalist or anti-corporate, very rarely do those in the movement identify themselves in opposition to globalisation as such. As Naomi Klein, one of the significant figures in the movement put it, writing shortly after Seattle, 'one thing is certain: the protesters in Seattle are not anti-globalization; they have been bitten by the globalization bug as surely as the trade lawyers inside the official meetings. . . . The faceoff is not between globalizers and protectionists but between two radically different versions of globalization. One has had a monopoly for the past ten years. The other just had its coming-out party' (2002: 4–6).

So, it is not entirely clear what 'anti' is really about and whether those who are accused of being 'anti' would plead guilty. We sometimes find the words 'anti-corporate' and 'anti-capitalist' used interchangeably, but others insist that objecting to corporations and objecting to capitalism are different albeit related matters. Nonetheless, it is often true that objecting to corporations and capitalism can combine in an overall objection to corporate capitalism, or as it is also called, **market managerialism**. In Chapters 7 and 8 of this book we analyse some of the dynamics of corporations and of capitalism, and outline the ways in which they both involve quite specific dynamics that deny or reduce the possibility of an open relation to the **Other**. In doing so, corporations and capitalism both involve risks to ethics, and this is basically, we suggest, why they frequently encounter so much resistance.

Yet, while the anti-capitalist and anti-corporate movements might appear at first glance to be negative and simply anti-, there is increasingly a recognition that, even if the movement does not have one ultimate **Utopian** solution (which previous revolutionary movements often did) that it is not purely a reaction. At meetings such as the World Social Forum and in many other locations, there is a growing understanding that there is much that is to be affirmed, and much that can be done outside of the bounds of corporate capitalism.

Aporia Aporia, like many other parts of thinking, is identified early on by Aristotle. In the *Topics*, he describes the way that thinking can get caught in tension between two paths, and he describes the trouble that this can cause. He writes: 'an equality between contrary reasonings would seem to be a cause of perplexity; for it is when we reflect on both sides of a question and find everything alike to be in keeping with either course that we are perplexed which of the two we are to do' (Aristotle, 1984f: 145b17–20). Later he defines aporia as 'a deduction that reasons dialectically to a contradiction' (162a15–17).

144

It might seem strange that anyone would want to make an argument *towards* aporia. Wouldn't thought be cleaner if eliminating aporias was the goal, rather than the other way around? Thought would then search out contradictions and resolve them into the unity of Knowledge.

This way of thinking about knowledege, in which the unity is good, is part of the **common sense** of the way that we think about thinking. It is part of a common sense that has been, in recent years, called into question by a number of thinkers, perhaps the most important of these being Jacques **Derrida**. In a variety of places, Derrida tries to think through aporias, and the peculiar nature of the double bind that results when we are drawn in two directions at the same time. He speaks, for example, of an 'aporia that paralyzes us because it binds us doubly (I must and I need not, I must not, it is necessary and impossible, etc.). In one and the same place, on the same apparatus, both hands are bound or nailed down. What are we to do?' (Derrida, 1993b: 22).

The crucial argument that Derrida makes about aporias is that when we find ourselves faced with an aporia we experience a question of 'not knowing where to go' (1993a: 12). I am drawn in two directions at once, and don't know which way to go. If I experience the demand from **the Other**, but am also drawn by an other Other, then I face the aporia of not knowing whom to give to (Derrida, 1995: Chapter 3). As you may imagine, then, this has significant importance for how we think about the very project of what **ethics** is about. Many have thought, over time, that ethics is a matter of knowing what to do. Ethics, on this view, would give a clear and decisive answer to the question 'how should I live?'. But Derrida argues that such clear and decisive arguments are more a matter of *morality*, the common sense of a restricted **community**. By contrast, if one is to experience the Other, then this will not be comforting, but will be disquieting and will involve the challenge of not knowing how to respond. This does not recommend inaction, or endless contemplation. But it does make clear that much of what is called 'ethics', when it fails the experience and experiment of aporia, denies the Other and denies the troubling and critical aspect of ethics. This is why Derrida argued that 'a sort of nonpassive endurance of the aporia was the condition of responsibility and of decision' (1993a: 16).

Aristotle (384–322 BC)   Many people refer to Aristotle as a Greek philosopher. In fact, he was not a Greek philosopher but a barbarian who sneaked into the philosophical academy, where he managed to become Plato's best student and critic. Following his master, he wrote many dialogues, but these were all lost for posterity. What we have of Aristotle are the inaccessible and somewhat scurrilous notes probably meant as a preparation for the dialogues. Nevertheless, these notes were brought together as a series of books that became classics for **philosophy**. Later in his life, Aristotle became the teacher of that other great un-Greek barbarian, Alexander the Great. In spite of his fame nowadays, he died as a poor and forgotten man.

Unlike Plato, who had a rather one-dimensional philosophical and mathematical nature, Aristotle also took an interest in scientific matters. In order to legitimate this interest, he had to defend the senses as one of two gateways to knowledge. According to Aristotle, the senses and the intellect (which is the second gateway) should match with each other when it comes to the human quest for knowledge. Plato always thought that the senses were an obstacle to real knowledge. They condemn human beings to a life of mere chatter, opinion (*doxa*), relativity. Aristotle could not accept a cleavage between knowledge and the world of the senses. He argued that there was only one world (rather than a true and a false world) and that we have, depending on the kind of object that we take an interest in, different ways of taking this world on. If we take an interest in nature, then we can become biologists, meteorologists or physicists. If we take an interest in human actions, we should study ethics and politics. If we take an interest in literature and language, we should become students of rhetoric and poetics. Aristotle engaged in all these intellectual undertakings. He was a universal man.

Yet, this division of intellectual activities also bears witness to his analytical rigidity. He sincerely thought that one who takes an interest in nature cannot be informed by insights from poetics or ethics. No doubt this is the reason why he felt no ethical hindrance whatsoever to deny women the status of humanity or to describe human beings as featherless bipeds. So his universality is quite strange, but his impact on the history of science and philosophy has been profound. Even today, we still work with categories that can be traced back to Aristotle: dynamics, potency, **possibilities**, actualisation, energy, and other notions that are so exciting to the **business** managers of our times.

Bauman, Zygmunt (1925–) Polish sociologist who has worked in England for most of his life and writer of a highly influential book titled *Modernity and the Holocaust* (1989). In it Bauman argued that it was **bureaucratic** forms of organisation that made both the technical efficiency and moral blindness of the **holocaust** possible. This was not an entirely new idea (see, for example, Merton, 1940 and Arendt, 1963), but it was expressed by Bauman as a cautionary lesson for the twentieth century. The century of organisation, of mass transportation, production and consumption had also become the century of mass extermination. In the book, Bauman explores the various distancing mechanisms that allowed ordinary Germans to (actively and passively) be complicit in one of the many horrors of the twentieth century. Though his arguments have been criticised (du Gay 2000), the book is perhaps best understood as an attempt to radicalise Max **Weber's** deep scepticism about the effects of bureaucratic reason on forms of legitimate authority.

In some of the books that immediately followed this one, Bauman explores the more general ways in which modern life tends to displace senses of belonging and responsibility. *Postmodern Ethics* (1993) frames this as a problem which might be addressed through paying attention to **Levinas's** arguments about the face and responsibility to the **Other**. For Bauman, such a 'postmodern' ethics would not seek the certainties of codes and prescriptions but would instead seek to allow the 'moral impulse' to find expression. In a way that echoes many of the arguments in this book,

Bauman seeks to explore the radical possibility of ethics, just as he acknowledges that so much of what passes for ethics is a form of disguised organisational or market-based coercion.

Bentham, Jeremy (1748–1832) British philosopher who is widely assumed to be the founder of **utilitarianism**, but did not invent the term himself. His early understanding of utilitarianism was reformist. He saw it as a form of thought that would be able to rationally disprove the 'nonsense on stilts' that passed for government in England at that time. His major works were combinations of rationalist ethical and political analysis, combined with stinging polemic against the key figures and institutions of his day. In some sense, he can also be seen as one of the key figures in the development of social science itself since his method was to use empirical analysis in order to bring about various changes in social organisation that would benefit the greatest number. His writings concerned pretty much all of what we would now call social science, with important interventions in the legal system, criminal justice, theories of markets, democratic institutions, and so on. Under the influence of James Mill (John Stuart **Mill**'s father), Bentham's liberalism became increasingly radical later in life. He died with a considerable international reputation, even if utilitarianism was regarded with extreme suspicion by the English establishment of the time.

Nowadays, Bentham's radicalism is often forgotten, and utilitarianism is presented as a dry managerialist theory of human nature. For some economists, he justifies a version of the 'economic man' as a creature driven by selfish wants. For cultural elitists, his insistence that the values of all are more important than the pleasures of a few is a view that questions the obviousness of ideas of character, beauty and truth. For business ethicists, he is the progenitor of a **rule**-based ethics that can be turned into stakeholder theory for managers. Bentham's ideas can certainly be characterised like this, but their translation two hundred years later also tells us something rather important in itself. What was radical in late eighteenth century England now looks somewhat conservative. Whether this is because the world has changed or opinions on utilitarianism have solidified is not clear. Representing Bentham's restless intelligence for a twenty-first century reader is therefore difficult, but we doubt that he would have been positive about the excuses that utilitarianism provides within **business ethics**.

Bureaucracy To call someone a 'bureaucrat' is to suggest that they care so much about the ends that they do not ponder them anymore and instead focus on the means. In other words, they merely follow orders. Indeed, the early origins of the word express pretty much the same sentiments. *Bureaucratie*, rule from the desk, was coined (according to Baron de Grimm in a letter dated 1 July 1764) by Vincent de Gourney in the middle of the eighteenth century. De Gourney saw bureaumania as an 'illness', an impediment to the proper exercise of market freedom, and this view echoes down the centuries to the present concern of the World Trade Organisation to 'liberate' trade from regulation. However, the most influential author for our contemporary understandings of bureaucracy was undoubtedly Max **Weber**, whose

Economy and Society was first published in 1921. Weber saw the advance of bureaucratisation as inevitable but tied it to a larger sociological thesis about the development of forms of legitimacy. He argued that, in every sphere of social life, from music to war, charismatic and traditional forms of authority are increasingly routinised into legal-rational, or bureaucratic, authority (for a contemporary version of these ideas, termed McDonaldisation, see Ritzer, 1996).

Weber was ambivalent about bureaucracy (see Chapter 7) and his melancholy diagnosis echoes through the twentieth century. Indeed, much organisational sociology and psychology after the Second World War was concerned with various ways in which the authoritarian Fascist version of bureaucracy could be better understood and avoided. Contemporary organisational behaviour on MBA courses still reflects this, with descriptions of authoritarian and bureaucratic personality types, accounts of experiments on the willingness of subjects to obey people in white coats or conform to crowd norms, and versions of the inefficiencies and dys-functions of bureaucracy. In *The Organization Man*, William Whyte described the 'social ethic' (which 'could be called an organization ethic, or a bureaucratic ethic') as a pervasive form of dull conformity (1956: 11). For Whyte, this is a climate that prevents individual initiative and imagination, a diagnosis shared by later writers such as Arendt (1963), MacIntyre (1981) and **Bauman** (1989). However, as du Gay (2000) points out, bureaucracy is itself an ethic that is intended to guarantee fair and equal treatment. The sense that bureaucracy distorts ethical reasoning is pervasive, but may simply ignore the importance of legal and procedural elements to running an organisation. It is all very well to be 'against bureaucracy', as any politician knows, but if the alternative is unrestrained **market managerialism** or some sort of heroic **individualism** in which all law and precedent is swept away, then perhaps red tape begins to look more appealing.

Business In an older sense, someone's business was the task that they were engaged in. It has been suggested that it may be etymologically derived from the busy-ness of the bee, and it certainly implies a certain hustle and bustle. Nowadays, the word has contracted in its meaning and is now largely assumed to refer to activities that result in private profits. Though there have certainly been a series of attempts to 'business' (in the verb sense) the public sector, the opposition between the *ethos* of service to clients versus profit for shareholders (or owners) is still a powerful one. It is this tension which provides one of the legitimations for **business ethics**. The supposed difference between 'business' and everything else requires a special sort of ethics to deal with it. (Perhaps in order to excuse it?) Yet it would be quite possible to cut the cake in a different way. If instead we assumed that the special sort of ethics should be applied to organisations more generally (both public and private), then perhaps the subject might properly be called 'organisational ethics'. Or if we assumed that the ethics of the public sphere more generally (everyone you do not regard as family and friends) are different to those that apply in the private sphere, then perhaps the discipline might have become 'public ethics'.

The point is that there is nothing obvious about the word 'business', and it is a little misleading to suggest that businesses can be clearly separated from other organisations in the public sphere that are not businesses. Many businesses are owned by families, many public sector organisations are oriented to notions of profitability, and many employees and managers move backwards and forwards across the so-called 'boundary'. Rather than searching for a definition of what is, and is not, business (and hence what is, and is not, business ethics), it might be more helpful to think about business as a word that has a particular ideological function. It marks a certain distinction between the hard reality of the market, and the warm nanny state comfort of those it protects. Without business, it claims, where would we be? And how could you write books like this? To which we might respond, following Oscar Wilde, that knowing the price of everything does not mean that you know the value of anything. Which is not, in some stupid way, to line up on the other side of the opposition as 'against business.' We would like you to ask, what does the concept 'business' do? What sort of ideas and actions does it make possible? And what does it hide behind its **common sense**?

Business ethics The idea that 'business ethics' might be available for definition in a few words should, if you have agreed with anything we have written in this book, make you laugh. After all, this whole book is about what business ethics is and what it might be. So, to presume that there is a single definition that is universally held would be frippery. Business ethics means many things, and it is the intersection and overlay of those different meanings that is the cause of great confusion in any discourse in which mention is made of business ethics. We propose not to deny these difficulties, but rather to draw them out, clarify them and understand them.

Most obviously, business ethics refers to the moral and ethical aspects of the practices of business. This is the matter of the *ethical questions of business*, that is, the kinds of questions we might ask in a commonsensical way about what takes place in the world of business – questions such as 'is bribery wrong?', 'should I always obey my boss?', and so on. But 'business ethics' also refers to a discipline of academic inquiry, an area that came to prominence in the late 1970s and early 1980s. This is why we also used the words '**business**' and '**ethics**' to refer to this academic discipline and to ideas and debates in that area and the journals, books and conferences in which these ideas circulate. This might be described as the *discipline of business ethics*. Third, we can see, and sometimes in response to the first and the second meanings of business ethics, the applied practices of business ethicists, those who work in and consult for business organisations specifically as business ethicists. These people are sometimes educators who explain the legal and ethical issues to employees; they sometimes write ethical codes and conduct ethics audits; and sometimes they are just part of the marketing department. These activities together could be described as *applied business ethics*.

From what we have said in this book, it should be clear that ethical questions are being asked about business, and that today there is a sense that the answers that have been given in the past are not adequate. We have also argued that both the discipline of business ethics and applied business ethics hold great promise, and we have affirmed that promise unequivocally. But at the same time, it would be naïve to think that business ethics (discipline or applied) is anything like adequate in the way they are currently thought or practised. This is why we have written this book – to invite those who are concerned with ethical questions of business to get involved in a project of reconfiguring the discipline and the possible spaces of engagement around business ethics. We are for business ethics precisely because of this promise that it holds for a critical consideration of the practices of business. It is too easy to dismiss business ethics, or to joke that business ethics is an oxymoron, a contradiction in terms. To do so is to ignore the **possibility** that business ethics, which is currently rather compromised, might itself be subject to change, and that this glossary entry might become wrong.

Capitalism   At the most simple, capitalism is a set of economic relations organised around the accumulation of capital and the sale and purchase of wage-labour. That being said, there are many different ways in which capital can accumulate and in which wage-labour can be bought, sold and organised. Although some, such as the historian Fernand Braudel, use the word capitalism to describe the rise of markets and trades that have existed for several centuries, others suggest that capitalism takes on its recognisably modern form in the eighteenth and nineteenth centuries with the emergence of competitive and industrial organisations that have private aims. It is possible to see a change in the operation of capitalism in the early twentieth century, with the concentration of capital, the rise of the welfare state and the Fordist organisation of production. Many have suggested that, since the 1970s, the 'monopoly' stage of capitalism has been giving way to post-industrial, post-modern or 'late' capitalism, with changes in the state form, the organisation of production and global relations. In spite of all these historical changes and adaptations, only a few people seem to unconditionally endorse capitalism. This is a major paradox. We all seem to live our lives under conditions about which many are thoroughly cynical whereas nobody seems to be able to conjure up real alternatives. Indeed, to be '**anti**' or **utopian** are the surest signs of otherworldliness.

Character   This word stems from the Greek *charassein*, which means 'to sharpen' or 'to carve in'. There is a relationship with letters that are carved in on a table. Or with tattoos, if you like. This indicates that a character is something very solid and permanent. If you have it, it will not easily go away. Aristotle defined character as an ensemble of attitudes and behaviours that make us who we are. In studying character, **Aristotle** was especially interested in, firstly, the relationship of the individual towards emotions. Are we able to govern or control our emotions? Secondly, he wrote about habit formation (*ethismos*). Does the **community** to which we belong allow us to develop the proper emotions and desires? Thirdly, he thought about reason. Can we reason correctly and are we logical?

Aristotle does not believe that a positive answer to these questions lies in the hands of individuals alone. The community to which they belong needs an entire system of education and laws in order to make the rise of noble characters possible. Talent or disposition, however, is also important. In fact, it is a peculiar combination of nature and nurture that allows noble characters to come to the fore. The notion of 'character' is still very much with us today. It gained serious momentum in leadership studies and the same debates that were once Aristotle's concern are rekindled again and again. In fact, the elections in many countries nowadays focus more and more on the characters of the politicians involved. When, during the campaigns, candidates start to debate whether they were heroes during a war that took place long ago, then we know that this is really about character or, if you like, personality. Particularly in the USA, this obsession with the character of the country's leaders – in **business** as well as in **politics** – is rather conspicuous. The debate is hardly ever about the capacity of leaders to reason logically or to show any understanding of complex situations. As many commentators have pointed out, intelligence is not what counts in contemporary society. To be made of the right moral stuff is deemed to be more important. Moral sensibility is, after all, much more evenly distributed in our society than IQ. So, we are still Aristotelians in the sense that we praise character, but we have also forsaken it in the sense that we do not relate character anymore to logic and reason. Against Aristotle, we have come to think that morality is not about logic and reason.

Commodity fetishism   Commodity fetishism is a concept developed by Marx in Chapter One of Volume One of his major work *Capital*. At its most simple, commodity fetishism refers to a tendency, in capitalist economies with massive output of products, to see only the physical and apparently objective characteristics of those commodities, and to fail to see the conditions in which commodities are produced. Commodity fetishism is a metonymic reduction, in which a part is seen as the whole. In this way, it is similar to the sexual fetishist who is only turned on by leather boots. The leather boot fetishist emphasises this one part as if it were the whole of sexual activity, as if this part represented the whole. In the same way, commodity fetishism refers to seeing only one part (the product that results from production) as the whole (which would include the social relations under which that commodity was produced).

One major question regarding commodity fetishism is whether or not it is **possible** to avoid it. Philosophers such as Louis Althusser and Etienne Balibar have argued that commodity fetishism is not a simple perceptual error, as if it were the subjective error of an **individual**. They argue that commodity fetishism is a necessary form of appearance in capitalist societies characterised by exploitative work practices and proliferations of commodities. Commodity fetishism is, as Althusser puts it, a 'purely objective "illusion"' (1968b: 191; cf. Balibar, 1995: 60–61).

In Chapter 8, however, we discussed some practices that question the objectivity and independence of commodities, and explicitly make clear their conditions of production, through labelling, for example. Given that these practices exist today, in so-called capitalist economies, are Althusser and Balibar wrong to argue that commodity fetishism is a necessary part of capitalism? Or, on the other hand, do

151

these practices actually question one of the features of capitalism to date, which is that the social relations involved in production of commodities have been masked from view? If so, then these challenges to commodity fetishism might be involved in what has been called a 'communism of capital' (see Virno, 2004), in which the most advanced capitalist economies increasingly emphasise the social and cooperative nature of commodity production, and in which commodities are recognised not simply as things, but as results of global systems of cooperative social production.

Common sense This is what **philosophers** set out to take issue with. Common sense, after all, denies paradox and paradox is what philosophers like to indulge in. They will always try to show that reality has two sides, two directions so to speak. This is exactly what common sense denies. In doing so, it unfolds a strategy which, according to Gilles Deleuze (1969), consists of four steps. First, common sense ignores the double nature of direction. It is always hoping for a *one-way street*. Only in such a street is the quest for optimal measures imaginable; counting becomes the same as knowing; and we have a simple method to judge what is true and untrue, good and bad, and so on. Second, one should divide the world in parts that we refer to as 'objects'. These objects are given a well-defined place so that chaos and boundlessness are kept at bay. Common sense always operates on a principle of distribution: this belongs here and that belongs there. The order that is gained in this way is perhaps dull and senseless and there is always an insane desire to break it. This desire is what common sense sets out to repress.

Third, common sense creates a kind of *neutral zone* where all difference evaporates and where each event is brought to a standstill. An example is the balancing out of debt and credits. Accountants and bookkeepers know that zero is the number that allows them to resolve the inequality of the involved parts on both sides. Here, common sense is always keen on compensation. We always expect and hope that figures will finally cancel each other out. This is the harsh logic, not only of accountancy, but, more generally, of common sense itself. Finally, we should ponder the question of who is going to be in control of the neutral zone (there is always politics involved after all). These should be people who have a sense for the common and for commonality. Only the ability to make inequality and difference common allows you to play disparate objects and disparate people off against each other and to immerse them in the neutral zone where the principle of distribution and the principle of compensation reign supreme.

It is the sense for the common that permeates **business** and management. Both are based on the idea of forcing events, transactions, actions, and so on, in the direction of some neutral zone. Management thinking is therefore neither contemplative nor active for it refuses paradox and uncertainty. It merely looks ahead, always keen on finding future compensation. And it has good reasons, albeit not **philosophical** or **ethical** ones, to do so.

Community In a very important sense, human beings only become human in communities. This is a central aspect to **virtue** theory, and to the various forms of neo-**Aristotelian** (MacIntyre, 1981) and communitarian (Etzioni, 1993) thought. Oddly, or not, the words commerce, commercial and company have the same root. This demonstrates something rather important about the way that community-oriented thinking works. The suggestion is that people are always inescapably shaped by their context, their nurture, their relationships. No-one is an island, because the very concepts of self and other are ones that we learn from others. If these assertions are correct, then even those activities which are supposedly most autonomous are actually also inextricably social. Commerce involves being with others, and complying with a particular set of **rules** which involve notions of trust and reciprocity. So the idea of the market as a set of rules which is somehow outside community then begins to look a little odd. 'Market' is merely the name we give to a particular set of rules for commerce. Further, there are different rules, depending whether your commerce involves selling strawberries by the road side, or oil price futures via the internet (Callon, 1998). These are not the same things, and to suggest that they are is to suggest that all rules for exchange are the same, when they are not.

But if everything is shaped by community, then is community always a good thing? This is an easy trap to fall into, but consider the difficulty with such a position. If the people around you say that something is good, does that make it good? It would certainly be foolish not to listen to them, but if ethics simply involves doing as others do, then it is difficult to see where ethics comes in at all. In Rome, do as the Romans do, even if it involves feeding non-Romans to the lions. In business, follow the company code of social **responsibility**. The problem is that ethics and community must always be in a certain tension. **Ethics** could not exist without a birth in some sort of community, but if all it does is to rehearse the **common sense** of that community then it is not ethics in the sense we want to sponsor in this book. The struggle, the ambiguity of not knowing what to do, of being beyond the rules of the community, are all in some sense constitutive of ethics. Community might be a warm word, a word that smells of motherhood and apple pie, but it is sometimes the chill of cold air and hunger that makes us really think.

Critical theory In a broad sense, a critical theory is a thinking that asks questions about assumed definitions of the ends or goals of social action. While certain forms of knowledge are committed to improving the **efficiency** of a system, critical theory poses questions of the ends towards which systems are put. In doing so, critical theory is not concerned principally with efficiency or understanding, but in freedom from imposed systems of thought and practice. Defined in this way, we can see that there is a long tradition of critical theory, of thinking about how to escape from ends imposed externally, and from systems that do not allow us to discuss ends. Also, in so far as **ethics** is a reasoned debate about the ends of social systems and the meaning of the good life, there is an intimate link between the tradition of critical theory and the tradition of ethical theory. Any ethical theory that asks the question of the meaning of the good life in a profound way will find itself implicated in critique.

153

In addition to referring to a long tradition of critical thought, the expression Critical Theory (here with capitals) also refers to the work of the Institute for Social Research established at the University of Frankfurt in 1931, and the work that was developed by this 'Frankfurt School of Critical Theory'. The Frankfurt School was a particularly productive group of researchers committed to asking questions about the tendencies of advanced **capitalist** societies, and summarising the work of this group or even giving an adequate definition of critical theory is not possible here (Held, 1980; Horkheimer, 1937; Jay, 1973).

In this book we have drawn specifically on the work of Theodor Adorno (1906–1969) and Jürgen Habermas (1929–), who are arguably the two figures from this group to most explicitly reflect on ethics. Without getting into detailed debates about their ideas and the criticism and development of their ideas, we have drawn on one major idea from each thinker. From Adorno, and particularly at the end of Chapter 8, we discuss his insistence that ethics is a matter of dissatisfaction with what 'is' and therefore it always involves a *critical* attitude to the present, and a hopefulness about a different future. We discuss the writings on ethics of Habermas in Chapter 9, and take from him particularly his emphasis on the way that ethics is a matter of communicative action, of discussion and disagreement about what counts as the good life.

Adorno and Habermas were both highly critical of **technocratic** reason, and of the way that, in modern societies, decisions about the good life and the things we should strive for are often made without any social or democratic deliberation. The good life is imposed upon us in the workplace by managers who control our work and in the social sphere by advertisers who seek to turn all social life into commodities. Both thinkers argue for a reasoned critique of **market managerialism** and argue for spaces in which discourse about the good life could take place. In this book we argue that one of the **possible** spaces in which such discourse could take place is in relation to questions of **business ethics**, and this is one of the great achievements of business ethics. Because of the possibility that business ethics could, if it is true to its work, produce a public sphere in which disagreements about the meaning of the good life could take place, we are for business ethics.

Deontology Deontologists are those who believe that **ethics** is about duties and about the intentions with which you do them. *Deontos* literally means 'what is necessary' or 'what is fitting'. So what we have here is a theory of duty and necessity. Oftentimes, this theory is linked to Immanuel **Kant**, but the expression 'deontology' is in fact Jeremy **Bentham**'s. At the end of his life, Bentham wrote a text called *Deontology*, a text he never finished. Initially, Bentham seems to have thought that the notion nicely captures the science of ethics as such. Later, however, he used it in a more specific sense to denote the doctrine of duty. In the opening lines of his essay we find a classic description of the deontological philosopher: 'A man, a moralist, gets into an elbow-chair and pours forth pompous dogmatisms about duty and duties. Why is he not listened to? Because every man is thinking about his own interests' (Bentham,

1983:12). It seems therefore that Bentham's use of the term is, at least in this quote, rather satirical or condescending. He did not fancy an ethical theory that not only seemed to ignore the consequences of human actions but that also ignored the individual's own interests.

But what about Kant? Was he a deontologist? And was he one in the sense that Bentham might have had in mind? We are not sure about this. There is no doubt that duties are important for Kant, and he stresses that virtue is in fact an inner disposition to do them. But he also stresses that this should never become a habit for this would undermine the **individual**'s autonomy and free will. Contrary to some deeply entrenched opinions about Kant's ethical system, he explicitly condemns any form of social coercion carried out in the name of duties. In the *Metaphysics of Morals*, he states over and over again that autonomy, not duty, is the highest moral principle. His ethics is in fact an invitation to us all to formulate our own goals, to make our own plans, and to do this, if possible, in a reasonable way.

So, then, who is a deontologist? You may consult your search engine on the web and key in words like 'contractualism', 'duty', 'deontology', and so on and you will find some names of more or less well-known philosophers. But even here, you will never find an unconditional embracement of full-blown deontology. In other words, most philosophers are not keen to accept that ethics consists solely of doing your duty. Hence, the deontologist described by Bentham might be a phantom in the history of **philosophy**. However, we suggest that you may encounter this phantom now and then in business organisations where deontology is more and more frequently linked to professionalism or to rules of conduct. Take, for example, the following 'deontological code' of a Dutch banking company:

1   Abidance by legal and regulatory obligations
2   Professionalism and requirement of confidentiality
3   Reliability and respect for customers
4   Loyalty to the company
5   Mutual respect for people and opinions

This is deontology at work. Doctrines of duty are tempting in business organisations for these are definitely not the places where people are supposed to be autonomous and to exercise their own free will. Eichmann's excuse, the duty to follow orders, is always lurking. But even so, in this case the deontological code did not work too well since the company above was involved in one of the biggest financial scandals in Dutch banking history. It seems that Bentham was, at least in one respect, right: 'Every man is thinking about his own interests.'

Derrida, Jacques (1930–2004) Jacques Derrida is famously associated with 'deconstruction' and has been linked, along with other Parisian philosophers of his generation such as Michel **Foucault** and Gilles Deleuze, with a tendency often described as 'poststructuralism'. All manner of peculiar things have been said about Derrida (on this, see Jones, 2004). Perhaps the most odd are the ideas that Derrida is a **relativist**, thinking that any claim to knowledge is as good as any other, and that Derrida is an idealist, thinking that the only things that exist are words. These kinds of claim are usually made by those who do not read, and do not want to carefully consider the writings of this important philosopher.

Any effort to simplify Derrida's work into a glossary entry will fail, especially given that one of the things that Derrida is so often keen to show us is how things are more complicated than they seem. He shows, in detailed readings of texts, how words and concepts are profoundly implicated in contexts. These contexts escape the text in question, even if the text seeks to deny this. He seeks to demonstrate how these implications complicate the text, disrupting the unity that it imagines or claims. In a way, this is what we have done to **business ethics** in this book. In the first half of this book, we work with the classic texts of business ethics, but show how these texts exceed themselves and hence open the way to a different idea of business ethics. In the second half of this book, we take the claims of ethics seriously by following the expansion already implied by the claims for business ethics. Put in Derrida's terms, we have read the text of business ethics deconstructively, that is, affirmatively, showing how many of the claims of business ethics confront themselves, and in doing so showing how business ethics is in a continual process of deconstruction. This deconstruction is not something we have imposed from outside, but rather something already taking place, to which we have given some order.

In addition to offering a powerful way of thinking about how we read and analyse texts, in recent years Derrida has also written specifically on questions of ethics. Elaborating and complicating the ethics that we inherit from **Kant** and **Levinas**, he has insisted on the irreducibly aporetic nature of ethics. Ethics always involves a duty (Kant), which is felt in terms of a demand from the **Other** (Levinas), but this is rarely a comfortable or easy demand. Indeed, ethics is, for Derrida, the very difficulty of being torn by a demand to which one does not know how to **respond**. When one begins to deal with an **aporia** like this, being demanded of in two directions at once, one is not immobilised or reduced to inaction. On the contrary, Derrida argues, if I know what path to follow, I am, as we put it in this book, following **common sense** in only one direction, and am acting as a puppet or automaton. Action begins, paradoxically, when I do not know how to act. Then, I am forced to decide, actively, which way to go. Then, and only then, can we say that one has made a decision and is acting ethically.

Efficiency Business organisations work efficiently if they do not spill resources. So, efficiency is a very good thing. A **virtue**, indeed. When people talk about efficiency measures in their companies, then you would expect that something good is going on. However, the problem is that efficiency is a very context-specific concept. In other words, what might be efficient to the organisation or to some people in an organisation is not necessarily efficient for some other members of the organisation, or for society more generally. Sacking people or polluting environments are two obvious examples. Here, efficiency boils down to an externalisation of costs, or making someone else pay. Other human or non-human agents, in other words, have to take the burden for the benefits that result from the measures. If 'efficiency' is, as some people have suggested, a hooray-word among leaders in **politics** and **business**, then we have very good reasons to be sceptical. Here, like nowhere else, virtuousness and viciousness are going hand in hand.

Essentialism   One of the traditional tasks of **philosophy** is seen as distinguishing the essential from the accidental. The essential or the essence is that unchanging and invariable part, while the accidental is that which is contingent and variable. For example, it is essential that a triangle have three sides, but not essential that the three sides be of the same length. Following this kind of demonstration, many thinkers, some of whom will take authorisation for this by referring to Aristotle's *Metaphysics*, have argued that the task of thinking is to identify the essential in any phenomenon and to distinguish it from the accidental.

In recent years, the idea that the essence of any phenomenon could be located and easily distinguished from the accidental has come under scrutiny. This is because it is often possible to show that the parts of a phenomenon that have been thought to be essential are in fact social or historical products and are therefore contingent. Many of the things that have been thought to be essential characteristics of particular social groupings have been exposed as contingent and therefore changeable. For this kind of reason, in philosophy and the social sciences today, appeals to essence are increasingly under fire, and 'essentialism' has become a term of abuse or accusation.

Turning to business ethics, would it be fair to say that most of business ethics is characterised by various forms of essentialism? Business ethicists have often assumed, for example, that **capitalist** business practices are essentially good, and that moral infelicities are contingent characteristics of **market managerialism**. But, given widespread pain and suffering and managerial wrongdoing, why not see corporate capitalism as essentially bad, and the little good in the world today as accidental to it? Or take another example of essentialism, perhaps even more radical than this one. Business ethicists have almost always imagined that there is, at bottom, a core thing called '**ethics**' on which they might be able to rest their arguments. It is a kind of unexamined notion of goodness that we can, if we really care to, agree upon. But why must this be so? Why should there be some ultimate essence of ethics and of the good? Rather than assuming that ethics is a 'thing' that could be discovered, by contrast an anti-essentialist position would explode the meaning of ethics and refuse any position that claimed to know, once and for all, what ethics was. An anti-essentialist business ethics would not rest on **relativism** (or on any other position), which would be to stop thinking and to stop talking. It would insist that ethics is a matter of instability and lack of certainty about whether this or that action is worthy of the name of ethics. This is perhaps what ethics is about.

Ethics   Like many interesting words, the word 'ethics' has many meanings. In most of them, to be 'ethical' is a good thing. Only someone who was a very calculating pragmatist could be impatient with ethics, since perhaps such scruples might get in the way of getting the job done. In a sense, this is an ethical requirement as well. Assuming, however, that it is not, might we not argue that ethics slows things down and makes decisions harder to take? And is such an argument not an argument about the unethical nature of ethics? This is not only a characteristically **philosophical** puzzle, but it suggests that there might be some very good reasons for people in **business** to be suspicious of ethics as well.

In other words, the question 'what do we have in mind when talking about ethics?' needs to be asked over and over again. Is it something about our intentions, or the consequences of our actions, or looking good in the eyes of others? Should we talk about rights, or law, or **responsibility**, or freedom? Or is it all of these things and more? And if we cannot say exactly what ethics is, then how can we continue to use the word with any confidence at all?

A common condemnation is that people who use the word do not realise the realities of the world that we live in, and neither do they really know what they are talking about anyway. To which it might be added that people who use the word a lot are really betraying their guilt by bragging about being good. A really good person would just be good, and not need to continually remind others, tugging at their coats saying 'look at me!' What this says about the three people who have just spent a year writing a book on ethics is something we would rather not explore. We are afraid that we might not measure up to the challenge of ethics. Ethics is a dangerous thing, but we cannot make it go away.

Ethos This is a very difficult word. It has so many connotations that one sometimes wonders whether it has a solid meaning at all. (Which might be a marvellous thing, in a glossary like this.) For human beings, Heraclitus believed, '*ethos*' is the divine or the demonic. It is the place where they can live and where the many can become one. The *polis*, the city-state, is an example of where the multiple becomes one. **Aristotle**'s understanding of *ethos* is also related to his understanding of the city-state: his ethics is a description of the citizens living there. He made a distinction between *ethos* in the sense of '**character**' and *ethos* in the sense of 'habit'. Both are, of course, linked to each other: your character may improve if you are able to develop habits that allow you to control your unruly passions. In the *Rhetoric* (1984e), Aristotle refers to *ethos* as the character of the orator, or more particularly, the kind of image that the orator intends to convey to the audience. So, here *ethos* has also an instrumental rather than ethical connotation.

Nowadays, we understand *ethos* not so much in a personal sense of the word as in a social sense. A quick scanning of internet dictionaries delivered the following results: (1) the character of a particular community or social institution; (2) the particular spirit that is behind manners, traditions, customs, and so on; (3) the ideal image of a **community** as it is expressed in a poem or a painting. All these different under-standings – from Aristotelian to contemporary ones – have something to do with the relationship between image and ideal. *Ethos* is often related to what is perceived as the real essence of individuals and communities. And essence, Plato taught us, is always beautiful. So, the *ethos* refers to the personal or the social at its very best. That is to say, if we follow, for example, du Gay (2000: 10) when he says that he wants 'to defend the *ethos* of the office from "unworldly" philosophical or managerial [*criticisms*]', then you deliberately sidestep everything that is nasty about **bureaucracy**. Focusing on *ethos* always involves a peculiar kind of social aesthetics, a search for some essential beauty.

Fashion   **Business ethics** is surely fashionable. But what is a fashion? The literature about management fashions is prolific. Fashion has become, if anything, fashionable in management thinking. Etymologically, the word derives from the French *façon*, which means 'way of doing', 'manner', but is also related to 'decency' or 'propriety'. Why would managers be interested in these kind of things? Why is it that they are willing to experiment with fashions such as business ethics? One reason, no doubt, is that management lacks a clear-cut professional identity and it is by no means clear what are sound management practices and what are unsound management practices. Of course, after the fact we can point our fingers to managers who have obviously done wrong, but that is only after the fact. What we have in mind here are not managers who are obviously engaging in misconduct or even crime. Rather, we think of the endless debates about whether managers should behave rationally or emotionally, whether they should focus on organisational interests or on the public good, whether ethical codes work or do not work, whether they should behave like entrepreneurs or **technocrats**, and so on. These are by no means settled issues in management thought and this is why many commentators have claimed that management lacks a settled professional identity.

Here, we do not have the space to argue for this more extensively, but we can provide you with a nice and intuitive argument. Go and ask a child what kind of job they want to do as a grown-up and you will notice soon enough that several real professions are conjured up: fireman, vet, pilot, truck-driver, nurse or football-player. The point is that you probably will not hear a thing about management (unless there is something very disturbing about the child in question). We know that there is a lot of management education that is intended to rectify this lamentable state of affairs, but so far nobody has been able to define what management is really about.

Yet, the strange thing about people lacking straight identities is that they engage in a variety of identity experiments. As a result, they become vulnerable to fashion, for fashion is, if anything, what allows you to experiment with your identity (which is actually the reason why those who claim to be sure about their identities can only look down on followers of fashion). Quite analogously to teenagers who, in their quest for identity, experiment with a variety of lifestyles, managers are willing to experiment with their professional lifestyles. What fancy apparel, piercing, tattooing or fantastic dance music might mean to a teenager, CSR and business ethics might mean to a manager. Indeed, perhaps one of the best defences of business ethics that

159

we can imagine is that it is a matter of managerial lifestyle – particularly if that also involves experimenting with beliefs, and imagining that things might be otherwise.

Foucault, Michel (1926–1984)   The work of the French philosopher and historian Michel Foucault is typically divided into three phases: (1) in the 1960s, an 'archae-ological' phase represented by historical studies of madness, medicine and the human sciences, which disrupted common sense notions of historical unity, progress and the human subject; (2) in the 1970s, a 'genealogical' phase represented by studies of the prison and the first part of his studies of sexuality, in which he transformed understandings of power, governance and the production of subjects; and (3) in the 1980s, an 'ethical' phase in which he investigated in detail the practices by which people turn themselves into subjects in relation to 'technologies of self'.

In these latter studies, which have the most obvious significance for business ethics, Foucault works out something that might be read as an **Aristotelian** concern with character or *ethos*. In particular, in the second and third volumes of his *History of Sexuality* (1984a; 1984b) he shows the way ancient Greeks practised a certain 'care for the self' in their bodily practices of diet, sexuality and pleasure. This involves a particular aesthetic cultivation in which one struggles with the desires of the flesh, and in taming them, or at least sublimating them, becomes one capable of being recognised as displaying a certain moral character.

When reading Foucault on ethics we should bear in mind that, no matter how original and interesting he is, he works in and in relation to a long philosophical tradition (see Jones, 2002). He identifies himself in direct relation to the critical tradition of philosophy following **Kant**, and as we have suggested throughout this book, there are clear resonances in their respective understandings of freedom. For both Kant and Foucault, **ethics** is about freedom, and hence about reflection on what Foucault calls 'multiple constraints', that is, power. Freedom does not involve escaping from power but recognising its operations in our basic everyday practices and, on reflection, changing these practices. We should also not think that Foucault conceives of an *ethos* of care for the self as an individual matter. He worked in the intellectual context of **Levinas** and **Derrida**, and in this light it is not surprising that he writes that the care for the self 'implies complex relationships with others insofar as this *ethos* of freedom is also a way of caring for others' (Foucault, 1997: 287).

Friedman, Milton (1912–)   Milton Friedman is a Nobel Prize-winning economist (1976) who became famous for his criticism of Keynes and his so-called monetarism. He is probably the most famous member of what is known as the Chicago School of Economics. By some people, he is considered to be the embodiment of evil. This is partly related to his alleged relationship with the Pinochet regime in Chile, a notorious violator of human rights. It is also related to his idea that the involvement of the government with economics should be minimised as much as possible, something which many critics condemn as downright cynical. In defence of Friedman, however, one must say that there is no proof that he entertained contact with the Chilean junta and that he also visited many communist countries (which obviously does not make him a supporter of Breznjev or Stalin). Friedman's perspective on the world is probably best characterised as libertarian. He has, for example, been a fierce defender of the legalisation of drugs and prostitution.

In the field of **business ethics**, Friedman is important for entirely different reasons. In 1970 he wrote a non-academic piece in the *New York Times Magazine* with the title: 'The social responsibility of business is to increase its profits'. For many business ethicists, this piece is a major source of reference; indeed, a downright stumbling block for it is that here we find the quintessential capitalistic defence of the profit motive and, in relation to this, a scepticism about social **responsibility**, and other ideas generally cherished by business ethicists. In Chapter 7, however, we have argued that Friedman's text requires close reading and deserves serious thought. His article is much more sophisticated than many business ethicists think it is. For all our problems with Friedman, his text betrays a deep concern for the relationship between democracy and business, an issue that is often ignored in business ethics. In general, if we wish to take issue with particular ideas then we are well-advised to render these ideas as convincingly as possible. Those with whom we disagree are generally neither stupid nor evil.

Future, the One of the substantial dangers of a narrow version of **business ethics** is that it would make the future look very much like the past. If various versions of moral philosophy are merely used to justify what we do already, then what is the point in the future being there at all? Business as usual, ethics as usual would leave the future closed like an unopened book or a missed opportunity. Surely what happens next is not merely about the passage of time, about the present reproducing the same as the next moment? It would be a conservative version of the future in which it is merely the comforting recognition of something that is already known. In accounts of decision science and certain sorts of business strategy, the passage of time is treated as a series of decisions that can be modelled in order to maximise the chances of getting from here to there. The fact that we then must already know what it looks like there is obvious enough, as is the fact that it must also (genealogically and alphabetically) contain here.

The accounts of ethics that we have developed in this book (following thinkers like **Levinas**, **Derrida**, and so on) rely on the future being radically other. On the future being quite different, open and miraculous. For if **ethics** is really to mean anything beyond following rules, then it must be suspicious of all rules, together with the way that they stretch out and tell us what the future must look like. The future has no 'must', no 'should' and no 'ought'. Yet it is the place that we are all going to live in, so we should take the greatest interest in how it is built.

Globalisation Contemporary ideas about globalisation are fast becoming one of the taken-for-granted assumptions of contemporary management and social science. But is globalisation new? Organisations like the Catholic Church, the Hanseatic league and the East India Company have been acting globally for far longer than the globalisation thesis has been around. Further, in academic terms, from at least the 1950s, a variety of futurologists have been arguing pretty much the same line. **Capitalism** has won, and (thanks to communication technologies) markets now roam unchallenged across the face of the world. This is the 'convergence thesis', Fukuyama's (1992) *The End of History and the Last Man*, the writings of Bell (1960), Toffler (1970), Drucker (1993) and the various 'post-industrial', 'post-modern', 'post-Fordist', 'post-capitalist' theorists (for an introduction to these ideas, see Kumar, 1995). Whilst there are internal differences, the emphasis is on a revolutionary kind of change. Knowledge and culture displace capital and economy, flexible organisation displaces rigid **bureaucracy**, multi-skilling displaces scientific management, and the global corporation displaces both the local and the state.

In its least problematic sense, globalisation is the description of an age in which time and space have largely been overcome by technology. However, it would be more accurate to say that this technology is only available to some. For members of the trans-national capitalist class, the globe is no longer an abstract concept but a lived reality of airport lounges and office blocks in certain parts of certain cities across the world. Simplistic versions of globalisation involve generalising the air-conditioned experience of these outposts, and ignoring the peasantry, shantytowns and refugee camps that are the local experience for many. Communication and commerce do not benefit all equally, and the word 'globalisation' has become emblematic of the political struggles of the early twenty-first century. For most neoliberals, globalisation is a process of social change that involves the breaking down of old boundaries and restrictions. It is a movement to personal and market freedom which is progressive in the sense that it confronts (often repressive) local traditions and attempts to replace them with consumerism, **individualism** and **capitalism**. However, for most neo-communitarians and socialists, globalisation represents the domination of the corporations of the North and the West. It results in cultural Coca-Colonisation and McDonaldisation, and the economic domination of the many by the few.

However, it is important not to simply suggest that all on the left are hostile to globalisation, and all on the right sponsor it. Far right 'patriots' and Islamic fundamentalists share a hostility to de-traditionalising forms of globalisation, whilst internationalist trade unionists and **anti**-corporate protesters are keen to develop alternative forms of globalisation. Being 'for' or 'against' globalisation is rather like being 'for' or 'against' ethics – it depends what you mean by globalisation in the first place. Against the universal view from Silicon Valley, the reader might want to think about the view from wherever it is that they live. Some classes of people, some places, some industries might be globalised – others are patently not. Some organisations might be acting globally, others are concerned with a few streets. And these are not merely matters of spatial economic connection – but of social mobility too. Further, in a globe where the vast majority of people have yet to make a telephone call, it is difficult to take seriously the idea that capital is being displaced by knowledge. So, who is globalisation for? Or to put that another way, what purpose might the story of globalisation serve for those who have much invested in it?

Golden mean   One of the ways to reduce **Aristotle**'s complex understanding of politics, ethics and community to a code-based ethics is to focus overmuch on the golden mean. In writing about different sorts of virtues and characters, Aristotle notes that **ethical** and **political** problems are often associated with an excess of a particular characteristic. Too much courage ends up as recklessness, too little as timidity. Sticking to principles for too long is sometimes seen as stubbornness, whilst throwing them away too easily is unscrupulous. Striking a path between extremes, a perfect balance, is therefore most likely to produce a good character. However, Aristotle does not think that this is a final state of affairs, but that it is actually an endless task for practical wisdom. In any case, since different virtues are valued in different places, then the golden mean is not a rule that can be applied in the same way in all places. Aristotle's list of virtues is what MacIntye (1967: 67) describes as 'the code of a gentleman' in Athenian society, not advice for all humans in all times and places. Some people seem to think that the golden mean is an antique version of 'Becoming Happy and Wealthy in One Easy Lesson' (Solomon, 1993). Whilst some of Aristotle's insights might be relevant for such a project, his insistence that morality can only be understood in a specific historical context makes any generalised application of the golden mean more likely to reveal differences rather than universal similarities.

Holocaust   In 1946, Hermann Göring, once commander-in-chief of the Nazis and second in the hierarchy only to Hitler himself, now prisoner and suspect during the Nuremberg trials, exclaimed to his psychologist that he 'had never been cruel' (Hilberg, 1992: 1). Here, Göring displayed at least a vague sense of morality. Good is what is not cruel. One may wonder what **Kant**, with all his lofty disdain for happiness and desire, would think of that. More importantly, the catastrophe that we now know as the holocaust would probably not have been possible if the perpetrators had only been people who delighted in cruelty. Indeed, cruelty is probably a very inefficient way of doing what the German leadership at the time thought was necessary. Functionaries and bureaucrats did the most important job. The very fact that **bureaucracy**, for all its undeniable importance in modern society, made something like the holocaust possible is reason enough to be suspicious about this particular form of organisation (Bauman, 1989). It allows you to engage in unfathomable cruelty without any desire whatsoever to do so. And also, we would hasten to add, without drowning in feelings of guilt. The labour of division characteristic of bureaucracies entails that moral responsibilities are divided up in very small 'bits of responsibility' so as to make the idea of any individual **responsibility** that stretches beyond the desire to abide by rule and order totally meaningless.

Following Hannah Arendt, Giorgio Agamben (1999b: 94–95) has observed that for post-war Germans of all ages it was much easier to cope with the idea of collective guilt than to cope with the idea that at least some Germans might have had an individual responsibility for the unimaginable. In complex circumstances, when ethical problems cannot be easily mastered, the idea of collective guilt often pops up as a kind of escape valve. Agamben alerts us to the work of Primo Levi, a famous Italian novelist and survivor of Auschwitz, who has always claimed that talk about collective guilt is utterly senseless simply because one cannot be guilty (in a meaningful sense of the term) for what others have done – parents, friends, neighbours, compatriots. This is perhaps what makes Levi's writing so strangely immune to resentment about nationalities or ethnicities that have engaged in genocide. Nonetheless, he insists that the only guilt he can conceive of is personal guilt: 'One must answer personally for sins and errors, otherwise all trace of civilization would vanish from the face of the earth' (see Agamben, 1999b: 95). Now bureaucracy has often been seen, quite rightly, as a crucial feature of modern civilization (du Gay, 2000). But would somebody like Levi have agreed? Would he really believe that rule-abiding functionaries are the gatekeepers of civilization? Perhaps there is also always something that escapes the bureaucrat, something that is not quite captured in an organisational use of words like responsibility or justice, which might involve breaking **rules** rather than following them.

Hygiene-machine One of the incredible achievements of human beings is their ability to plan and design organisation on a massive scale. They are able to design magnificent social machinery and then execute this in the world. But the problem is that the world is not always the same as it appears in the plans, and then the humans have a problem. Should they design plans that include the variation, inconsistency and frivolity of other humans, or should those others be made to fit into the plan?

In a book called *The Hygiene-Machine*, the Dutch philosophers René ten Bos and Ruud Kaulingfreks have argued that contemporary culture in general and contemporary organisations in particular display a tendency towards the hygienic (Kaulingfreks and ten Bos, 2005a; 2005b; ten Bos, 2004; 2005; ten Bos and Kaulingfreks, 2001; ten Bos and Rhodes, 2003). This is to say, modern culture is infused with the idea of the possibility of achieving perfect cleanliness, if only everyone would follow the plan and get organised. Ordering means that the world itself should move towards the Idea of the perfectly systematic and organised. However, if we compare the fragmentary nature of the world and its inhabitants, we sadly often find that they will never live up to the purity of our Idea. It is always the world that is the problem. The hygiene-machine is characterised by 'hosophobia', a fear of dirt and the impure (Kaulingfreks and ten Bos, 2005a). If this hosophobic tendency is what makes modern organisation so powerful, it is also what makes it so dangerous.

One might think that ethical thinking could cause problems for the hygiene-machine. After all, **ethics** is about asking difficult questions about difficult things. Ethics is a matter of values and politics, about conflicts and **aporias**. So ethics is perhaps the thing that will stop the hygiene-machine, right? Wrong. The hygiene-machine, being a rather powerful thing, has an incredible ability to capture even the things that threaten it (laughter, love, desire, ethics) and turn them towards its own ends. And when we think about **business ethics**, much of it is nothing more than hygiene. It is a matter of cleaning up the worst excesses of corporate **capitalism**, or if that is not possible, then at least appearing to do so by putting the worst of the dirt behind the furniture.

But remember, ethics always contains the unpredictable, and business ethics can bite back. Even the hygiene-machine cannot clean up that which exceeds it, which refuses to find a settled place within rules. Which is why we are for business ethics.

Individualism   We are all individuals. You, reading these words, wherever you are, are locked in your head. Of course you are an individual, someone who cannot be divided, or added up with others to make a mass. When you decide, it is you that decides, following your conscience and your reason. You have no reason to doubt that, because you think and therefore you are. For some other individual to come along and tell you that you are not what you think you are would simply be foolish.

So how was it possible for you to read that last sentence? You are looking at something that contains these words – a book, a photocopy or a computer screen. Without those technologies, you would not have been able to read those words. The possibility of reading has required something outside you, in order that your inside can do what it has just done. But this is not the end of this problem, because you also had to have been able to read to a certain ability, and this was not something that was always within you. Your understanding of nouns and verbs and sentences and paragraphs and chapters and books has relied on all of those people who you have been taught by, whether deliberately or not. Even the very word and idea 'individual' is one that you also had to learn from others, in order that you could recognise it on paper and in yourself. Of course having books and being able to read is not the same as understanding, and that understanding must itself also rely on some sort of relationship between what we meant by these words, and what they mean to you. Those might not be exactly the same things, but for there to be any connection between us we must also share a universe of comprehensibility in which we know what words like good and bad might mean. You must be able to see, however dimly, what the world looks like for the **Other**. But it doesn't even end here, because the books and teachers that allowed for reading, language and understanding were themselves the product of ink and paper, schools and parents. And on it goes, with each individual only being possible because of all of the technologies, ideas and relationships that assisted them to come into being.

None of this is likely to change the fact that you probably do feel like an individual, and that when you do something that relates to **ethics**, you feel that it is you who are doing it and not all those other histories, technologies and ghosts that we mentioned in the last paragraph. However many sociologists insist that individualism is a relatively new way of thinking (Abercrombie et al., 1986), or moralists insist that it is destroying **community** (Etzioni, 1993), or philosophers proclaim that heroic agency is a fiction (Foucault, 1966), this is unlikely to stop you from feeling **responsible** for your actions. But why would we want to persuade you not to feel responsible? If you felt divided, and multiple and irresponsible 'you' would probably find it difficult to imagine what ethics would look like, and consequently difficult to write a glossary entry that explained what ethics was.

Kant, Immanuel (1724–1804) A very serious man. He lived in an outer province of Prussia from where he taught his contemporaries that there are very good reasons to become reasonable. He believed that science could save mankind from the hell it has so often created. For Kant, the hallmark of science was mathematics. He believed that good **philosophy**, be it ethics, epistemology or whatever, takes mathematics as its natural centre. Note what he writes about the putative origin of philosophy:

> A new light broke upon the first person who demonstrated the isoceles triangle (whether be he called 'Thales' or had some other name). For he found that what he had to do was not to trace what he saw in this figure, or even trace its mere concept, and read off, as it were, from the properties of the figure; but rather he had to produce the latter from what he himself thought into the object and presented (through construction) according to a priori concepts, and that in order to know something securely a priori he had to ascribe to the thing nothing except what followed necessarily from what he himself had put into it in accordance with its concept.
>
> (Kant, 1781: Bxi–Bxii)

What is being said here is that to understand the world mathematically, you need not necessarily immerse yourself in empirical observations. It is enough for you to make a reasonable thought experiment out of whatever it is that you want to study. You construe it yourself and you will notice soon enough that other people who rely on reason too will arrive at similar understandings. Moreover, you will be able to formulate a critique that is clear as it can possibly be and that is not impaired by the muddy debates about interpretations or meanings of arbitrary perceptions. Mathematicians and philosophers are, for all their differences, the 'technicians of reason'.

It is, we think, crucially important to bear this mathematical propensity in mind when we discuss Kantian ethics. It is not an ethics from the real world that contains flesh and blood humans. Rather, it beckons to us from a lofty and idealistic world, a world in which only technicians of reason can rejoice. But is there any good reason to think that ethics should be easy?

Levinas, Emmanuel (1905–1995) A Jewish philosopher, born in Lithuania, Levinas worked in France in the generation that preceded thinkers such as **Derrida** and **Foucault**. Levinas argued that Western thought has been characterised by a thinking of the Same, at the expense of the **Other**. As such, the task of thinking became one of identity. More specifically, it should ask questions about theories that assume that consistency and correspondence are more important than difference and otherness. This is a problem, Levinas argues, because we live in a world with other people, and because ethics is a matter of how we relate to those others. Western thought has largely been insufficient to the task of a thinking of ethics, which is a thinking of the Other. Levinas believes that I am drawn to respond to the Other and in doing so am myself called into question.

It is telling that, despite the existence of a large, rich and controversial work, almost all translated into English, and being one of the major influences on discussions of ethics in philosophy in the second half of the twentieth century, Levinas has been almost totally avoided by the discipline of business ethics (cf. Jones, 2003a; Roberts, 2001; 2003).

Market managerialism The two most common features of contemporary organising are a faith in the 'market', combined with a celebration of the practices and occupation of 'management'. Following broadly classical economic understandings of supply and demand, 'markets' are claimed to be the best way to stimulate efficiencies of production, distribution and quality. This understanding is now taken to apply to both the private and public sectors, to goods and services, and even to inform 'ethical' choices in **business**. 'Management' is a modern form of thinking about organising which stresses the strategic capacities of a small cadre of high status co-ordinators, and celebrates them accordingly. Managers are often argued to be a class of people who can best understand the tides of the market. Perhaps they can see further because of their elevation within organisational hierarchies, or perhaps these claims are made (by gurus, business schools, professional associations, and so on) because they all want to be paid well.

Though many marketers and managerialists would like to claim that this is the one best way to organise, Parker (2002a) treats market managerialism as an ideology which is engaged in a contest for legitimacy with other social movements. **Anti**-corporate protest, for example, is generally hostile to market managerialism. Certain elements of business ethics, particularly virtue ethics and elements of **Kantian** reasoning, might also be hostile to market managerialism. However, the majority of **business ethics** assumes and normalises a particular understanding of market exchange, and a hierarchical sense of organisation. Not only does this restrict understandings of exchange to narrowly **capitalist** ones (when many other forms exist, see Williams, 2004), it also fails to recognise the many alternative ways that organising can be done, inspired variously by **utopias**, feminism, anarchism, environmental movements, and so on (see Parker et al., forthcoming). Alternatives such as these might reveal market managerialism to be neither **common**, nor sensible.

Marx, Karl (1818–1883) Karl Marx is one of the most widely debated figures in the history of human thought. This is perhaps unsurprising if we understand that he was an ardent critic of the philosophy and political economy of his time, and rarely turned down the opportunity for an intellectual scrap. Both an astounding intellect and an engaged political writer, he offended a great number of people in power and therefore was effectively chased from his homeland in what is now Germany, exiled in France and Belgium, and then from 1849 he lived and worked in London. He spent

167

more than thirty years working on the proposed six-volume work *Capital*, which was never completed.

If Marx was writing today we would call him 'interdisciplinary'. He was an economist, political theorist, philosopher and journalist, and also a great classical scholar and lover of literature. Perhaps because of his critical nature and his vast array of different influences, it is unsurprising that Marx has been treated in so many different ways. If you are new to Marx but have heard of something called 'Marxism', then you should probably remind yourself of the comment that Marx made to his son-in-law, Paul Lafargue. One day, on hearing what was being said about him and his works, Marx remarked that 'If anything is certain, it is that I am no Marxist!'

The point we are trying to make is that Marx has a great deal to say about our world, as long as it remains a capitalist one, but in the same way as you should not trust Bowie on **Kant** or Solomon on **Aristotle**, we need to tread carefully when it comes to someone such as Marx, who has been the subject of so much (often uninformed) chatter. The only solution is to read him yourself.

Mill, John Stuart (1806–1873) John Stuart Mill, like his father's friend, Jeremy **Bentham**, wrote and thought about a wide range of theoretical and practical matters. His writings on scientific method, and the difficulty of studying human beings had a major influence on the development of British sociology. His writings on the position of women, constitutional reform, economics and education developed utilitarian thinking in directions that are ultimately more liberal and less radical than Bentham. Mill argued that some forms of happiness are more worthwhile than others, and that some principles that tend to generate happiness should be generalised as good. For example, that the pleasure of playing a game is not as good as the pleasure of reading a great piece of poetry. Or, since Mill believed that 'liberty' and 'toleration' tended to produce the maximum utility, then liberal social principles that defended such notions should be supported.

In an odd sense, though they both claim the title '**utilitarian**', much of Mill's generalised elitism seems to contradict Bentham's clear-eyed reformism. Perhaps one way to understand the difference is simply to see Mill as a liberal utilitarian who was influenced by romantic conceptions of human nature. For Mill, it was not enough to simply work towards the greatest good of the greatest number because this ignores all the varieties of good that human beings can identify – from freedom to poetry. Most of the obvious criticisms of hard-nosed utilitarianism were well understood by Mill (see 1962), and his defences are better than most. He alerts us to the problems with using utility as the measure of all things, but eventually ends up defending social and economic freedom above all else. Ironically, and perhaps influenced by the 35 years he spent working for the neo-colonial East India Company, his version of utilitarianism ends up looking much more elitist and managerial than Bentham's.

Nietzsche, Friedrich (1844–1900) While he is renowned for his scathing and wide-ranging critique of Western philosophy, in this book we have drawn on only two ideas from Nietzsche. First, we draw on Nietzsche's trenchant and uncompromising criticism of empty talk of ethics, and of abstract moralising. This appears throughout his work, but can be found in *Human, all too Human* (1878, Chapter 2); *Daybreak* (1881); *Beyond Good and Evil* (1886) and in particular in *The Genealogy of Morals* (1887). Second, Nietzsche is an unfailing optimist, an exemplar of affirmation, joyfulness and laughter. In the same way that Nietzsche railed against negativity and hoped for **philosophy** to become a joyful or 'gay science', we might imagine a joyful business ethics that would puncture all pretensions and deflate grand words. A kynical ethics perhaps. Needless to say, Nietzsche is not very widely read by 'business ethicists'!

Other, the   The Other defies definition precisely because it does not obey the logic of 'is' that governs definition and glossaries (even like this one). The Other is perhaps best approached, therefore, by what it is not. The Other is not the Same. The Other is not reducible. The Other is not identical to anything. The Other is not enclosable. The Other is not me, even if it makes me. The Other is not a thing. If it appears as a thing (a face, for example), then that is only the material manifestation (the 'plastic form') of the Other. Perhaps the Other is the **future**. The Other is invention. The Other takes me away from where I am. The Other discomforts. Without discomfort, I have probably reduced the Other to something I know, something the same as me. The Other, therefore, is not merely other but is radically Other. 'The absolutely other is the Other' (Levinas, 1961: 39). The Other does not comfort me. The Other is what I am called on to comfort. The Other demands a response. But will not punish me if I do not respond. The Other asks for hospitality. Without condition. If there are conditions then *I* must not impose them on the Other. The Other is dangerous, but if there is an Other then there will be that risk. Besides denial, besides **hygiene**, besides pseudo-morality, there will be the Other. The Other, for Levinas, is the ontological condition of ethics.

Phenomenology   A stream in **philosophy** that is oftentimes related to the work of Edmund Husserl, even though there are many philosophers who used the term earlier than he did. Phenomenology is the study of so-called **essences**, in Husserl's case the essence of our consciousness. Crucial in determining this essence is an understanding that consciousness encounters the world and that the world encounters consciousness. The human mind is believed to be directed to the world by dint of so-called 'meanings' (remembering, appearances, perceptions, and so on). In other words, this mind has a particular kind of openness to the world and is, as a consequence, influenced by it. Consciousness and world engage in an infectious relation, even though this is clearly not a term that many phenomenologists would use themselves.

Apart from Husserl, some other great names from philosophy are related to phenomenology: Hegel, Heidegger, **Levinas**, Sartre, Gadamer, Merleau-Ponty, all of whom developed their own insights and ideas. What they have in common is that they are deeply suspicious of grand metaphysical systems of speculative thought since they refuse to acknowledge that one can talk sensibly about unobservable entities.

They prefer to talk about evidence. Be this as it may, never think that reading phenomenologists is easy: some of the mentioned authors have produced the most inaccessible prose ever. Even turning to the concrete, to the things themselves, does not mark the end of complex and speculative thinking.

Philia This is the word that **Aristotle** used to indicate 'friendship', but he understood friendship in an entirely different way to our current interpretation. The word is closely related to *'philos'*, which means 'loved' or 'dear'. What is loved or dear to a person? According to Aristotle, you may think of the **community** of which you are a part. The members of this community can be friends. They form a community of friends. Importantly, Aristotle thinks that friendship is not confined to people with whom we only maintain an emotional relationship: you can also become friends with people with whom you entertain an opportunistic or instrumental relationship which is, for example, the case in business relations. Friendship is about friendliness, about the ability to get along with each other, about reasonability and cordiality, and so on. These are, we suggest, all features that need not be excluded from business relations, though the **bureaucrat** would like it if they were. Yet, we should not infer from these warm words that friendship is something easy. As **Derrida** (1997: 6) has noted, in Aristotelian friendship there is always a certain kind of aristocracy involved: one cannot be a friend of the many, one cannot be a friend without trial, one cannot be a friend without conditions. As we have indicated in Chapter 5, friends are also people with whom you can have serious conflicts. It is true, there have been business books with funny titles such as *How to Win Friends and Influence People* (Carnegie, 1936) suggesting that friendship is not difficult. For those among you, dear readers, who really think that friendship is an easygoing affair, we recommend that you read Aristotle or Derrida.

Philosophy What are we doing when we philosophise? Some people would argue that we are thinking. But thought is clearly not a monopoly of philosophers. Artists think, scientists think, managers think, many people think. In other words, if philosophers claim that they are experts in thought, they probably have a kind of thinking in mind that is rather strange. But what is this strangeness?

It is certain that philosophers are, for example, engaged in the practice of reasoning. They are interested in valid arguments and it might be said that some philosophers, most notably logicians, are more interested in validity than in empirical adequacy or felt truth. But this certainly does not hold for all philosophers. Logicians are, after all, a very special type of philosopher. And apart from this, it is difficult to think of a scientist who does not take any interest in sound reasoning.

Others would claim that philosophy is very much about dialogue and communication. To be sure, many philosophers are engaged in constant – and oftentimes spurious – twaddle. Two philosophers meeting in a pub or marketplace are not likely to stop once they have started talking. But then again, would two artists or scientists be likely to stop when they hit upon the right theme? And what about managers? Their existence is very much about talking and communication too.

170

Perhaps, then, we should say that philosophers aspire to wisdom whereas others aspire to beauty, knowledge or profit. Philosophers are, after all, the self-declared friends of wisdom (**philia** and *sophia* here mean 'friend' and 'wisdom', respectively). This implies a kind of humbleness: the philosopher does not possess wisdom but merely desires it in a way that you can desire friendship or love. This humility, however, puts him or her in the right position to question received wisdom, to question **common sense**, to ask painful questions about the taken-for-granted.

The domain of the philosopher is the paradox: he or she always goes against (*para*) generally accepted opinion (*doxa*). This is why philosophers often appear as rather obnoxious people who cast doubt on what all other people are keen to accept. Let us therefore put it this way: philosophers, like it or not, are people who use paradox to alert others that thinking is a task that never stops – even in definitions of philosophy in glossaries that claim to know what philosophy is.

Polis This word is usually translated as 'city-state', which is, as is the case with many Greek words, delusively simple. It is usually understood as the *ethos* of the many, that is to say, the dwelling place where many citizens can be one (and therefore also partake in the divine). This dwelling place can be thought of as an island in the wilderness or, as we are talking about Greece, an island on an island in the sea. This means that there is always a problem with other islands or city-states.

The world for the citizens of the city-state is irredeemably agonistic, but in order to cope with its threats they have to open up to what lies outside. Hospitality is an indispensable feat of the *polis*. It allows the *polis* to digest the multiple and the **Other** while simultaneously staying one. It cannot be emphasised enough that the idea of strangers with diminished rights, or even no rights at all, is a very recent one in the history of European culture (and takes us back, in some sense, to a savage prehistory). In the *polis*, the stranger (but also other non-citizens such as women, slaves or children) encounters a world of divinely inspired laws. In it, citizens and non-citizens engage in a world of *logos* and of law. To deny the forces of both would be an intolerable violation. The *polis*, in sum, is therefore an answer to the problem of uniting the many with the one.

Now, the multiple is not only a threat that lies outside the city-state, that is, in the wilderness where barbarians roam. Strangeness has always been in the heart of the city-state. Why would that be the case? The very idea of a *polis* is the result of a struggle to gain autonomy from the community (*oikos*) from which it originally arose. This community is still the silent heart of all city-states. *Polis* is organisation, civil society, discussion, public, openness and masculinity; *oikos* is disorganisation, silence, inward-orientation, privacy and femininity. In the *polis*, male citizens try to emancipate themselves from the womb that is the *oikos*. This battle lies at the heart of each *polis*. For the Greeks it seemed that the battle is painful, for those who are engaged in it know in their heart of hearts of the womb's indelible superiority. Everywhere in Greek literature (which was almost entirely produced by men) you can read that women know forms of belonging and solidarity that men are incapable of. As soon as you need *logos* (in the sense of reason and words) to establish your community, you have already lost the battle even though you must carry on. This is what makes the battle so painful.

The *oikos* from which male citizens try to escape by reason and philosophy remains silent as ever in the heart of the *polis* and it is therefore ultimately uncanny and strange. Yet, in an odd doubling, it is exactly the strangeness in the heart of the *polis* that allows its citizens to cope with the strangeness outside.

Politics   Whenever you talk to managers of hospitals, ministerial departments, police organisations, prisons and **businesses**, you will soon find out how resentful these people are about politics. Why would that be the case? A suggestion is that politicians, those who are supposed to do politics, are often considered to be untrustworthy and unprofessional. They talk too much, they are not aware of the details that pervade daily practice and they are so addicted to the media that they say whatever the public wants them to say. In short, politicians have no sense for quality and detail. No wonder that business people, unencumbered as they are by political traditions, are often inclined to involve themselves with politics in order to correct its various wrongs. While it goes without saying that they have understood that politics matters to their various businesses, we would also like to suggest that business-minded persons sincerely think that politics can be done much more efficiently than is usually the case. This is why they want to infuse politics with business-like **virtues** such as transparency, action-orientation and unassailable targets. Hence, a kind of managerial idealism characterises their perspective on politics. As a consequence, politics gets depoliticised. Politics is increasingly regarded, even by politicians themselves, as plain work and parliament is understood as the business organisation where politics is produced.

But do we really need to enrich politics with organisational virtues or business virtues? Would it not be a noble task of business ethics to take more seriously the limitations of the virtues it seems to espouse and to protect politics from business or management? To us, politics seems to be a domain where good intentions and transparency simply collapse. We think that politicians should not be organisational **technocrats** who specialise in means, but servants of the polity, meaning all members of our society. This bewildering variety of people do not share the same goals or the same values. The managerial illusion that this is possible is endangering politics, in the sense of endless passionate debate about ends.

Organisations suffer from this illusion too. Even in these relatively self-contained spheres, at least some politics is, like it or not, inevitable. Why then should we want society itself to surrender to this illusion? As if conflict would, one day, simply end, and all that would be left is puppets and **rules**.

Possibility   The **business** world is a world of possibility. The most preferred talk in this world circles around notions such as dynamism, capacity, potency, talent, and so on. There is always an understanding that something very interesting might be happening in the near or far **future**, something better, something redeeming, something more perfect. The ultimate principle of business in a **capitalistic** world is compensation and where can one find compensation if not in the future? The business world is therefore crammed with plans, for a plan is an event in the head that anticipates a future event in the world. The philosopher Hegel believed in a world where events in the head would eventually coincide with events in the world, something which he referred to as 'absolute spirit'. We are not sure whether such a spirit is possible, but it is definitely a possibility that has obsessed those who like to plan. The idea that the world is a place that matches thought is indeed an enthralling one.

It is for this reason that the business world cannot tolerate possibilities to remain possibilities. Unrealised possibilities are, if anything, unfulfilled promises. So, the interest in possibility is not in open possibility as such but in its actualisation. It is all for the betterment of the world and of the organisation and, in the end, of ourselves that we are or should be in business. Those who are not actualised, the idle and awkward who remain unfulfilled promises have no place here. Such is the harsh logic of business.

Relativism The strange thing about relativism is that it is so obviously true, and so obviously frightening. The idea originates with the contrary notion, that of a fixed point. If anything has a foundation, a certain ground, then all the other things can be arranged in relation to that point. Like a **bureaucratic** organisation chart, some things can be equivalent, higher or lower, and the order of things is clear and uncontested. Archimedes was supposed to have said that if he could find the ultimate fixed point, the fulcrum, he could move the entire world. This geometric metaphor has been widely applied, with the search for foundations and essences being deemed to be the holy grail of knowledge. Find the philosopher's stone and all sorts of power becomes possible.

Now we might want to argue that atoms, genes and galaxies are fixed points in some sense, but what fixed points might we find on the human scale? The answer so far seems to be none. The very multiplicity of ideas about human nature, progress, utopia, beauty and so on that we find across history and between ourselves tells us something rather significant about the impossibility of certain human knowledge. All these ideas are relative to each other, and relate to each other, but none could be said to be a foundation or fundament. (Unless you are a fundamentalist, in which case you believe that one thing – Book, God, Truth – simply explains all the others and makes them wrong. You may be right, or you may be wrong.) So for a post-foundationalist, truth, on the human scale, is a relative matter. Truth is better treated as a relation to a particular body of knowledge and social context or, as **Nietzsche** had it, 'A moveable host of metaphors, metonymies, and anthropomorphisms: in short, a sum of human relations which have been poetically and rhetorically intensified, transferred, and embellished, and which, after long usage, seem to a people to be fixed, canonical, and binding. Truths are illusions which we have forgotten are illusions' (1873: 84). Truth, in other words, is **common sense**.

Yet, if we apply these ideas to ethics, we glimpse the alarming possibility of being beyond good and evil. Perhaps, all the attempts to provide foundations in intentions, consequences, virtues, rights, duties, decisions and faith end up as so much hot air, so many preferences. For some, this is such a frightening possibility that they try to shut it out altogether and label it 'nihilism' — a dark philosophy of nothing. For others, the very absurdity of the human being in a meaningless universe provokes rather more joyful reactions. Existentialists, such as Jean-Paul Sartre, suggested that we were condemned to be free, and hence should attempt to make our choices present to ourselves as much as we are able. The relativity of human judgements is precisely what enables such freedom, since if there were reliable foundations all we would need to do is follow the rules that we deduce from them. For others, such as Nietzsche, the overcoming of a cow-like attitude to ethics was only possible once ethics was recognised as just a set of stories, fables and moralising injunctions. Indeed, for many philosophers of the past century, being part of the herd, staying close to the warm heart of the **community**, is not **ethics** at all. It is an excuse for an ethics that rehearses the idea that following orders and staying within traditions is itself a good. And if the twentieth century has taught us anything, it must be that following orders does not always result in the good. In a much more positive meaning of the term, if things are relative to each other they can be moved around.

Ethics no longer becomes the articulation of a good that is self-evident from a first or universal principle, but an endless struggle to make sense or, what amounts to the same, to do good *and* to do evil. By relating different traditions to each other, or relating the self to the **Other**, we open up a range of ethical possibilities. Relativism can thus also be understood as the truthful beginning of ethics or as the particular situation of truth in which we find ourselves. And if we can be truthful to this situation, we may be able to finally understand that good is not simply opposed to evil, that ethics does not allow us to simply judge about what is good and evil, or that evil is excluded by all the good that we are doing. As Badiou (2002: 61) beautifully argued, if evil exists, it is an 'unruly effect of the power of truth'.

Responsibility   An interminably difficult concept. Perhaps, even the most impenetrable concept in current discourse amongst business ethicists. The lack of explicit discussion in business ethics about the difficulties of this concept should not fool a critical reader; it probably says a lot more about the discipline of **business ethics** than it does about the concept of responsibility. Does it suggest an irresponsibility with regard to concepts, thought and reason amongst business ethicists? Why do business ethicists refuse to respond to recent thinking about responsibility? Amongst recent thinking on responsibility, noteworthy is the work of Jacques **Derrida**, who has noted the difficulty yet centrality of this concept. Derrida argues that the question 'What is responsibility?' is always urgent, even if it has been unanswered (1993b: 16). Even further, the question might be unanswerable.

Although the concept of responsibility lacks coherence, Derrida notes that this

> has never stopped it from 'functioning' as one says. On the contrary, it operates
> so much better, to the extent that it serves to obscure the abyss or fill in its absence

of foundation, stabilizing a chaotic process of change in what are called conventions. Chaos refers to the abyss or the open mouth, that which speaks as well as that which signifies hunger. What is thus found at work in everyday discourse, in the exercise of justice, and first and foremost in the axiomatics of private, public, or international law, in the conduct of internal politics, diplomacy, and war, is a lexicon concerning responsibility that can be said to hover vaguely about a concept that is nowhere to be found.

(1995: 84–85)

Responding to talk of responsibility, to its contradictions and **aporias** and practical political consequences, is therefore an urgent task for business ethics, but one that has only just begun (see Chapter 8).

Rules It is impossible to imagine organisations without some sort of rules, but what about business, and what about **ethics**? In some accounts, business cannot be a rule-governed activity at all, since it simply reflects the survival of the fittest and the hidden hand of proper selfishness. In markets, there are no rules, only choices. Running in parallel with this formulation, we have a view of ethics as that form of thought and action that imposes a rule on business. **Business ethics** is about stopping businesses from doing things they would otherwise rather like to do. If markets are about untrammelled desire, then ethics is about the calculation that follows from conscience.

This sort of interpretation is fairly common in business ethics. **Kant**'s philosophy is represented as following the rules of the categorical imperative; **utilitarianism** is understood as a sort of managerial calculus which can ensure that all stakeholders have their wants optimised; and **virtue** theory becomes the listing of characteristics that need to be cultivated within wise business people. By following these rules, the three steps to happiness, you can be good (and perhaps even wealthy too). But let us reverse this description. Rather than thinking that the unruly market is best left ungoverned whilst the heart is best ruled, perhaps the opposite might be true? Markets are sets of rules after all. They determine who can buy and who can sell, what can be bought and what can be sold, where these things can be bought and sold, how the parties establish some mechanism of exchange and expectations of information, acceptable levels of monopoly sellers or monopsonistic buyers, the degree of formalisation or professionalisation, the level of state intervention, the commonly expected time horizons and (perhaps most importantly) definitions of success or failure. To think of markets, in their wide diversity, as being unruly is actually deeply misleading. But perhaps so too is the rather repressive idea that ethics must be about rules, about prescriptions that are intended to determine certain forms of behaviour. After all, if they are merely rules, then what makes ethics any different from playing a game, or adhering to the law? Simply because someone did not cheat at chess, and never drove above the speed limit does not make them ethical, any more than following orders is always ethical.

175

So perhaps the economy of ethics governing **market managerialism** might be productively rethought as ethics being constrained by market managerialism. It is precisely the formal and informal 'rules' by which business and organisations operate that ethics questions, and attempts to open up to alternatives. That we are so often ruled by these rules, and do not question the common sense of the bottom line or the legitimacy of hierarchical authority, seems to reflect a loss of ethical nerve. This is not to suggest that we can somehow do without rules. That would be a very odd conclusion, and one that would make all forms of organisation (including language) somehow unethical in themselves. Rules, for markets, for organisations and for behaviour are clearly necessary. Society must be defended, yet the moment that ethics stops questioning these rules, it stops being ethics and becomes mere puppetry.

Techne Famously, **Aristotle** suggested that art imitates nature (1984b: 194a22) and 'art' is the usual translation of the Greek word '*techne*'. Other possible translations are 'craft', 'skill', and so on. Popular words such as technique or technology have their etymological origin in *techne*. Aristotle's claim is not as straightforward as it seems. It is true, *techne* imitates nature, but later he also claims that *techne* 'in some cases completes what nature cannot bring to a finish, and in others imitates nature' (1984b: 199a15–17). The relationship between both is therefore quite complex (as always in philosophy): if *techne* would merely imitate nature, then it would be subservient to it. It is, however, bringing nature to a completion. What does this mean?

The idea is not that *techne* stands for the production or manufacturing of something out of nothing. It is rather that it allows something in what is already there (that is, nature) to come to the fore in all its truthfulness. What lies hidden can now be seen. Martin Heidegger often claimed that this is what truth (in the Greek sense at least) is all about: what lies concealed should be brought out in the open. This process of 'unconcealment' is exactly truth. Insofar as *techne* is able to bring about this process, it is closely related to truth.

This is remarkable. For many of us, words like technique and technology have hardly any relation with truth. They refer to what is instrumental and, some would argue, inauthentic. A neo-Aristotelian, however, would probably claim that technique and technology have lost their *techne* for they have lost their truth. For Aristotle himself, many human activities can be described as *technai*. In other words, when a person exercises his skills in science, in rhetoric, in reasoning, and so on, then something truthful and authentic about this person will be brought to light. And what about ethics? Ethics is also an art. Only in this sense is ethics rooted in truth. This is an understanding that we, citizens in the contemporary corporate **capitalist** world, have almost lost completely when we discuss ethics.

Technocrat(ic) Max **Weber** made an important distinction between two sorts of rational action. Instrumentally rational action is based on a calculation about the best way to achieve a particular goal, whilst value rational action is based on the overriding importance of a particular set of ideas. Most complex tasks, such as building bridges and running universities, require both. A decision has to be made concerning the value of the bridge or university, and then many **bureaucratic** and technical decisions need to be made to make it happen. Hence, one of the consequences of complex organisation (from the pyramids to the concentration camps) is that many people may be involved in a project but have little knowledge or understanding about the values that originally animated it.

The word 'technocrat' would generally be applied to those manager-technicians who apply their knowledge to such projects, and nowadays it implies a certain narrow arrogance. (Though in the USA in the 1920s a technocracy of experts was seen as a progressive opposition to a government of lackeys for big **business**.) In an important sense, all but the most senior managers could be termed technocrats, since they rarely set their own goals, and instead apply their knowledge to action motivated by the values of others.

A technocratic society would be a society of bureaucrats, of people who follow specific sets of rules that apply to their domain. Though it is important not to simply dismiss rule following as somehow unethical, to only follow rules without thinking about them turns you, as **Kant** has suggested, into a puppet or an automaton. In that sense, it is difficult to see the technocrat as opening up any space for ethical decision since they are primarily concerned with a narrow sense of technique. Not that this is a new problem. Plato, in the *Statesman*, has Socrates engaged in a conversation with a stranger. The stranger has been discussing various arts and crafts (*techne*) such as navigation, medicine, generalship, painting, carpentry, divination, draught-playing, rearing horses, and so on:

> Stranger: 'I say, if all these things were done in this way according to written regulations, and not according to art, what would be the result?'
> Socrates: 'All the arts would utterly perish, and could never be recovered because enquiry would be unlawful. And human life, which is bad enough already, would then become utterly unendurable'.
>
> (Plato, 1999: 299)

Technique is essential in all matters if they are to be done well, but writing a book on ethics would be pointless if technique was all that was required. Business ethics has often been keen on the idea of ethical codes and statements that present a technocratic solution to the problem of ethics (Willmott, 1998). But can ethics be reduced to conformity with a code? Can a great work of art be made by reading a 'how to' book?

Textbooks In its original meaning, a textbook was a classic work with wide spaces in between the lines in order to allow for explanatory comments to be written in the spaces. Like a textile, the words of the author and of the commentator were woven together, in tension with each other. Nowadays, the texture of textbooks is altogether more tightly woven. Multinational publishing conglomerates make very large amounts of money by selling texts, and in order to do so they must insist (in their marketing at least) that this is the book that will tell you everything you need to know. There will be no spaces for the reader to think in, or if they do exist they will be 'self study questions' which are tightly framed in case thought should escape from its box. This textbook is not a textbook. Paradox. Think for yourself.

Utilitarianism   This can be defined in three ways:

1. A radical and far-reaching form of thought that encourages us to rid ourselves of **common sense** assumptions about 'good' and instead concentrate on making the maximum number of people happy. A sharp challenge to anyone who would put some value over another in the name of 'natural law' or 'human nature'. Never mind about the waffle, what can we do and what are the likely consequences? If business ethicists were really utilitarians, then they would immediately begin to question much of what passes for business ethics. (Particularly its various attempts to defend the interests of managers and shareholders, as if they were more important than those of workers and **communities**.)

2. An anti-human administrative ethic that ignores all the distinctive ways in which human beings construct their own sense of what it is to be good. An ethics for monkeys who can count, and who are deluded enough to believe that the application of rules is the same as being good. An obsession with social engineering using 'facts', when facts are always contested and all forms of paternalist intervention are doomed to fail. If business ethicists really understood utilitarianism they would immediately recognise that its Machiavellian doctrines should have no place within a discipline that attempts to encourage hard thinking about intentions, character and generosity.

3. A highly contested ethical-political doctrine, associated with **Bentham** and **Mill**, and generally summarised as the search for the greatest good of the greatest number.

Utopia   Thomas More's (1516) book *Utopia* coined a word that was based on a pun. Utopia is both 'no-place' (*outopia*) and 'good-place' (*eutopia*). It is somewhere we might want to be and somewhere that doesn't exist. To call someone a utopian is often to brand them as unrealistic and impractical. Yet, history is littered with utopian schemes and plans. From the grandiose dreams of Soviet and Chinese communism, European fascism and capitalist versions of globalisation, the attempt to remake the world according to some sort of blueprint seems to have been a characteristic feature of modern life. Smaller utopian settlements have abounded too, whether these were the factory villages of industrialists like Robert Owen or attempts to found alternative economies and societies (see Kumar, 1987; Parker, Fournier and Reedy, forthcoming). Many of these alternatives have represented different understandings of organising, democracy, exchange, and so on and are hence of great interest as a counter to uncritical celebrations of **market managerialism**.

The paradox of utopianism is nicely expressed by Oscar Wilde: 'A map of the world that does not include Utopia is not even worth glancing at, for it leaves out the one country at which Humanity is always landing. And when Humanity lands there, it looks out, and, seeing a better country, sets sail' (in Carey, 1999: 314). As with so many fictional utopias, they seem pleasant until you begin to think about living there. In some sense, then, rather than being impractical, utopias are often rather too practical. In providing the recipes and instructions for the good life, they end up delivering a **technocratic** version of **ethics** and **politics**, one in which choices and freedoms are variously circumscribed or delineated in the name of a greater good (ten Bos, 2000). But the promise of utopia still remains, and much utopian thinking grows from a restlessness with the present and the hope that things might be different. Hence our discussion at the beginning of Chapter 9 concerning the difference between (capitalised) Utopias that are closed and utopias that are open. Much like the rainbow's end, or the horizon, utopia is somewhere best kept in mind but never arrived at. If it did exist, we would not want to be there. By the way, Thomas More was very much aware of this.

Virtue The word virtue has masculine connotations. *Vir* is man. The road between virility and virtue has therefore always been a short one. People like Plato and **Aristotle** simply did not think about women when they were talking about the good and the bad. **Business ethics**, however, is politically correct enough to remedy this. Even business women can be virtuous nowadays and business men who do not believe this are clearly not virtuous (although they think of themselves as virile). But what does this word – virtue – mean? And how does it relate to duty?

Aristotle claimed that virtuousness is a quality that you can achieve by means of exercise. Exercises will help you to develop your natural capacities. **Kant** would not deny this, but he would hasten to add that morality as such is not a matter of training and exercise but a matter of doing your duty (which he has formulated in terms of the categorical imperative). The problem is that Aristotle suggests that by doing exercises a person can go from a lesser state of virtuousness to a higher state of virtuousness. Okay, says Kant, but this is not to say that you will improve your morality. Doing your duty is not so much a matter of degree as a matter of all or nothing: either you do your duty or you do not do it. Morality is obedience and not mere exercise.

For Aristotle, virtuousness and desire should be in line with each other. Kant does not rule this out, but he would simply claim that desire is morally irrelevant. Admittedly, it is possible that desire and duty can go hand in hand with each other, that is to say, that you desire to do your duty, but it is also possible that duty goes against what you desire. And this possibility does not make the duty in any way whatsoever less important or less absolute. Any reasonable mind (rather than a desiring mind) understands this. And it also understands that it is reason alone that makes human beings equal and not emotion, desire, tradition or habit. If we want a universally acceptable ethics, we would be well-advised to opt for reason.

Virtuousness, Aristotle believes, is a quality for which the person will be praised and honoured. It is very important to understand that in Aristotle virtuousness is something that can be seen and that is open to the public. Kant believes that this is very unwise. If the public claims that something is morally acceptable, is it then morally acceptable? At the heart of Kant's strictures is an understanding that morality, if it is worthy of the name, can never be relative to particular groupings or traditions. After all, the public may vary. The mafia has its virtues. So do street gangs in Los Angeles, business people in Silicon Valley, and business ethicists like Solomon and Bowie. According to Kant, however, all these people do not tell the reasonable mind anything about how to conduct a morally good life. For Kant, the public are not the same as our own innermost conscience and reason. What counts is the inner disposition.

For Aristotle, virtuousness is a way of actualising the self. It is, in other words, a one-way road to happiness. Kant would say that morality is not about happiness and once more he offers a perfectly lucid (albeit deeply Christian) argument for this: if morality would be about happiness, then the unhappy person has no reason to abide by it and this cannot be true.

Is all this to say that Kant simply wants to jettison the idea of a virtue? No, but he claims that the concept can only be morally relevant if it is freed from any link to emotion, habit, public or training. In Kant's own words, ethics is only morally relevant if it is freed from anything 'heteronomous'. Virtuousness is not what others think is good about my behaviour or what feels good to me but about what I autonomously decide and wish. For Kant, virtue is the inner disposition to abide by duties that I rationally comprehend and endorse. Whether this is still a masculine conception of virtuousness, we would like to leave to you to decide.

Weber, Max (1864–1920) Max Weber is often given credit, along with Emile Durkheim and Karl **Marx**, of being one of the founders of modern sociology. He is widely known in **business** studies for his list of the characteristics of **bureaucracy**, which sets out the terms of routinised domination carried out on the basis of rational-legal (as opposed to traditional and charismatic) authority (see Weber, 1948: 196–244). Weber is perhaps less well known to students of business for his analysis of the emergence of modern **capitalism**, which appears in a very accessible and short book called *The Protestant Ethic and the Spirit of Capitalism* (Weber, 1930). In this book Weber also describes the process of rationalisation which is associated with bureaucracy, and argues that a specific **character** ('the protestant ethic') is significant in the emergence of capitalism. Weber is often treated as if he were either a defender of bureaucracy and capitalism, or as if he simply thought that these were necessary evils. A more subtle reading suggests that Weber is ambivalent or dialectical in his approach, seeing both sides to the issue. Such a reading enables us to understand how Weber marvels at bureaucracy, proclaiming its 'technical superiority over any other form of organization', and that 'bureaucracy inevitably accompanies modern mass democracy' (1948: 214, 224), while at the same time finding rationalisation responsible for the 'disenchantment of the world' and bureaucracy becoming an 'iron cage' (1948: 155; 1930: 181).

180

From the point of view of **business ethics**, perhaps the most important reader of Weber today is Paul du Gay, whose book *In Praise of Bureaucracy* (2000) offers a powerful argument against those who dismiss bureaucracy out of hand. Du Gay's arguments are also important because of the way that he stresses that any social organisation, including bureaucracy, involves a specific ***ethos***, a way of living in the world, and that the bureaucratic *ethos* involves some quite specific moral values, some of which we may want to defend.

Be this as it may, for us it remains difficult to see how bureaucratic life might enthuse people. To put it more bluntly, why would we want to *praise* (rather than *defend*) a necessary evil?

◪ Further reading

WHY READ?

It is customary for textbooks to include a section at the end in which the authors recommend some books which students could read. There are several purposes for this kind of thing. Sometimes, this is a chance for the author to show how clever they are, by making a massive list of books that they might or might not have read. In fact, because suggestions for further reading often look like this, the three of us disagreed about whether we should offer further reading or not.

Obviously, in the end we decided to offer some suggestions for further readings, but we wanted to make clear why we are doing this. We insist that the purpose of this list is to give you some ideas of what you could read if you wanted to follow up on the ideas that we explore in each of the chapters of the book. But most importantly, we have been arguing throughout this book that reading is a highly contested matter. We have shown, for example, that it is possible to read writers such as Bentham, Mill, Kant, Aristotle, Friedman, Solomon and Bowie in ways that are very different. We have, at our boldest, tried to offer the possibility of reading business ethics itself in a different way.

When we say this, we are not saying that you can read books in any old way that you like. There are protocols of scholarship which we do not propose to abandon, and we hope that we have not strayed too far from these in our book. If we have, then there is no doubt that reviewers or readers or any other commentator will let us know. Scholarship always involves a contesting of the ideas of others, and hence trying to find different ways of reading texts and understanding things. In recent years, in particular since the Second World War, there has been a lot of talk across the social sciences about what 'reading' means. Writing in the 1960s, Louis Althusser wrote:

> I venture to suggest that our age threatens to one day appear in the history of human culture as marked by the most dramatic and difficult trial of all, the discovery and training in the meaning of the 'simplest' acts of existence: seeing, listening, speaking, reading.

(1968a: 15)

Perhaps Althusser is a bit melodramatic, but he puts in stark terms the radical nature of a reflection on the meaning of reading. And certainly a lot of thought has been put into thinking about the meaning of reading. We want to make three points here about reading, which might be useful to understanding how we are making arguments in our book. These points might also be useful when you are reading, and when you think about reading.

First, reading involves a relation to alterity, that is, to otherness. When you read you discover things about the world and you discover concepts that you never could have formulated yourself. Even when you sit alone in your room reading, reading is a radically social act. It involves immersion in a culture of books, and involves prior knowledge of a lot of things that are outside you. Reading also can, quite literally, transport you to other places, even from the comfort of your armchair. It can invite you to see the world from the eyes of an Other. It can invite you to see the world of others. It can invite you to see as an Other.

Second, and as a consequence of the first point, there is something about reading that is fundamentally a matter of ethics. If ethics is, as Levinas argues, a relation of openness to the Other, reading is one of the ways that we can encounter the Other. It is not the only way. We can see others on the television, or we can go out into the wide world and see for ourselves. But by reading we are involved, some have argued, in a crucially ethical relation – a relation with others and other ideas which threaten to unsettle our convictions and take us somewhere else. The German philosopher Peter Sloterdijk (2001) has argued that a book somehow resembles a message that is put in a bottle and given to the ocean in the hope that one day an unknown friend will find it and open it. He even claims that the possibility of books to turn strangers into friends is a key element of all communitarian and humanitarian ethics.

Third, a relation of openness to the Other requires that we put aside many of our assumptions before we read. If we think that we know what a book will say before we open it, we should not even bother opening it, and we should not pretend that we know anything about what it contains. If we want to read, we have to have a disposition of openness to the Other that we will encounter in that book. We have to be prepared to be caught off our guard, to have our mind changed. Partly what we have been trying to do in this book is to create the possibility of thinking about business ethics in a different way. This involves setting aside a set of assumptions. The assumption that business ethics is necessarily a good thing, for example. If we can work on that task of setting aside assumptions, and put our common sense to one side, we can see that there are other paths less travelled but ones that can be explored.

It is with the intention of inviting you on that path that we suggest the following books. But more important than which books you read is the matter of *how* you read them – hopefully, with a mind open to paradox and with a readiness to be unsettled by the friend who comes out of the pages.

CHAPTER 1 – INTRODUCTION: AGAINST BUSINESS ETHICS

If you are starting out on business ethics, standard textbooks in the area include Beauchamp and Bowie (2004), Boatright (2003), Crane and Matten (2004), De George (2004) and Petrick and Quinn (1997).

You can get an introduction to the field by looking at edited collections, such as Bowie (2002), Frederick (1999), Shaw (2003) and White (1993), or the more critically oriented Parker (1998).

There are now also a range of collections looking at business ethics in relation to specific topics, such as the natural environment (Crane, 2000), information technology (De George, 2003), accounting (Duska and Duska, 2003) and computers (Erman, Wiliams and Shauf, 1997).

Instructors may find it useful to consult collections of case studies, such as Beauchamp (2004) and Beauchamp and Bowie (2004) and the reflections in Megone and Robinson (2002).

For an introduction to some of the broad philosophical sources that we draw on throughout this book, you may wish to consult Adorno (2000), Gibbs (2000) and Wyschogrod and McKenny (2003).

CHAPTER 2 – COMMON SENSE BUSINESS ETHICS

If you want to know something about the general history of the business organisation, from a fairly conventional point of view, have a look at Micklethwait and Wooldridge (2003). More contemporary and critical accounts can be found in Bakan (2004), Beder (2000) and Frank (2000).

Adam Smith's *The Wealth of Nations* (originally published in 1776) is often said to be the founding text of the common sense of business. However, if you read it you will see just how ambivalent Smith was about the virtues of big business. One might also read *The Wealth of Nations* in the light of Smith's earlier major work *The Theory of Moral Sentiments* (originally published in 1759).

The common sense of business ethics is perhaps best understood by beginning with Carr (1968) and Friedman (1970), and then having a look at Bowie (1993) or Arthur (2003).

Ideas about the cultural representation of business can be found in Hassard and Holliday (1998), Parker (2002a), Rhodes (2001; 2002; 2004) and Rhodes and Westwood (forthcoming).

On science and the relationship between truth claims and different scientific methods, see Chalmers (1999). For a general and popular introduction to philosophy, see Hospers (1996), and for an argument as to why philosophy might matter, see Adorno (1998). On the relationship between philosophy and organisation, see Jones and ten Bos (forthcoming).

184

For clear and short introductions to conventional ethical philosophy see Blackburn (2001), Graham (2004) or MacIntyre (1967).

CHAPTER 3 – 'BUSINESS ETHICS' I: CONSEQUENCES

Mary Warnock's collection *Utilitarianism* (1962) brings together many of the key writings, particularly Mill's essay on Bentham. Short accounts of the key ideas can be found in Pettit's chapter in the useful collection edited by Singer (1991) or in Snoeyenbos and Humber's chapter in the collection edited by Frederick (1999). See also Arrington (1998) and Graham (2004). More detailed considerations can be found in Lyons (1965), Parfit (1984) and Smart and Williams (1973).

For more general commentaries on the meanings and limits of utilitarian logic and its connections with market managerialism, see Bauman (1989), MacIntyre (1981) and Poole (1991).

Freeman (1984; 1994) and Carroll (1979; 1991; 1998) are useful sources for stakeholder theory, and a good summary of the field appears in McEwan (2001). Milton Friedman (1962; 1970) is typically set up as the nemesis of stakeholder theory, but after reading Chapter 8 of our book, you might think critically about this set up.

CHAPTER 4 – 'BUSINESS ETHICS' II: INTENTIONS

The starting point for any discussion of duty, intention and deontological ethics is the work of Immanuel Kant. Kant's work is available in several editions, but the best single collection of his ethical writing in English is the Cambridge University Press volume *Practical Philosophy*, which contains the major ethical works as well as several other shorter pieces. The same publisher has now produced a comprehensive collection of Kant's lectures on ethics, from transcriptions by his students (Kant, 1997).

The major representative of Kantian business ethics, who we criticised in Chapter 4, is Norman Bowie, who has published a series of essays and a book which presents what he calls 'Kantian business ethics'. In our book, we have commented critically on Bowie's work, but we hope you will consult his work and make up your own mind. See, for example, his book (Bowie, 1999a) and the articles (Bowie, 1993; 1998; 1999b; 2000).

You will find numerous introductory books on Kant's ethics, which might also be a useful place to start. You might consult, for example, the provocative and highly readable discussion by Cummiskey (1996). For useful sources that provide a sophisticated rendering of Kant's view on ethics and morality, see the essays in the useful collection edited by Timmons (2002). Taking these ideas further, we would also recommend a reading of Adorno's (2000) lectures, which are based around a discussion of Kant's ethics and an assessment of the relevance of this to modern organised life.

185

Advanced readers may consult the second chapter of Deleuze (1984). See also the beautiful speculative meditations on Kant in Lingis (1998). On the conflict between two categorical imperatives, Derrida (1995) is a useful source. On the relation between Kant and Levinas, see Llewelyn (2000).

CHAPTER 5 – 'BUSINESS ETHICS' III: VIRTUES

The starting point for virtue ethics is Aristotle, and the crucial book is the *Nichomachean Ethics*; although it is useful to refer to the *Eudemian Ethics*, the attributed *Magna Moralia*, and related works such as the *Politics*. The best version of these in English is the Jonathon Barnes' *Complete Works of Aristotle*, but many cheaper paperbacks are also available.

There are plenty of excellent books on Aristotle. We suggest Bartlett and Collins (1999) and Nussbaum (1994, especially Chapters 2 and 3).

In the field of business ethics, you should read the work of Robert Solomon (1992; 1993; 1999b; 2004). Also important as a starting point is MacIntyre (1981) and Iain Mangham (1995) and the responses to him in an issue of *Organization* (1995).

For the most exciting contemporary thinking on community, see the powerful work of Agamben (1993b) and Nancy (1991). You may also wish to read works such as Rancière's *Short Voyages to the Land of the People* (2003), Derrida (2000; 2001) and the essays in Part Three of Derrida (2002). Finally, there are important considerations on community and the commonality in Hardt and Negri (2004).

CHAPTER 6 – THE MEANING OF ETHICS

Thinking about the way that objects present themselves to consciousness, you might well start with Bachelard's *Psychoanalysis of Fire* (1938), thinking about the way that the obstacles to the understanding of fire by chemists are related to the understanding of ethics by business ethicists.

For an introduction to phenomenology, see Moran (1999) and also the reader edited by Mooney and Moran (2001). You should use these as starting points to guide you into the vast area of phenomenology.

We have found it useful in this book to introduce the question of the meaning of ethics through the work of Levinas. For an accessible way into his work, you might want to begin with collections of interviews such as Levinas (1985; 2001). His key books are *Totality and Infinity* (1961) and *Otherwise than Being* (1974).

For a useful introduction to Levinas, see Davis (1996) and for explanation and critique see Peperzak (1993; 1998; 2002).

The most important development of Levinas' work in recent years is that of Derrida, whose early criticism (1964) and later work rest heavily on Levinas (see Derrida, 1995; 2000). Writing directly on Levinas, also see Derrida (1991; 1999). In relation to business ethics and corporate social responsibility following Levinas and Derrida, see Roberts (2001; 2003) and Jones (2003a).

CHAPTER 7 – DENYING ETHICS I: BUREAUCRACY

Arendt's book *Eichmann in Jerusalem* (1994) and then Bauman's (1989) *Modernity and the Holocaust*, both beautifully written pieces of social commentary, cover many of the issues in this chapter. Also see Arendt (2003) and Bauman (1993). MacIntyre (1981) articulates similar issues but from within a neo-Aristotelian approach. The various editions of Ritzer (1996) also illustrate the Weberian aspects of these ideas in a very accessible way, as does Power (1998).

Paul du Gay (2000) probably provides the best critique of Bauman and MacIntyre, and does much to show what an important and perceptive writer Max Weber was. The best short collection of Weber's writing is *From Max Weber* edited by Gerth and Mills (Weber, 1948), but a more comprehensive edition is the Roth and Wittich edition of *Economy and Society* (Weber, 1978).

On the effects of bureaucracy, see Whyte (1956) and Marcuse (1964). On the connections between bureaucracy and utilitarianism, see Poole (1991). On Milgram's experiments, see Milgram (1974) and for a commentary and account of their wider context, see Slater (2004).

CHAPTER 8 – DENYING ETHICS II: GLOBAL CAPITAL

For information on the protests against the WTO in Cancún and other cities, there is much information available online. You will find vastly differing accounts of these events, and you will find interesting repetition (often of incorrect information) even in the major and apparently respectable media. The only solution is to read carefully and critically, and in addition to major news sources (such as the BBC, which has archives at www.bbc.org), you should also read the reports of organisations such as Food First (www.foodfirst.org) and Global Exchange (www.globalexchange.org). The Independent Media Centre is a must (www.indymedia.org).

Debate over the responsibility of business is normally set up in a debate between Friedman (1962; 1970) and various representatives of stakeholder theory, of which Freeman (1984) is a classic source (see also Freeman, 1994). It is essential that you read these original sources rather than relying on commentators because, as we argue in Chapter 8, there is more to these texts than is often noticed.

There are now numerous books including critiques of neoliberalism. As a way into these debates, accessible sources include Bello (2002), Callinicos (2003) and Chomsky (1999). On Seattle and Genoa, respectively, see Yuen, Katsiaficas and Burton-Rose (2001) and One-Off Press (2001), and for a more general overview, see Yuen, Katsiaficas and Burton-Rose (2004). For introductions of the movement in general, see Klein (2002) and Kingsnorth (2003). If you take an interest in what all these writers rail against, you should visit the various websites of the World Bank (www.worldbank.org), IMF (www.imf.org) and WTO (www.wto.org).

On commodity fetishism, read Marx (1976: 163–177) and the commentary in Balibar (1995: Chapter 3). For excellent discussions, see Agamben (1993a: Chapters 6–10) and Žižek (1997: Chapter 3).

In relation to Critical Theory and ethics, see Adorno (2000) and Horkheimer (1993). For statistics on the situation of the global economy, you will find useful information in the World Bank's annual *World Development Indicators*, which are summarised in the *World Development Report*. Other useful sources include the *World Economic Outlook* published twice a year by the International Monetary Fund, *Vital Signs* published annually by the Worldwatch Institute (www.worldwatch.org) and *LABORSTA* prepared by the International Labor Organization (www.ilo.org).

CHAPTER 9 – BUSINESS ETHICS TODAY

On community, see Chapter 5 and also the suggestions for further reading related to that chapter above.

On trust, see Fukuyama (1995). For a more serious discussion of trust, see O'Neill (2002) and in relation to business, see Kramer (2003) and Sievers (2003).

On whistleblowing, see Punch (1996) and Perry (1998). On the way that we approach whistleblowing in this chapter, see Foucault (2001) and, in relation to this, Jack (2004). See also the interviews in Foucault (1996).

On responsibility, see Derrida, (1993b; 1995), Jonas (1984) and Keenan (1997). You may also consult the vast amount of literature on corporate social responsibility.

On cynicism, see Sloterdijk's important *Critique of Cynical Reason* (1988). See also Žižek (1989) and Bewes (1997). On communication, ethics and the public sphere, see Habermas (1990; 1992; 1993; 1998).

On whether or not one should keep ethics, see Nietzsche (1887) and Caputo (1993) and the editorial introduction and conclusion to Parker (1998).

CHAPTER 10 – CONCLUSION: FOR BUSINESS ETHICS

Business ethics is, if anything, a management fashion. See, for two entirely different kinds of discussion of management fashions Micklethwait and Wooldridge (1996) and ten Bos (2000). Since Foucault plays a rather important role in this chapter, we hope you will start reading his works. There is plenty of his work available in English, but you may wish to start with biographies about his work (for two contrasting examples, see Macey, 1993 and Halperin, 1995). The temptation to mention many more texts than we have is strong, but by now, at the very end of this book, we are sure that we have mentioned far too many titles. Ethics, after all, is something you *do* rather than merely read about. We just hope that the realms of reflection and action will, in the best Aristotelian tradition, have an impact on each other.

References

Abercrombie, Nicholas, Stephen Hill and Bryan Turner (1986) *Sovereign Individuals of Capitalism*. London: Allen and Unwin.

Adorno, Theodor (1973) *Negative Dialectics*, trans. E B. Ashton. London: Routledge.

Adorno, Theodor (1974) *Minima Moralia: Reflections from Damaged Life*, trans. E. F. N. Jeffcott. London: Verso.

Adorno, Theodor (1998) 'Why still philosophy?' in *Critical Models*, trans. Henry Pickford. New York: Columbia University Press.

Adorno, Theodor (2000) *Problems of Moral Philosophy*, trans. Rodney Livingstone. Oxford: Polity.

Adorno, Theodor and Max Horkheimer (1969) *Dialectic of Enlightenment*, trans. John Cumming. New York: Continuum.

Agamben, Giorgio (1993a) *Stanzas: Word and Phantasm in Western Culture*. Minneapolis: University of Minnesota Press.

Agamben, Giorgio (1993b) *The Coming Community*, trans. Michael Hardt. Minneapolis: University of Minnesota Press.

Agamben, Giorgio (1999a) *Potentialities: Collected Essays in Philosophy*, trans. Daniel Heller-Roazen. Stanford, CA: Stanford University Press.

Agamben, Giorgio (1999b) *Remnants of Auschwitz: The Witness and the Archive*, trans. Daniel Heller-Roazen. New York: Zone Books.

Althusser, Louis (1968a) 'From "*Capital*" to Marx's philosophy' in Louis Althusser and Etienne Balibar, *Reading* Capital, trans. Ben Brewster. London: Verso.

Althusser, Louis (1968b) 'The Object of *Capital*' in Louis Althusser and Etienne Balibar, *Reading* Capital, trans. Ben Brewster. London: Verso.

Arendt, Hannah (1963/1994) *Eichmann in Jerusalem: A Report on the Banality of Evil*. London: Penguin.

Arendt, Hannah (2003) *Responsibility and Judgement*, ed. Jerome Kohn. New York: Random House.

Aristotle (1984a) 'Eudemian Ethics' in Jonathon Barnes (ed.) *Complete Works of Aristotle* (vol. 2). Princeton, NJ: Princeton University Press.

Aristotle (1984b) 'Metaphysics' in Jonathon Barnes (ed.) *Complete Works of Aristotle* (vol. 2). Princeton, NJ: Princeton University Press.

Aristotle (1984c) 'Nicomachean Ethics' in Jonathon Barnes (ed.) *Complete Works of Aristotle* (vol. 2). Princeton, NJ: Princeton University Press.

Aristotle (1984d) 'Politics' in Jonathon Barnes (ed.) *Complete Works of Aristotle* (vol. 2). Princeton, NJ: Princeton University Press.

Aristotle (1984e) 'Rhetoric' in Jonathon Barnes (ed.) *Complete Works of Aristotle* (vol. 2). Princeton, NJ: Princeton University Press.

Aristotle (1984f) 'Topics' in Jonathon Barnes (ed.) *Complete Works of Aristotle* (vol. 1). Princeton, NJ: Princeton University Press.

Arrington, Robert (1998) *Western Ethics: An Historical Introduction*. Oxford: Blackwell.

Arthur, Alex (2003) 'A utility theory of truth' *Organization*, 10(2): 205–221.

Bachelard, Gaston (1938/1964) *The Psychoanalysis of Fire*, trans. Alan Ross. Boston, MA: Beacon.

Badiou, Alain (2002) *Ethics: An Essay on the Understanding of Evil*, trans. Peter Hallward. London: Verso.

Bakan, Joel (2004) *The Corporation: The Pathological Pursuit of Profit and Power*. New York: Free Press.

Balibar, Etienne (1995) *The Philosophy of Marx*, trans. Chris Turner. London: Verso.

Bartlett, Robert and Susan Collins (1999) *Action and Contemplation: Studies in Moral and Political Thought of Aristotle*. Albany: State University of New York Press.

Bauman, Zygmunt (1989) *Modernity and the Holocaust*. Cambridge: Polity.

Bauman, Zygmunt (1993) *Postmodern Ethics*. Oxford: Blackwell.

Beauchamp, Tom (ed.) (2004) *Case Studies in Business, Society, and Ethics* (fifth edition). Englewood Cliffs, NJ: Pearson Prentice Hall.

Beauchamp, Tom and Norman Bowie (2004) *Ethical Theory and Business* (seventh edition). Upper Saddle River, NJ: Pearson Education.

Beder, Sharon (2000) *Selling the Work Ethic: From Puritan Pulpit to Corporate PR*. London: Zed Books.

Bell, Daniel (1960) *The End of Ideology: On the Exhaustion of Political Ideas in the Fifties*. Glencoe, IL: Free Press.

Bello, Walden (2002) *Deglobalization: Ideas for a New World Economy*. London: Zed Books.

Bentham, Jeremy (1983) *Deontology, Together with A Table of the Springs of Action and Article on Utilitarianism*. Oxford: Clarendon Press.

Bentham, Jeremy (1789/2001) 'An introduction to the principles of morals and legislation' in *Selected Writings on Utilitarianism*. Ware: Wordsworth.

Berlin, Isaiah (1969) *Four Essays on Liberty*. Oxford: Oxford University Press.

Bewes, Timothy (1997) *Cynicism and Postmodernity*. London: Verso.

Bierce, Ambrose (1911) *The Devil's Dictionary*. London: Bloomsbury.

Bird, Frederick Bruce (1996) *The Muted Conscience: Moral Silence and the Practice of Ethics in Business*. London: Quorum.

Blackburn, Simon (2001) *Being Good*. Oxford: Oxford University Press.

Boatright, Joan (2003) *Ethics and the Conduct of Business* (fourth edition). Englewood Cliffs, NJ: Prentice Hall.

Borgerson, Janet (2004) 'Learning from feminist ethics: Relationships, responsibility and experience'. Paper presented at the Inter-Disciplinary Corporate Social Responsibility Conference, Nottingham, 22–23 October.

Bové, José and François Dufour (2001) *The World is Not For Sale: Farmers Against Junk Food*, trans. Anna de Casparis. London: Verso.

Bowie, Norman (1993) 'The ethics of bluffing and poker' in Thomas White (ed.) *Business Ethics: A Philosophical Reader*. London: Macmillan.

Bowie, Norman (1998) 'A Kantian theory of meaningful work' *Journal of Business Ethics*, 17: 1083–1092.

Bowie, Norman (1999a) *Business Ethics: A Kantian Perspective*. Malden, MA: Blackwell.

191

Bowie, Norman (1999b) 'A Kantian approach to business ethics' in Robert Frederick (ed.) *A Companion to Business Ethics*. Oxford: Blackwell.

Bowie, Norman (2000) 'A Kantian theory of leadership' *The Leadership & Organization Development Journal*, 21(4): 185–193.

Bowie, Norman (ed.) (2002) *The Blackwell Guide to Business Ethics*. Oxford: Blackwell.

Braverman, Harry (1974) *Labor and Monopoly Capital*. New York: Monthly Review Press.

Brewer, Kathryn (1997) 'Management as a practice: A response to Alasdair MacIntyre' *Journal of Business Ethics*, 16(6): 825–833.

Callinicos, Alex (2003) *An Anti-Capitalist Manifesto*. Oxford: Polity.

Callon, Michel (ed.) (1998) *The Laws of the Markets*. Oxford: Blackwell.

Caputo, John (1993) *Against Ethics: Contributions to a Poetics of Obligation with Constant Reference to Deconstruction*. Bloomington, IN: Indiana University Press.

Carey, John (ed.) (1999) *The Faber Book of Utopias.* London: Faber and Faber.

Carnegie, Dale (1936) *How to Win Friends and Influence People*. New York: Simon and Schuster.

Carr, Albert (1968) 'Is business bluffing ethical?' *Harvard Business Review*, January/February: 143–153.

Carroll, Archie B. (1979) 'A three-dimensional conceptual model of corporate social performance' *Academy of Management Review*, 4(4): 497–505.

Carroll, Archie B. (1991) 'The pyramid of corporate social responsibility: Toward the moral management of organizational stakeholders' *Business Horizons*, July–August: 39–48.

Carroll, Archie B. (1998) 'The four faces of corporate citizenship' *Business and Society Review*, 100/101: 1–7.

Chalmers, A. F. (1999) *What is this Thing Called Science?* Buckingham: Open University Press.

Chomsky, Noam (1999) *Profit Over People: Neoliberalism and Global Order*. New York: Seven Stories Press.

Crane, Andrew (2000) *Marketing, Morality and the Natural Environment*. London: Routledge.

Crane, Andrew and Dirk Matten (2004) *Business Ethics: A European Perspective*. Oxford: Oxford University Press.

Cummiskey, David (1996) *Kantian Consequentialism*. New York: Oxford University Press.

Danaher, Kevin (2001) *10 Reasons to Abolish the IMF & World Bank*. New York: Seven Stories Press.

Daston, Lorraine and Katherine Park (1998) *Wonders and the Order of Nature, 1150–1750*. New York: Zone Books.

Davis, Colin (1996) *Levinas: An Introduction*. Oxford: Polity.

De George, Richard (ed.) (2003) *The Ethics of Information Technology and Business*. Oxford: Blackwell.

De George, Richard (2004) *Business Ethics* (sixth edition). Englewood Cliffs, NJ: Prentice Hall.

Deleuze, Gilles (1968/1994) *Difference and Repetition,* trans. Paul Patton. New York: Columbia University Press.

Deleuze, Gilles (1969) *Logic of Sense*, trans. Mark Lester. London: Continuum.

Deleuze, Gilles (1984) *Kant's Critical Philosophy: The Doctrine of the Faculties,* trans. Hugh Tomlinson and Barbara Habberjam. London: Athlone.

192

Derrida, Jacques (1964/1978) 'Violence and metaphysics: An essay on the thought of Emmanuel Levinas' in *Writing and Difference*, trans. Alan Bass. Chicago, IL: Chicago University Press.

Derrida, Jacques (1991) 'At this very moment in this work here I am', trans. Ruben Berezdivin, in Robert Benasconi and Simon Critchley (eds) *Re-reading Levinas*. London: Athlone.

Derrida, Jacques (1993a) *Aporias: Dying – Awaiting (One Another at) the 'Limits of Truth'*, trans. Thomas Dutoit. Stanford, CA: Stanford University Press.

Derrida, Jacques (1993b) 'Passions: "An oblique offering"', trans. David Wood in *On the Name*. Stanford, CA: Stanford University Press.

Derrida, Jacques (1995) *The Gift of Death*, trans. David Wills. Chicago, IL: University of Chicago Press.

Derrida, Jacques (1997) *Politics of Friendship*, trans. George Collins. New York: Verso.

Derrida, Jacques (1999) *Adieu to Emmanuel Levinas*, trans. Pascale-Anne Brault and Michael Naas. Stanford, CA: Stanford University Press.

Derrida, Jacques (2000) *Of Hospitality: Anne Dufourmantelle Invites Jacques Derrida to Respond*, trans. Rachel Bowlby. Stanford, CA: Stanford University Press.

Derrida, Jacques (2001) *Of Cosmopolitanism and Forgiveness*, trans. Mark Dooley and Michael Hughes. London: Routledge.

Derrida, Jacques (2002) *Negotiations: Interventions and Interviews, 1971–2001*, trans. Elizabeth Rottenberg. Stanford, CA: Stanford University Press.

Desmond, John (1998) 'Marketing and moral indifference' in Martin Parker (ed.) *Ethics and Organizations*. London: Sage.

Dickens, Charles (1854/1994) *Hard Times*. London: Penguin.

Diderot, Denis (ed.) (1751–1765) *Encylopédie, ou, dictionaire raisonné des sciences, des art et des métiers* (36 vols). Paris: Briasson.

Druker, Peter (1993) *Post-Capitalist Society*. New York: HarperBusiness.

du Gay, Paul (2000) *In Praise of Bureaucracy: Weber, Organisation, Ethics*. London: Sage.

Duska, Ronald and Brenda Duska (eds.) (2003) *Accounting Ethics*. Oxford: Blackwell.

Engstrom, Stephen (2002) 'The inner freedom of virtue' in Mark Timmons (ed.)*Kant's Metaphysics of Morals: Interpretative Essays*. Oxford: Oxford University Press.

Erman, David, Mary Williams and Michele Shauf (eds.) (1997) *Computers, Ethics, and Society* (second edition). Oxford: Oxford University Press.

Etzioni, Amitai (1993) *The Spirit of Community*. New York: Crown.

Fisher, Colin and Alan Lovell (2003) *Business Ethics and Values*. Harlow: Pearson Education.

Flaubert, Gustave (1880/1994) *Dictionary of Received Ideas*, trans. Geoffrey Wall. London: Penguin.

Forsyth, Donelson (1992) 'Judging the morality of business practices: The influence of personal moral philosophies' *Journal of Business Ethics*, 11(5): 461–470.

Foucault, Michel (1966/1970) *The Order of Things: An Archaeology of the Human Sciences*, trans. A. Sheridan Smith. London: Routledge.

Foucault, Michel (1984a/1985) *The Use of Pleasure: The History of Sexuality, Volume 2*, trans. Robert Hurley. London: Penguin.

Foucault, Michel (1984b/1986) *The Care of the Self: The History of Sexuality, Volume 3*, trans. Robert Hurley. London: Penguin.

Foucault, Michel (1996) *Foucault Live: Collected Interviews, 1961–1984*, ed. Sylvère Lotringer. New York: Semiotext(e).

Foucault, Michel (1997) *Ethics: Essential Works of Foucault, 1954–1984, Volume One*, ed. Paul Rabinow. New York: New Press.

Foucault, Michel (2001) *Fearless Speech*. Los Angeles, CA: Semiotext(e).

Fournier, Valérie (2002) 'Utopianism and the cultivation of possibilities: Grassroots movements of hope' in Martin Parker (ed.) *Utopia and Organization*. Oxford: Blackwell.

Frank, Thomas (2000) *One Market Under God: Extreme Capitalism, Market Populism and the End of Economic Democracy*. London: Secker & Warburg.

Frederick, Robert (ed.) (1999) *A Companion to Business Ethics*. Oxford: Blackwell.

Freeman, R. Edward (1984) *Strategic Management: A Stakeholder Approach*. London: Pitman.

Freeman, R. Edward (1994) 'The politics of stakeholder theory: Some future directions' *Business Ethics Quarterly*, 4(4): 409–422.

Freeman, R. Edward and Robert Phillips (1999) 'Business ethics: Pragmatism and postmodernism' in Robert Frederick (ed.) *A Companion to Business Ethics*. Oxford: Blackwell.

Friedman, Milton (1962) *Capitalism and Freedom*. Chicago, IL: University of Chicago Press.

Friedman, Milton (1970) 'The social responsibility of business is to increase its profits' *New York Times Magazine*, 13 September.

Fukuyama, Francis (1992) *The End of History and the Last Man*. London: Penguin.

Fukuyama, Francis (1995) *Trust: The Social Virtues and the Making of Prosperity*. New York: Free Press

Garsten, Christina and Christopher Grey (1997) 'How to become oneself: Discourses of subjectivity in post-bureaucratic organizations' *Organization* 4(2): 211–228.

Gibbs, Robert (2000) *Why Ethics? Signs of Responsibilities*. Princeton, NJ: Princeton University Press.

Godfrey, Richard, Gavin Jack and Campbell Jones (2004) 'Sucking, bleeding, breaking: On the dialectics of vampirism, capital and time' *Culture and Organization*, 10(1): 25–36.

Graham, Gordon (2004) *Eight Theories of Ethics*. London: Routledge.

Griseri, Paul (1998) *Managing Values: Ethical Change in Organisations*. London: Macmillan.

Habermas, Jürgen (1990) *Moral Consciousness and Communicative Action*, trans. Christian Lenhardt and Shierry Weber Nicholsen. Oxford: Polity.

Habermas, Jürgen (1992) *The Structural Transformation of the Public Sphere: An Inquiry into a Category of Bourgeois Society*, trans. Thomas Burger and Patrick Lawrence. Oxford: Polity.

Habermas, Jürgen (1993) *Justification and Application*, trans. Ciaran Cronin. Oxford: Polity.

Habermas, Jürgen (1998) *The Inclusion of the Other: Studies in Political Theory*, trans. Ciaran Cronin. Cambridge, MA: MIT Press.

Halperin, David (1995) *Saint Foucault: Towards a Gay Hagiography*. New York: Oxford University Press.

Hardt, Michael and Antonio Negri (2004) *Multitude: War and Democracy in the Age of Empire*. New York: Penguin.

Hassard, John and Ruth Holliday (eds.) (1998) *Organization/Representation: Work and Organizations in Popular Culture*. London: Sage.

Heidegger, Martin (1927/1962) *Being and Time*, trans. John Macquarrie and Edward Robinson. Oxford: Blackwell.

Heidegger, Martin (1978) 'What calls for thinking?' trans. David Farrell Krell, in David Farrell Krell (ed.) *Martin Heidegger: Basic Writings*. London: Routledge.

Held, David (1980) *Introduction to Critical Theory: Horkheimer to Habermas*. Oxford: Polity.

Held, David (2004) *Global Covenant: The Social Democratic Alternative to the Washington Consensus*. Oxford: Polity.

Hilberg, Raul (1992) *Perpetrators, Victims, Bystanders: The Jewish Catastrophe 1933–1945*. New York: Harper Collins.

Hofstadter, Richard (1963) *Anti-Intellectualism in American Life*. New York: Vintage.

Horkheimer, Max (1937/1972) 'Traditional and Critical Theory' in *Critical Theory: Selected Essays*, trans. Matthew O'Connell. New York: Continuum.

Horkheimer, Max (1993) 'Materialism and morality' in *Between Philosophy and Social Science: Selected Early Writings*, trans. G. Frederick Hunter, Mathew S. Kramer and John Torpey. Cambridge, MA: MIT Press.

Hospers, John (1996) *An Introduction to Philosophical Analysis*. London: Routledge.

Hutcheson, Francis (1725/2004) *An Inquiry Concerning the Original of our Ideas of our Ideas of Virtue or Moral Good in Two Treatises*, ed. Wolfgang Leidhold. Indianapolis, IN: Liberty Fund.

Jack, Gavin (2004) 'On speech, critique and protection' *ephemera: theory and politics in organization*, 4(2): 121–134.

Jack, Gavin and Alison Phipps (2005) *Tourism and Intercultural Exchange: Why Tourism Matters*. Clevedon: Channel View.

Jackall, Robert (1988) *Moral Mazes: The World of Corporate Managers*. New York: Oxford University Press.

Jay, Martin (1973) *The Dialectical Imagination: A History of the Frankfurt School and the Institute for Social Research, 1923–1950*. London: Heinemann.

Jonas, Hans (1984) *The Imperative of Responsibility: In Search of an Ethics for the Technological Age*, trans. Hans Jonas and David Herr. Chicago, IL: University of Chicago Press.

Jones, Campbell (2002) 'Foucault's inheritance/Inheriting Foucault' *Culture and Organization*, 8(3): 225–238.

Jones, Campbell (2003a) 'As if business ethics were possible, "within such limits". . .' *Organization*, 10(2): 223–248.

Jones, Campbell (2003b) 'Theory after the postmodern condition' *Organization*, 10(3): 503–525.

Jones, Campbell (2004) 'Jacques Derrida' in Stephen Linstead (ed.) *Organization Theory and Postmodern Thought*. London: Sage.

Jones, Campbell and Steffen Böhm (2003) 'From . . . to . . .' *ephemera: critical dialogues on organization*, 3(2): 90–94.

Jones, Campbell and René ten Bos (eds.) (forthcoming) *Philosophy and Organization*. London: Routledge.

Kant, Immanuel (1781/1998) *Critique of Pure Reason* (Cambridge Edition of the Works of Immanuel Kant), trans. Paul Guyer and Allen Wood. Cambridge: Cambridge University Press.

Kant, Immanuel (1784/1996) 'An answer to the question: What is enlightenment?' in *Practical Philosophy* (Cambridge Edition of the Works of Immanuel Kant), trans. Mary Gregor. Cambridge: Cambridge University Press.

Kant, Immanuel (1785/1996) 'Groundwork of the metaphysics of morals' in *Practical Philosophy* (Cambridge Edition of the Works of Immanuel Kant), trans. Mary Gregor. Cambridge: Cambridge University Press.

195

Kant, Immanuel (1788/1996) 'Critique of practical reason' in *Practical Philosophy* (Cambridge Edition of the Works of Immanuel Kant), trans. Mary Gregor. Cambridge: Cambridge University Press.

Kant, Immanuel (1790/2000) *Critique of the Power of Judgement* (Cambridge Edition of the Works of Immanuel Kant), trans. Paul Guyer and Eric Mathews. Cambridge: Cambridge University Press.

Kant, Immanuel (1795/1996) 'Toward perpetual peace' in *Practical Philosophy* (Cambridge Edition of the Works of Immanuel Kant), trans. Mary Gregor. Cambridge: Cambridge University Press.

Kant, Immanuel (1797/1996) 'The metaphysics of morals' in *Practical Philosophy* (Cambridge Edition of the Works of Immanuel Kant), trans. Mary Gregor. Cambridge: Cambridge University Press.

Kant, Immanuel (1997) *Lectures on Ethics* (Cambridge Edition of the Works of Immanuel Kant), trans. Paul Heath and J. B. Schneewind. Cambridge: Cambridge University Press.

Kaulingfreks, Ruud and René ten Bos (2005a) 'Are organizations bicycles? On hosophobia and neo-gnosticism in organizational thought' *Culture and Organization*, 11(2): 83–96.

Kaulingfreks, Ruud and René ten Bos (2005b) 'In praise of blowjobs' in Joanna Brewis, Stephen Linstead, David Boje and Tony O'Shea (eds.) *The Passion of Organizing*. Copenhagen: Abstrakt.

Keenan, Thomas (1997) *Fables of Responsibility: Aberrations and Predicaments in Ethics and Politics*. Stanford, CA: Stanford University Press.

Kersting, Wolfgang (1993) *Wohlgeordnete Freiheit: Immanuel Kant's rechts- und Sozialphilosophie*. Frankfurt: Suhrkamp

Kingsnorth, Paul (2003) *One No, Many Yeses: A Journey to the Heart of the Global Resistance Movement*. London: Free Press.

Kingwell, Mark (1998) *Better Living: In Pursuit of Happiness from Plato to Prozac*. Toronto: Viking.

Klein, Naomi (2000) *No Logo*. London: Flamingo.

Klein, Naomi (2002) *Fences and Windows*. London: Flamingo.

Knights, David and Darren McCabe (1998) 'What happens when the phone goes wild? Staff, stress and spaces for escape in a BPR telephone banking work regime' *Journal of Management Studies*, 34(3): 371–388.

Korten, David (1995) *When Corporations Rule the World*. London: Earthscan.

Kramer, Roderick (2003) 'The virtues of prudent trust' in Robert Westwood and Stewart Clegg (eds.) *Debating Organization: Point-Counterpoint in Organization Studies*. Oxford: Blackwell.

Kumar, Krishan (1987) *Utopia and Anti-Utopia in Modern Times*. Oxford: Blackwell.

Kumar, Krishan (1995) *From Post-Industrial to Post-Modern Society: New Theories of the Contemporary World*. Oxford: Blackwell.

Lawrence, Felicity (2004) *Not on the Label: What Really Goes Into the Food on Your Plate*. London: Penguin.

Legge, Karen (1995) *Human Resource Management: Rhetorics and Realities*. Basingstoke: Palgrave Macmillan.

Levinas, Emmanuel (1961/1969) *Totality and Infinity*, trans. Alponso Lingis. Pittsburgh, PA: Duquesne University Press.

Levinas, Emmanuel (1974/1981) *Otherwise than Being, or, Beyond Essence*, trans. Alponso Lingis. Pittsburgh, PA: Duquesne University Press.

Levinas, Emmanuel (1985) *Ethics and Infinity*, trans. Richard Cohen. Pittsburgh, PA: Duquesne University Press.

Levinas, Emmanuel (1999) *Alterity and Transcendence*, trans. Michael Smith. New York: Columbia University Press.

Levinas, Emmanuel (2001) *Is it Righteous to Be? Interviews with Emmanuel Levinas*, ed. Jill Robbins. Stanford, CA: Stanford University Press.

Limbs, Eric and Timothy Fort (2000) 'Nigerian business practices and their interfaces with virtue ethics' *Journal of Business Ethics*, 26(2): 169–179.

Lingis, Alphonso (1998) *The Imperative*. Bloomington, IN: Indiana University Press.

Llewelyn, John (2000) *The HypoCritical Imagination: Between Kant and Levinas*. London: Routledge.

Lukes, Steven (1985) *Marxism and Morality*. Oxford: Oxford University Press.

Lyons, David (1965) *Forms and Limits of Utilitarianism*. Oxford: Clarendon Press.

Macey, David (1993) *The Lives of Michel Foucault*. London: Vintage.

MacIntyre, Alisdair (1967) *A Short History of Ethics*. London: Routledge and Kegan Paul.

MacIntyre, Alisdair (1981) *After Virtue*. London: Duckworth.

Mangham, Iain (1995) 'MacIntyre and the manager' *Organization* 2(2): 181–204.

Marcos, Subcommandante (1996) 'Fourth declaration from the Lacandón jungle' in Tom Hayden (ed.) (2002) *The Zapatista Reader*. New York: Thunder's Mouth Press.

Marcuse, Herbert (1964) *One Dimensional Man*. London: Routledge and Kegan Paul.

Margalit, Avishai (1996) *The Decent Society*. Cambridge, MA: Harvard University Press.

Marx, Karl (1847/1955) *The Poverty of Philosophy*. London: Martin Lawrence.

Marx, Karl (1859/1970) *A Contribution to the Critique of Political Economy*. Moscow: Progress Publishers.

Marx, Karl (1867/1976) *Capital: A Critique of Political Economy, Volume One*, trans. Ben Fowkes. London: Penguin.

McEwan, Tom (2001) *Managing Values and Beliefs in Organisations*. London: Financial Times and Prentice Hall.

McGregor, Douglas (1960) *The Human Side of Enterprise*. New York: McGraw-Hill.

Megone, Chris and Simon Robinson (eds.) (2002) *Case Histories in Business Ethics*. London: Routledge.

Merton, Robert (1940/1957) 'Bureaucratic structure and personality' in *Social Theory and Social Structure*. Glencoe, IL: Free Press.

Micklethwait, John and Adrian Wooldridge (1996) *The Witch Doctors: What the Management Gurus are Saying, Why it Matters and How to Make Sense of It*. London: Heinemann.

Micklethwait, John and Adrian Wooldridge (2003) *The Company: A Short History of a Revolutionary Idea*. London: Weidenfeld and Nicolson.

Milgram, Stanley (1974) *Obedience to Authority: An Experimental View*. New York: Harper and Row.

Mill, John Stuart (1861/1972) 'Considerations on Representative Government' in H. B. Acton (ed.) *Utilitarianism*. London: Dent & Sons.

Mill, John Stuart (1869a/1962) 'Bentham' in Mary Warnock (ed.) *Utilitarianism*. London: Collins.

Mill, John Stuart (1869b/1997) *The Subjection of Women*. New York: Dover.

Mill, John Stuart (1873/1989) *Autobiography*. London: Penguin.

Mittal, Anuradha (2003) 'September 10, 2003: Daily report from Cancún #4' Food

First: Institute for Food and Development Policy. Online at: http://www.foodfirst. org/wto/reports/2003-09-11AM.php Accessed 20 July 2004.

Mooney, Tim and Dermot Moran (2001) *The Phenomenology Reader*. London: Routledge.

Moran, Dermot (1999) *Introduction to Phenomenology*. London: Routledge.

More, Thomas (1516/1965) *Utopia*. London: Penguin.

Murphy, Patrick (1999) 'Character and virtue ethics in international marketing: An agenda for managers, researchers and educators' *Journal of Business Ethics*, 18(1): 107–125.

Nancy, Jean-Luc (1991) *The Inoperative Community*, trans. Peter Connor, Lisa Garbus, Michael Holland and Simon Sawhney. Minneapolis: University of Minnesota Press.

Nancy, Jean-Luc (1997) 'What is to be done?', trans. Leslie Hill, in Phillipe Lacoue-Labarthe and Jean-Luc Nancy, *Retreating the Political*, ed. Simon Sparks. London: Routledge.

Nietzsche, Friedrich (1873/1979) 'On truth and lies in a nonmoral sense' in *Philosophy and Truth: Selections from Nietzsche's Notebooks of the Early 1870's*, trans. Daniel Breazale. Atlantic Highlands, NJ: Humanities Press International.

Nietzsche, Friedrich (1878/1986) *Human, all too Human*, trans. Richard Schacht. Cambridge: Cambridge University Press.

Nietzsche, Friedrich (1881/1982) *Daybreak: Thoughts on the Prejudices of Morality*, trans. R. J. Hollingdale. Cambridge: Cambridge University Press

Nietzsche, Friedrich (1886/1966) *Beyond Good and Evil: Prelude to a Philosophy of the Future*, trans. Walter Kaufmann. New York: Vintage.

Nietzsche, Friedrich (1887/1956) 'The geneaology of morals' in *The Birth of Tragedy and the Geneaology of Morals*, trans. Francis Golffing. New York: Anchor Books.

Nietzsche, Friedrich (1889/1990) *Twilight of the Idols/The Anti-Christ*, trans. R. J. Hollingdale. London: Penguin.

Nussbaum, Martha (1994) *The Therapy of Desire. Theory and Practice in Hellenistic Ethics*. Princeton, NJ: Princeton University Press.

O'Neill, Onora (2002) *A Question of Trust*. Cambridge: Cambridge University Press.

One-Off Press (2001) *On Fire: The Battle of Genoa and the Anti-Capitalist Movement*. oneoffpress.com

Parfit, Derek (1984) *Reasons and Persons*. Oxford: Oxford University Press.

Parker, Martin (ed.) (1998) *Ethics and Organizations*. London: Sage.

Parker, Martin (2000) *Organizational Culture and Identity*. London: Sage.

Parker, Martin (2002a) *Against Management: Organization in the Age of Managerialism*. Oxford: Polity.

Parker, Martin (ed.) (2002b) *Utopia and Organization*. Oxford: Blackwell.

Parker, Martin (2003a) 'Business, ethics and business ethics: Critical theory and negative dialectics' in Mats Alvesson and Hugh Willmott (eds.) *Studying Management Critically*. London: Sage.

Parker, Martin (2003b) 'Ethics, Politics and Organising', *Organization* 10(2): 187–203.

Parker, Martin, Valérie Fournier and Patrick Reedy (eds.) (forthcoming) *The Dictionary of Alternative and Utopian Organisation*. London: Zed Books.

Peperzak, Adriaan (1993) *To the Other: Introduction to the Work of Emmanuel Levinas*. West Lafayette, IN: Purdue University Press.

Peperzak, Adriaan (1998) *Beyond: The Philosophy of Emmanuel Levinas*. Evanston, IL: Northwestern University Press.

Peperzak, Adriaan (2002) 'Giving' in Edith Wyschogrod, Jean-Joseph Goux and Eric Boynton (eds.) *The Enigma of Gift and Sacrifice*, New York: Fordham University Press.

Perry, Nick (1998) 'Indecent exposures: Theorising whistleblowing' *Organization Studies*, 19(2): 235–257.

Peters, Tom and Robert Waterman (1982) *In Search of Excellence: Lessons from America's Best-Run Companies*. New York: Harper & Row.

Petrick, Joseph and John Quinn (1997) *Management Ethics: Integrity at Work*. London: Sage.

Plato (1954) 'The apology' in *The Last Days of Socrates*, trans. Hugh Tredennick. London: Penguin.

Plato (1999) *Statesman*, trans. Christopher Rowe. Indianapolis, IN: Hackett.

Poole, Ross (1991) *Morality and Modernity*. London: Routledge.

Power, Michael (1998) *The Audit Society: Rituals of Verification*. Oxford: Oxford University Press.

Punch, Maurice (1996) *Dirty Business: Exploring Corporate Misconduct*. London: Sage.

Rancière, Jacques (2003) *Short Voyages to the Land of the People*, trans. James Swenson. Stanford, CA: Stanford University Press.

Rhodes, Carl (2001) 'D'Oh: The Simpsons, popular culture and the organisational carnival' *Journal of Management Inquiry*, 10(4): 374–383.

Rhodes, Carl (2002) 'Coffee and the business of pleasure: The case of Harbucks vs Mr Tweek' *Culture and Organization*, 8(4): 293–306.

Rhodes, Carl (2004) 'Utopia in popular management writing and the music of Bruce Springsteen: Do you believe in the promised land?' *Consumption, Markets and Culture*, 7(1): 1–20.

Rhodes, Carl and Bob Westwood (forthcoming) *Critical Representations of Work and Organizations in Popular Culture*. London: Routledge.

Ritzer, George (1996) *The McDonaldization of Society* (revised edition). Thousand Oaks, CA: Pine Forge.

Roberts, John (2001) 'Corporate governance and the ethics of narcissus' *Business Ethics Quarterly*, 11(1): 109–127.

Roberts, John (2003) 'The manufacture of corporate social responsibility: Constructing corporate sensibility' *Organization*, 10(2): 249–265.

Rosenthal, Sandra and Rogene Bucholz (1999) *Rethinking Business Ethics: A Pragmatic Approach*. Oxford: Oxford University Press.

Roy, Arundhati (2004) 'Confronting empire' in Eddie Yuen, George Katsiaficas and Daniel Burton-Rose (eds.) *Confronting Capitalism: Dispatches from a Global Movement*. New York: Soft Skull Press.

Saint-Exupéry, Antoine de (1999) *The Little Prince*, trans. Katherine Woods. Harmondsworth: Penguin.

Saul, John Ralston (1994) *The Doubter's Companion: A Dictionary of Aggressive Common Sense*. New York: Free Press.

Schlosser, Eric (2002) *Fast Food Nation: What the All-American Meal is Doing to the World*. London: Penguin.

Schrijvers, Joep (2004) *The Way of the Rat: A Survival Guide to Office Politics*. London: Cyan Books.

Seabright, Paul (2004) *The Company of Strangers: A Natural History of Economic Life*. Princeton, NJ: Princeton University Press.

Seltzer, Mark (1992) *Bodies and Machines*. New York: Routledge.

Shanahan, Kevin and Michael Hyman (2003) 'The development of a virtue ethics scale' *Journal of Business Ethics*, 42: 197–208.

Shaw, William (ed.) (2003) *Ethics at Work: Basic Readings in Business Ethics*. Oxford: Oxford University Press.

Sievers, Burkard (2003) ' "Fool'd with hope, men favour the deceit", or, can we trust in trust?' in Robert Westwood and Stewart Clegg (eds.) *Debating Organization: Point-Counterpoint in Organization Studies*. Oxford: Blackwell.

Singer, Peter (ed.) (1991) *A Companion to Ethics*. Oxford: Blackwell.

Slater, Lauren (2004) *Opening Skinner's Box: Great Psychological Experiments of the 20th Century*. London: Bloomsbury.

Sloterdijk, Peter (1988) *Critique of Cynical Reason*, trans. Michael Eldred. Minneapolis: University of Minnesota Press.

Sloterdijk, Peter (1998) *Sphären I: Blasen*. Frankfurt am Main: Suhrkamp.

Sloterdijk, Peter (2001) 'Regeln für den Menschenpark. Ein Antwortschreiben zu Heideggers Brief über den Humanismus' in *Nicht Gerettet Versuche nach Heidegger*. Frankfurt am Main: Suhrkamp.

Smart, J. J. C. and Bernard Williams (1973) *Utilitarianism: For and Against*. Cambridge: Cambridge University Press.

Smith, Adam (1759/2000) *The Theory of Moral Sentiments*. New York: Prometheus Books.

Smith, Adam (1776/ 1952) *An Inquiry Into the Nature and Causes of the Wealth of Nations*. Chicago, IL: University of Chicago Press.

Solomon, Robert (1992) 'Corporate roles, personal virtues: An Aristotelian approach to business ethics' *Business Ethics Quarterly*, 2: 317–339.

Solomon, Robert (1993) *Ethics and Excellence: Cooperation and Integrity in Business*. Oxford: Oxford University Press.

Solomon, Robert (1999a) *A Better Way to Think about Business*. Oxford: Oxford University Press.

Solomon, Robert (1999b) 'Business ethics and virtue' in Robert Frederick (ed.) *A Companion to Business Ethics*. Oxford: Blackwell.

Solomon, Robert (2004) 'Aristotle, ethics and business organizations' *Organization Studies*, 25(6): 1021–1043.

Stiglitz, Joseph (2002) *Globalization and its Discontents*. London: Allen Lane.

ten Bos, René (2000) *Fashion and Utopia in Management Thinking*. Amsterdam: Benjamins.

ten Bos, René (2002) 'Machiavelli's kitchen' *Organization*, 9: 51–70.

ten Bos, René (2003) 'Business ethics, accounting and the fear of melancholy' *Organization*, 10(2): 267–286.

ten Bos, René (2004) 'The fear of wolves: Anti-hodological ruminations about organizations and labyrinths' *Culture and Organization*, 10(1): 7–24.

ten Bos, René (2005) 'On the possibility of formless life: Agamben's politics of the gesture' *ephemera: theory and politics in organization*, 5(1): 26–44.

ten Bos, René and Ruud Kaulingfreks (2001) *De hygiënemachine: Kanttekeningen bij de reinheidscultus in cultuur, organisatie en management*. Kampen: Agora.

ten Bos, René and Carl Rhodes (2003) 'The game of exemplarity: Subjectivity, work and the impossible politics of purity' *Scandinavian Journal of Management*, 19(4): 403–423.

ten Bos, René and Hugh Willmott (2001) 'Towards a post-dualistic business ethics: Interweaving reason and emotion in working life' *Journal of Management Studies*, 38(6): 769–793.

Thompson, Paul, Chris Smith and Stephen Ackroyd (2000) 'If ethics is the answer, you are asking the wrong questions: A reply to Martin Parker' *Organization Studies*, 21: 1149–1158.

Timmons, Mark (ed.) (2002) *Kant's Metaphysics of Morals: Interpretative Essays*. Oxford: Oxford University Press.

Toffler, Alvin (1970) *Future Shock*. London: Pan Books.

Verstraeten, Johan (ed.) (2000) *Business Ethics: Broadening the Perspectives*. Leuven: Peeters.

Vidal, John (1997) *McLibel: Burger Culture on Trial*. London: Pan Books.

Virno, Paulo (2004) *A Grammar of the Multitude: For an Analysis of Contemporary Forms of Life*, trans. Isabella Bertoletti, James Cascaito and Andrea Casson. New York: Semiotext(e).

Voltaire (1769/1972) *Philosophical Dictionary*, trans. Theodore Besterman. London: Penguin.

Warburton, Peter (2000) *Debt and Delusion: Central Bank Follies That Threaten Economic Disaster*. New York: Penguin.

Warnock, Geoffrey (1971) *The Object of Morality*. London: Methuen.

Warnock, Mary (ed.) (1962) *Utilitarianism*. London: Collins.

Watson, Tony (1994) *In Search of Management: Culture, Chaos and Control in Managerial Work*. London: Routledge.

Weber, Max (1930) *The Protestant Ethic and the Spirit of Capitalism*, trans. Talcott Parsons. London: Allen and Unwin.

Weber, Max (1948) *For Max Weber*, ed. H. H. Gerth and C. Wright Mills. London: Routledge and Kegan Paul.

Weber, Max (1978) *Economy and Society: An Outline of Interpretive Sociology*, ed. Guenter Roth and Claus Wittich. Berkeley: University of California Press.

White, Thomas (ed.) (1993) *Business Ethics: A Philosophical Reader*. New York: Macmillan

Whyte, William H. (1956) *The Organization Man*. Hammondsworth: Penguin.

Wicks, Andrew and R. Edward Freeman (1998) 'Organization studies and the new pragmatism: Positivism, antipositivism and the search for ethics' *Organization Science*, 9(2): 123–140.

Williams, Colin (2004) *A Commodified World? Mapping the Limits of Capitalism*. London: Zed Books.

Willmott, Hugh (1998) 'Towards a new ethics? The contributions of poststructuralism and posthumanism' in Martin Parker (ed.) *Ethics and Organizations*. London: Sage.

Wolfreys, Julian (2004) *Critical Keywords in Literary and Cultural Theory*. Basingstoke: Palgrave.

Wood, Allen (1999) *Kant's Ethical Thought*. Cambridge: Cambridge University Press

Wood, Allen (2002) 'The final form of Kant's practical philosophy' in Mark Timmons (ed.) *Kant's Metaphysics of Morals: Interpretative Essays*. Oxford: Oxford University Press.

World Bank (2004) *World Development Report*. New York: World Bank.

World Social Forum (2001) 'World Social Forum Charter of Principles' in William Fisher and Thomas Ponniah (eds.) (2003) *Another World is Possible: Popular Alternatives to Globalization at the World Social Forum*. London: Zed Books (also available online at www.forumsocialmundial.org).

Wray-Bliss, Edward (2002) 'Research subjects/Research subjections: Exploring the ethics and politics of critical research' *Organization*, 10(2): 307–325.

Wray-Bliss, Edward (2003) 'Abstract ethics, embodied ethics: The strange marriage of Foucault and positivism in labour process theory' *Organization*, 9(1): 5–39.

Wyschogrod, Edith and Gerald McKenny (eds.) (2003) *The Ethical*. Oxford: Blackwell.

Yack, Bernard (1999) 'Community and conflict in Aristotle's political philosophy' in Robert Bartlett and Susan Collins (eds.) *Action and Contemplation. Studies in the Moral and Political Thought of Aristotle*. Albany: State University of New York Press.

Yuen, Eddie, George Katsiaficas and Daniel Burton Rose (eds.) (2001) *The Battle of Seattle: The New Challenge to Capitalist Globalization*. New York: Soft Skull Press.

Yuen, Eddie, George Katsiaficas and Daniel Burton-Rose (eds.) (2004) *Confronting Capitalism: Dispatches from a Global Movement*. New York: Soft Skull Press.

Žižek, Slavoj (1989) *The Sublime Object of Ideology*. London: Verso.

Žižek, Slavoj (1997) *The Plague of Fantasies*. London: Verso.

Author index

Subject index

aesthetics 22–3, 72, 85

American Beauty 15

Ancient Greece 2–3, 21, 56–7, 60–2, 65, 70–2, 120–2, 140, 144–5, 171

anti- 74–6, 96, 100, 102–3, 105–6, 111, 113, 125, 130, 143–4, 157; capitalism 96, 100, 102–3, 105, 111, 113, 130, 143–4; corporate 103, 105–6, 111, 125, 130, 143–4, 167; essentialism 74–6, 157; globalisation 96, 100, 102–3, 111, 143–4

aporia 144–5, 156; and **the Other** 145; and unity 145

Arthur Andersen 6–7, 44

automaton/puppet 8, 32, 48–54, 58, 82–3, 91, 136–7; *see also* **techne**

bureaucracy 7, 67, 78, 82–95, 126–7, 146–8, 159, 162–4, 177, 180–1; and business ethics 7, 67, 78, 87, 91–5; and conformity 82–95, 148; and democracy 88–9, 93; end of 92–3; *In Praise of Bureaucracy* 92–5, 181; iron cage of 180; *McDonaldization of Society, the* 85–7, 148, 162; meaning(s) of 84, 180–1; and moral distance 86–95, 126–7, 146, 163–4; *Organization Man the* 83, 115, 148; and the Other 78, 90, 92, 94; and performativity 86, 94; technical advantages of 84, 93–4

business 2–7, 10–13, 57–60, 65–7, 81–2, 115–16, 148–9, 153; business communities 57–60, 65–7, 115–16, 153; emergence of 81–2; meaning(s) of 10–13, 148–9

business ethics 1–21, 23–4, 26, 41–7, 52, 55–68, 70, 78, 80, 87, 91–5, 97–100, 103, 105–6, 109–17, 121–31, 133–40, 149–50,

159–61; and bureaucracy 7, 67, 78, 87, 91–5; *Business Ethics Quarterly* 44; and common sense 1, 5, 8–13, 15–21, 24, 58, 87, 130, 133, 136; and community 115–6, 126; and Corporate Social Responsibility (CSR) 97–100, 109–11, 121–8, 133, 159–61; and cynicism 7, 117, 124–6, 130; and deontology 41–7, 52, 55; and discomfort 2, 7–8, 23, 43, 51, 53, 55, 63, 105, 128–9, 133–4, 136–40; emergence thereof 16–18, 130, 139; fashionability thereof 112–14, 130, 159; *Journal of Business Ethics, the* 44, 57; meaning(s) of 16–17, 70, 131, 149, 150; and politics 6–7, 25–6, 66–7, 80, 110–11, 131, 139; and the possibility of thought 134–40; and rules 8, 12, 14–16, 24, 135–6; Society of Business Ethics, the 44; and stakeholder theory 59, 68, 94, 97, 99, 106, 111, 123; textbooks 1–2, 7–8, 18–19, 138–9; and virtue ethics 56–68

capitalism 7, 11–13, 17, 19, 26, 33–6, 39, 58, 66, 78, 80–113, 120, 130, 132, 134, 140, 143–4, 151–2, 167; anti-capitalism 96, 100, 102–3, 111, 113, 143–4; *Capital* 33, 103–9, 151–2; *Capitalism and Freedom* 97–9; and **commodity fetishism** 103–9, 151–2; and consequentialism 26, 36; corporate capitalism, 7, 11–13, 17, 19, 36, 39, 58, 66, 78, 80–113, 120, 130, 132, 134, 140, 167; and democracy 102–3; and neo-liberalism 81, 96, 99–103, 109–10; and the Other 78, 97, 108

categorical imperatives 44–50, 55, 68, 92

206